PROVENCE

SPRING / SUMMER 2019

EUR 19 | CHF 29 | USD 25

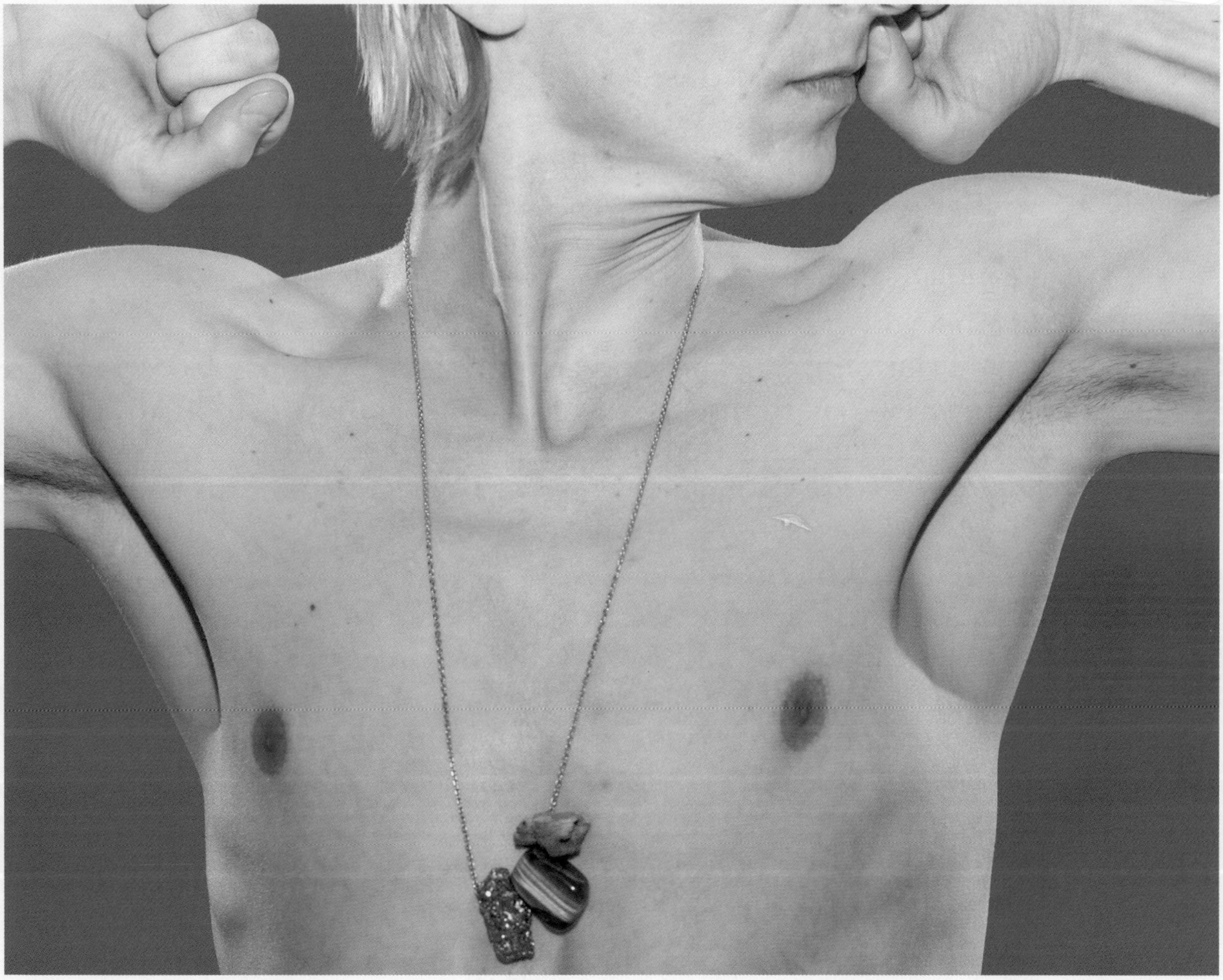

Marc Asekhame, Barbara Bleisch, Gisela Capitain, Mariuccia Casadio, Cinecittà, Bice Curiger, Bea Feitler, Femme Fatale, Spice Grrlz, Gorillaz Grrls, Edgars Gluhovs, Ursina Gysi, Katrin Hassler, Daniel Herleth, Nina Hollensteiner, Karl Holmqvist, Eva Illouz, Inka Meißner, Cady Noland, Catherine Opie, Boris Ovini, The New Pope, Stefanie Pretnar, Cinzia Ruggeri, Esther Schipper, Elisabeth Taylor, Bärbel Trautwein, Hannah Villiger, Cao Yu

PROVENCE

EDITORIAL

In 1977, Brazilian-born designer and art director Bea Feitler (1938–82) famously stated, "As for magazines, I think there is a need for a magazine that combines a *House & Garden* with *Vogue*, a magazine of elegance and lifestyle."

Reflections on printed matter and its formats has been a recurring theme throughout the history of PROVENCE. In the DESIGN section of this issue, Marte Eknæs's and Nicolau Vergueiro's contribution "The Power of Print" brings the work of Bea Feitler into focus. Feitler used printed matter as a vessel with which to address and shape social issues through editorial decisions, and is best known for her work with *Harper's Bazaar*, *Ms. Magazine*, *Rolling Stone*, and the modern *Vanity Fair*.

Furthermore, we are delighted to publish "A House to Start: Cinzia Ruggeri's Art around Life" by legendary Italian fashion critic cum curator Mariuccia Casadio. Here she reflects on the work of fashion pioneer Cinzia Ruggeri. The text is accompanied by photographs from Ruggeri's 2018 exhibition at Galleria Federico Vavassori, which was curated by Casadio.

With "Takeovers, Joint Ventures, and Continuations—Three Gallerists in Conversation", PROVENCE continues the examination of the format of the contemporary gallery, which we initiated in our previous issue. This time, we speak with Gisela Capitain and Esther Schipper, as well as Daniel Herleth and Bärbel Trautwein of Galerie Barbara Weiss.

In the first of two editorials in this issue's fashion section, photographer Marc Asekhame and stylist Ursina Gysi offer their impression of ultra-fast fashion designer-replica Fashion Nova. The second editorial, by our fashion director Nina Hollensteiner, and photographer Boris Ovini, tells the story of a spiritual healing session gone supernaturally awry.

REPORT includes a feature on Cady Noland by artists Inka Meißner and Stefanie Pretnar, followed by a conversation with Beijing-based artist Cao Yu about her European debut "Femme Fatale", showing at Galerie Urs Meile in Luzern. Also, artist Edgars Gluhovs is reporting from the eternal city in "Don We Now Our Gay Apparel", where he shares his experiences from the set of *The New Pope*.

LITERATURE contains a series of shorter contributions, such as a poem by Karl Holmqvist, a review of Matias Faldbakken's 2018 novel *The Waiter* by curator and scholar Anne Gruber, and a book list on the theme of "The Violence of Gender".

This issue also comes with two PORTFOLIOS; artist Hannah Villiger's intriguing polaroids and a suite of photographs by LA-based photographer Catherine Opie documenting the possessions of Hollywood actress Elizabeth Taylor.

But, we begin with the rubric ISSUES, which includes a conversation between sociologist Eva Illouz, and philosopher Barbara Bleisch, who has also hosted the program "Sternstunde Philosopie" at the Swiss television station SRF, on Illouz's best-selling books *Why Love Hurts* and *Why Love Ends*, which interpret modern love, the deficiencies of love in a capitalist era and the "culture of lovelessness."

In "Prospecting Gendered Structures", sociologist Katrin Hassler supports her research on gender and power relations in the art world with an approach developed from Pierre Bourdieu's gender theory and his theory of the artistic field. Here, a paradox becomes evident, which proceeds from the juxtaposition of the empirical results and the visualization of the field's distance from the societal centers of power. The factual relative power of women in the art world—despite the existing asymmetries—can also be seen as a matter of dominance and subordination on the macro-level of the social sphere.

PROVENCE—always changing, always in a state of flux—is nothing without its contributors, artists, readers and "Aix". As of this year, our core team comprises Olamiju Fajemisin, Jean-Claude Freymond-Guth, Nina Hollensteiner, Tobias Kaspar, Philip Pilekjær, and Pascal Storz. This summer, PROVENCE bids farewell to Hannes Loichinger—after ten years as a collaborator and editor, he will be leaving his position. With this and recent changes—fiction and nightmares becoming true—PROVENCE's main office has moved to the Zürich-based tank to think through contemporary art, Longtang. We are also pleased to announce that as of now, PROVENCE will be published biannually.

As a small preview to PROVENCE AW 19/20, the fashion label FFIXXED STUDIOS created a new bag for PROVENCE: Goodbye Plastic!

PROVENCE. Biannual. Subscribe.

Please don't faint.

PROVENCE, May 2019

ISSUES

FASHION

PORTFOLIO

GALLERY

REPORT

LITERATURE

DESIGN

PROVENCE

TABLE OF CONTENTS

PROVENCE
SPRING / SUMMER
2019

Founder and
Executive Director
Tobias Kaspar

Editors
Olamiju Fajemisin
Philip Pilekjær

Contributing Editor
Hannes Loichinger

Fashion Editor
Nina Hollensteiner

Art Director
Pascal Storz

Managing Director
Jean-Claude Freymond-Guth

Copy Editor
Olamiju Fajemisin

Image Editing
Georgs Avetisjans

Printing and Binding
Studio RBB, Rīga

PROVENCE, Est. 2009 by Tobias Kaspar, Pascal Storz, Hannes Loichinger (2009–19), and Daiga Grantina (2009–11) in Nice, France

PUBLISHER

Published by
PROVENCE
Longtang e.V.
Hagenholzstrasse 106
CH–8050 Zürich
www.provence.st
mail@provence.st

PROVENCE is an independent entity of Longtang e.V. Switzerland

Co-published by
Spector Books
Harkortstrasse 10
D–04107 Leipzig
www.spectorbooks.com
mail@spectorbooks.com

DISTRIBUTION

Germany, Austria
GVA, Gemeinsame Verlags-auslieferung Göttingen GmbH & Co. KG, www.gva-verlage.de

Switzerland
AVA Verlagsauslieferung AG, www.ava.ch

France, Belgium
Interart Paris, www.interart.fr

UK
Central Books Ltd, www.centralbooks.com

USA, Canada,
Central and South America,
Africa, Asia
ARTBOOK | D.A.P.
www.artbook.com

South Korea
The Book Society, www.thebooksociety.org

Australia, New Zealand
Perimeter Distribution, www.perimeterdistribution.com

FOR SUBSCRIPTIONS AND BACK ISSUES

Bruil & van de Staaij
Postbus 75
7940 AB MEPPEL
The Netherlands
(T) +31-522-261303
www.bruil.info/provence
info@bruil.info

ACKNOWLEDGMENTS

Sandra Roth, Mathew Sova, Laura Salvo, Jia Cong, Eric Hattan, Egija Inzule, Thomas Schmutz, Anne Gruber, Emil Klein and Ludovica Parenti at Longtang, and especially to all the authors and collaborators for their contributions

CREDITS

The rubric title “Issues” is a loose adoption of castillo/corrales exhibition trilogy “The Issues of Our Time” (2013–14). castillo/corrales (2007–16) was a co-operatively run non-profit art space in Paris. Its independent publishing house, Paraguay Press, co-published *The PROVENCE City Guide: Nice* (2011), a hack into the Wallpaper City Guide series and an homage to PROVENCE’s hometown of Nice in the south of France.

SUPPORT

This publication was made possible with the generous support of Foundation Erna und Curt Burgauer. Longtang e.V. receives annual support by Migros-Kulturprozent, Fondation Nestlé pour l’Art; Kanton Zürich, Fachstelle Kultur; Genossenschaft “Mehr als Wohnen”; AGEMKTKLP, product subsidy and sponsoring by Axa Art; Bosshard + Co. AG; Ruckstuhl AG

ISSN: 2624-7682
ISBN: 978-3-95905-334-1

ISSUES

PROSPECTING GENDERED STRUCTURES

Text Katrin Hassler

A progressive discourse about art and gender falls short without a perspective based on a social theory. Katrin Hassler supports her research with an approach developed from Pierre Bourdieu's gender theory, and his theory of the artistic field. This approach unites a theoretical framework with empirical data. Gendered structures are analyzed at different levels, at both the symbolic and economic poles of the field, or through diachronic developments and different groups of actors, and are reflected in power-relationships in society as a whole. Here, a paradox becomes evident, which proceeds from the juxtaposition of the empirical results and the visualization of the field's distance from the societal centers of power. The factual relative power of women in the art world, despite the existing asymmetries, can also be seen as a matter of dominance and subordination on the macro-level of the social sphere.

SYMBOLIC AND ECONOMIC DIMENSIONS

Rank (symbolic capital)	All artists n	Female artists %
Top 10	10	10,0
Top 50	52	7,7
Top 100	103	12,6
Top 500	514	18,9
Top 1000	1037	22,9
Top 1500	1552	24,4
Top 2000	2079	24,9
Top 2500	2612	25,4

Top 2,500 artists in the international art field ranked according to symbolic capital

It is rare that gender asymmetries—connected to an extensive exclusion of women—are manifested as succinctly as they are in the art market: *Jimson Weed/White Flower No. 1* (1932) by Georgia O'Keeffe received a bid of 44,405,000 US dollars at Sotheby's in 2014, the highest price ever paid on the tertiary market for a work by a female artist.[1] The high mark for works by male artists is much greater, reaching a new dimension in 2017 with the sale of Leonardo da Vinci's *Salvator Mundi* (ca. 1500): 450,312,500 US dollars.[2] A 2017 study shows that observers value computer-generated pictures more highly when they are ascribed to a male artist, demonstrating how deeply entrenched gender differentiations are in our thinking.[3]

The field proves to be male dominated, not only at the economic level, but also at the symbolic pole, which refers to the currency of artistic reputation. Here too, female artists are underrepresented in numerical terms. Data on the leading 2,500 positions in the artistic field in 2010 illustrate that in this segment no more than 25.4% are women. Among the top 500,

Cindy Sherman, *Untitled #299*, 1994 / Chromogenic color print, 49 × 33 inches / Courtesy of the artist and Metro Pictures, New York

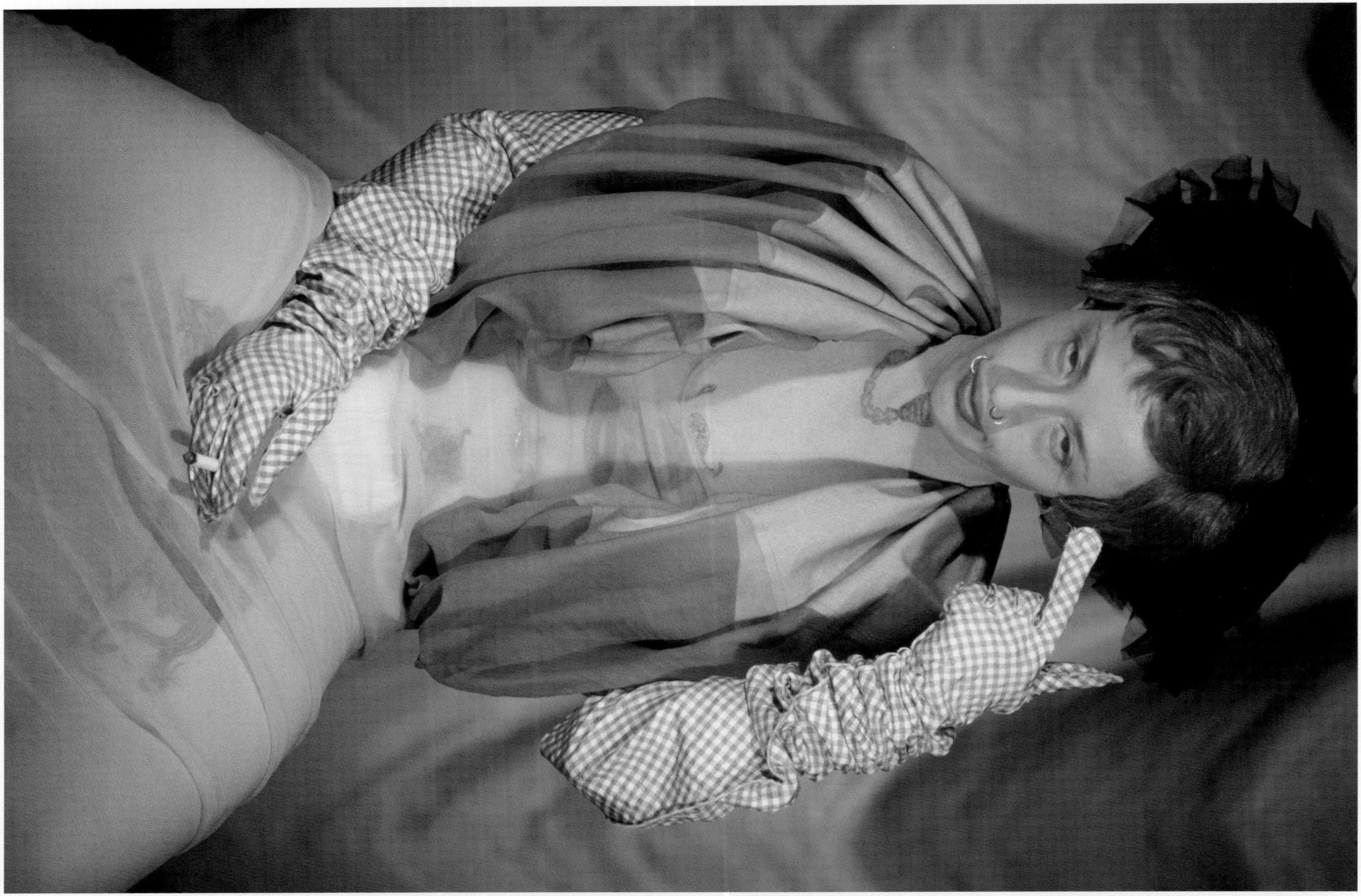

there are 18.9%, while the top 100 has only 12.6% and only one female representative, Cindy Sherman, ranks among the top 10.[4] A comparison with data from the current *Artfacts* ranking raises the number of women among the top 10 to two—Louise Bourgeois' rank moved up from 12 to 10. Among the leading 100 artists, sixteen female representatives register an increase to 14.4%.[5] When contrasted with the number of female students at art academies, these numbers seem even graver: their percentage has continually increased in recent years and is now substantially over 50% on average.[6]

TOP 100, VERTICAL INEQUALITY AND THE MECHANISMS OF EXCLUSION

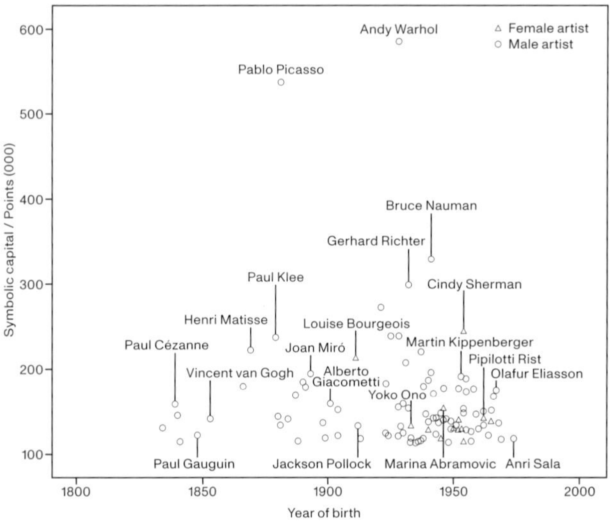

Top 100 artists in the international art world according to year of birth and symbolic capital (female and male artists by name with the highest points per decade [birth year])[7]

A visualization of the asymmetries is provided by the representation of the top 100 female artists according to *Artfacts.Net* by symbolic capital and year of birth. All female artists listed are found in a very limited area—in the lower right quadrant. While the male artists in this segment occupy a space ranging from the earliest birth years around 1830 and their highest point values are at around 600,000 (symbolic capital), all their female colleagues on the list were born after 1900 and fail to exceed a point value of 300,000. Bourgeois, born in 1911, is the oldest female artist in the top 100 segment; all the others were born between 1944 (Yoko Ono) and 1965 (Tacita Dean). Sherman, born in 1946, achieves the highest evaluation of all women in this field and is distinguished by a relatively large distance between her points and those of both the male and female artists in her age range. This includes Nan Goldin, Andreas Gursky, Martin Kippenberger, and Kiki Smith. Based on their evaluations, Bourgeois and Sherman have similarly exalted placements, or "star positions" in relation to the group of female artists, much as Andy Warhol and Pablo Picasso do in relation to the entire sample.

However, the female artists are distinguished by their significantly lower evaluation. This distinct, vertical inequality represents one of the characteristic structural features of fields of cultural production in which a few "winners" gain a markedly higher symbolic capital than the majority of artists.[8] The exclusive existence of male extremes must be emphasized; female representatives occupy similar positions only in relation to their female colleagues.[9] Seven male artists from the Impressionist circle and thus the consecrated avant-garde are in the top 100, including Vincent van Gogh, Paul Cézanne, and Paul Gauguin[10]—the complete absence of female Impressionist artists speaks for itself. Berthe Morisot and Mary Cassatt are considered the most successful women painters of the movement[11], they score among the top 2500, but have a relatively worse position than their male colleagues. Cassatt, born in 1844 ranks as number 551, and Morisot, born in 1841 places at number 224. In the case of these examples, attempts made by art historians to rehabilitate female artists have had little success.[12] However, the observations presented here indicate that there is a space of possibles for younger female artists to enter the top segment that was not available to the same extent in earlier generations.

Year of birth	All artists n	Female artists %
–1929	500	11,6
1930–1939	232	15,9
1940–1949	293	23,2
1950–1959	397	27,2
1960–1969	728	32,0
1970–1979	375	36,0
1980–	7	–
Total	2532	25,2

Top 2,500 artists in the international art field ranked according to year of birth

CONSECRATED AVANT-GARDE AND THE PERPETUATION OF ASYMMETRIES

The increased inclusion of younger female artists raises the following question: to what extent do the changes actually indicate a shift, an increasing alignment with the space occupied by male colleagues and, concomitantly, entry into the established avant-garde? In this regard, it is necessary to observe the developments in order to rule out that the shift is only an apparent one, with female artists succeeding in entering the top field as part of the avant-garde, but not making the transition to the established avant-garde and the resulting stabilization of their position.[13] In short, movements can be registered in the art world towards an increasing presence of female artists, including in top areas; but it cannot be said that their position is equalizing with that of their male colleagues. Despite different waves of the women's movement, notwithstanding the visibility of female artists such as the Guerrilla Girls or the efforts of gallerists such as Monika Sprüth and Philomene Magers, who have been actively discussing gender asymmetries in art for decades and pushing for their elimination, contra the attitude towards women as equal active subjects (e.g. in the media), a positioning independent of gender, especially at the top positions, neither exists nor seems to be possible in the foreseeable future. The perpetuation of unequal gender relationships in art and the persistence of male domination, as a process and object of grand attempts at revision, indicates the inability of a society that is conscious of the asymmetries to remove these inequalities and relationships of domination with the necessary forcefulness and usher in a true and lasting shift.

INTERVIEW

PROVENCE: Not long ago, I read in a text of yours about the aversion in the art world to quantitative studies, which are sometimes accompanied by a rejection of the results obtained. What do you attribute these reactions to?

Katrin Hassler: Despite the existence of studies measuring gender positions in the art field, many different issues arise in the discussions around such statistics because few take place in a transdisciplinary setting. This discourse debating gender in the art sphere on a statistical level can be recognized as a rather marginal one, often shaped by a lack of acceptance of the findings. Beneath individual aversions, an attitude rooted in the (hyper-)idealistic, constructivist and individualistic traditions of the field is discernible, which is apparent on the practical as well as academic side of things. Given the importance of differentiating between idiographic (particularity of a specific case) and nomothetic (general trends or "laws") approaches as a basis, the methodological foci of the academic disciplines predominantly concerned with the topic of gender in the arts—such as art history and partly gender studies—are principally associated with the former, and this proves to be one reason why insufficient data about gender relations in the art field has been gathered or analyzed, when compared to other economic or academic spheres, and especially concerning the international art field. In addition to this, art history continues to be based on case studies of artists, movements, and periods as well as national frameworks or studies of theories of visual representation. Although more recent trends towards studies with quantitative designs in liaison with digital humanities can be discerned in art history, these again rarely concern gender in their analyses. A certain kind of development concerning these questions is recognizable, and I propose not turning back to a position of "either ... or". Quantitative designs should be predominately seen as an addendum to methods classically included in art history. I see a big opportunity—rather than a challenge—in accepting them as a complement to the case-study model of practice and more idiographically oriented approaches.

PROVENCE: In your study, you speak of a paradox of the gender dichotomy. What is paradoxical about the result of your inquiries?

KH: Art critic Brian Boucher wrote that "girls run the world. That's arguably especially true in the art world."[14] This statement does not appear to have any basis in fact in terms of their role as artists in international rankings. In contrast, a more appropriate and differentiated position held by the sociologist Pierre Bourdieu within his gender analysis, *Masculine Domination*, declares that the cultural sector is one of the few professional areas where women can occupy leading positions. Bourdieu describes women as responsible agents for the conversion of economic capital into symbolic capital within the domestic unit, leading to the conclusion that the professional emancipation of women, among others in the cultural field, can accordingly also be seen as an extension of the traditional female role—even securing the submission of women to this domination.[15] This perspective becomes evident when contrasting data based on the *Artfacts.Net* ranking with data concerning the economic field, based on *Catalyst.org*. On the one hand, the field can—to the extent that the diagnosed developments continue—be regarded as one in which gender loses importance as as a structuring variable increasingly. At the same time, the strong and increasing presence of women in leading positions of this microcosm is evidence of a kind of gender segregation, and a continuation of the power relationships to be designated as male domination when it comes to the macrocosm of the social room. This paradoxical situation forces us to take these more-or-less hidden gendered (and therefore gendering) structures into account.

Rank (symbolic capital)	Artists (all) n	Female artists %	Museum directors (all) n	Female directors %	Gallerists (all) n	Female gallerists %
Top 10	10	10.0	10	10.0	11	27.3
Top 50	52	7.7	–	–	62	32.3
Top 100	103	12.6	–	–	129	37.2
Top 200	206	18.0	186	32.4	251	39.8

Data denoting share of women in different professional groups in the international top field

PROVENCE: If you look at various professional groups in the art world, are there differences? Or are the inequalities among artists, curators, and gallerists equally distributed?

KH: My research shows that this situation of discrimination does not only apply to artists, but also to other agents in the art field, such as directors of leading museums and galleries. According to this, female gallerists display a share of approximately 40.0% of women in the top 200 positions; the directors show 32.4%, whereas female artists occupy 18.0%. In addition to this, the data reveal a differentiation between the professions of art production and art mediation with the former showing a much stronger asymmetrical distribution of gender than the latter. This comparison also indicates an exceptionally high visibility for female gallerists, also apparent when measured by assessments of the top 10 in which women form slightly more than a quarter (27.3%) of those listed. For both groups, artists as well as museum directors, only 1 in 10 of the listed agents are female at this absolute peak. Looking at the top 50 and top 100 rankings, artists and gallerists clearly differ in the percentages of women when compared to men (no specifications can be made for the museum directors): only 7.7% of the top 50 positions are occupied by female artists, whereas female gallerists make up 32.3% of the top 50 rankings. While the proportion of women at the top 100 level show 12.6% for artists and 37.2% for gallerists.[16] A change is becoming apparent for both artists and museum directors leading to a stronger inclusion of women in the younger age cohorts. For gallerists, an analogous transformation cannot be discerned: rather, the professional group shows a largely balanced gender representation even for the older cohorts, whereas for galleries founded in the 1980s and later, the figures indicate a considerable asymmetry in favor of the male agents. In galleries founded between the years 1990 and 1999, 12.4% of the leading positions were occupied by women.

PROVENCE: How can these differences be explained?

KH: An explanation for the differentiation between productive and mediating positions can be found in the conceptualization of artistry and its persistent, mythical and naturalized *topoi* of the male genius. Interestingly, despite the claims about the "disappearance of the author," the "blurring of the boundaries between art and life," and the "reformulation of the concept of artistic work" that have been taking place for forty years, the consistency of mythical characterizations in which creative excellence is based in individual, male genius remain visible in the data presented. Additionally, the issue raised as to why more women enter and sustain careers in the mediation side of the field—especially in the gallerist profession—can be further elucidated by taking a closer look at some historical and even literary figures and salonnieres, as is also observed by Pierre Bourdieu in *The Rules of Art*, such as Princess Mathilde Bonaparte as an example from nineteenth-century Paris or, in reference to Flaubert's *Sentimental Education*, Madame Arnoux and Madame Dambreuse. However, the sociologist didn't explicitly determine aspects of gender in his field analyses. To briefly illustrate one example, Princess Mathilde Bonaparte acted as a prominent mediator in artistic fields—a protector as well as patron of the arts—and invested her fairly high social and economic capital for these very purposes. Bourdieu accentuates her endeavoring to acquire benefits and protection for her friends, such as the *Légion d'honneur* for Flaubert or the prize of the *Académie Francaise* for George Sand. Her inherited capital allowed her to adopt a (powerful) position of public influence—particularly on cultural issues—at a time when women were usually denied public prominence. From this perspective, the salons can be declared spaces of possibles for bourgeois women, giving them the ability to receive *some* official recognition in the nineteenth century; albeit the space remains restricted to the cultural field, and is mostly accompanied by an exclusion from positions of political and economic power. This structure of dominance continues to exist today, albeit in a much more moderate form, and its influence becomes partly visible in the data given above. As mentioned before—even if women still occupy powerful positions in the art field less frequently than their male counterparts, they acquire a relative inclusion in this sphere in comparison to the economic field. The particularly high share of female gallerists can also be concisely explained insofar as it concerns an occupation, known for its relative informality, neither requiring a set career path nor a specific academic education—thus being much more permeable.

PROVENCE: Can your study be related to investigations that, for example, delve more deeply into the relationship between center and periphery and the differences connected to that? What results do you see from a more international comparison?

KH: I consider analyzing the relationship between center and periphery in studies using data to be very important—even with regard to a field that operates globally according to the participants' self-understanding. So, it plays no small role within my study. I focused on it using the geographical origins of the artists, and revealed a tendency according to which the inclusion of women decreases the closer we get to the Western-dominated center of the field. This can be seen for example in the cases of Africa, the Middle East and Eastern Asia. It can be explained on a basic level by the degree of reputation afforded to a professional position of that kind in society, and how attractive it therefore is for men.

PROVENCE: In what way do the results of your study become "effective?" In other words, are there moments that place your analysis in relationship to a critique of the existing inequalities that can be made operational? And do you, with your critical analysis of gendered structures, form a coalition with other ways of approaching mitigating societal inequality?

KH: In seminars and talks on this issue—in a university context, at art academies, but also at UNESCO, in other words on a stronger level of cultural policy—I have led many multifaceted discussions about this. This issue is very prominent right now, in the media, in the art studies discourse, and also in politics, and we can see that at various levels people are becoming sensitized to it, which I see as being foundational in order for it to become operational. I recently discussed it with a group of international students in Italy and once again realized how important these kinds of data are with regard to attaining a clear perspective about the status quo and (gradual) change, but also for detaching the discourse from an emotional framework that can become extreme. Here, data allow us to demonstrate the status quo in a factual way. It would be good to have a stronger interdisciplinary openness in which artistic practice along with curatorial, scientific, and cultural-policy discourse makes use of the places where they overlap, and make the diverse methodological approaches productive. To return to your question, my analysis does not offer a way to make it operational, but it absolutely can—or is intended to—be a point of reference and the basis for a critique that can be made operational. My central concern was to create a "gender mapping," that gives insight into and an overview of the gendered and gendering structures of the field, closes at least some of the data gaps, and in so doing also shines a light on perspectives where critique of that kind can begin.

Translated by Laura Freeburn

The preceding contribution uses excerpts from Katrin Hassler's *Kunst und Gender. Zur Bedeutung von Geschlecht für die Einnahme von Spitzenpositionen im Kunstfeld* (Bielefeld: transcript, 2017), "On Gender Statistics in the Art Field and Leading Positions in the International Sphere," published in *n.paradoxa*, 39 (January 2017): 48–55 and "Zur Krise der Geschlechterverhältnisse in der Kunst" in *Bildpunkt* (Summer 2018): 22–25.

1 See http://www.sothebys.com/en/auctions/ecatalogue/2014/american-art-n09229/lot.11.html, accessed May 05, 2019.
2 Cf. Roman Kräussl, "Die Avantgarde der Frauen. MM-Kunstindex," *Manager Magazin* 05 (2018): 92.
3 The analysis of 1.5 million auction data points from 1970 to 2013 furthermore describes an asymmetry according to which female artists only attain 47.6% of the profits of their male colleagues on the international auction market, see Renée B. Adams et al., "Is Gender in the Eye of the Beholder? Identifying Cultural Attitudes with Art Auction Prices," December 6, 2017, https://ssrn.com/abstract=3083500.
4 The data presented here show an excerpt of the analyses of different segments of the international field published in the book *Kunst und Gender. Zur Bedeutung von Geschlecht für die Einnahme von Spitzenpositionen im Kunstfeld* (Bielefeld: transcript, 2017) by Katrin Hassler. The symbolic capital presented here is based on the Artfacts ranking (for the most part *ArtFacts.Net* 04/2010) and includes factors such as presence and exhibitions, institutional ranking, and peer group connection; economic success does not factor into the valuation.
5 See *Artfacts.Net* 01/2019. Regarding the discussion over using rankings in an art studies context, see Hassler 2017.
6 See Andrea Löther, "Hochschulranking nach Gleichstellungsaspekten 2017," cews.publik, 21, GESIS-Leibniz-Institut für Sozialwissenschaften CEWS, 2017, 79.
7 Data source: *ArtFacts.Net* 04/2010; source: Hassler 2017.
8 See also Mark Lutter, "Soziale Strukturen des Erfolgs: Winner-takeall-Prozesse in der Kreativwirtschaft," MPIfG Discussion Paper 12/7, 2012, 1.
9 On the power-law distribution see Nassim Nicholas Taleb, *The Black Swan* (New York: Random House, 2007), 229–52.
10 On the consecrated avant-garde see Pierre Bourdieu, *The Rules of Art* (Stanford: Stanford University Press, 1996), 149–54.
11 Cf. Ulf Wuggenig, "The Artist and the Dealer: The Roles of Gustave Caillebotte, Mary Cassat and Paul Durand-Ruel in 19th Century Revolutionary Art," in *PROVENCE*, Issue O (June 2010): 44–49.
12 Linda Nochlin discussed these kinds of rehabilitation strategies as early as 1971 in her trailblazing text for feminist art history "Why have there been no great women artists?", first published in Vivian Gornich et al. (eds.), *Woman in Sexist Society: Studies in Power and Powerlessness* (New York: Basic Books, 1971). While she believes this practice is essential for expanding the knowledge of art history about female artists, she criticizes a failure to question the assumptions of exclusion. Currently, with Art+Feminism, a large-scale international project is taking place to register female artists in the (art history) memory and especially in Wikipedia. With the involvement of various art institutions such as the Museum of Modern Art, New York and the Tate London, edit-a-thons regularly take place which so far have led to over 11,000 Wikipedia articles; see http://www.artandfeminism.org, accessed March 20, 2019.
13 Over time a corresponding decrease in the number of female artists would be evident; their success would not be evaluated as a long-term one as it was for their male colleagues.
14 Brian Boucher, "25 Women Curators Shaking Things Up," *ArtnetNews*, March 17, 2015, https://news.artnet.com/exhibitions/25-women-curators-on-the-rise-276386. Also the reference to "girls" suggests a rather limited ability of gender-theoretical reflection.
15 See Pierre Bourdieu, *Masculine Domination* (Stanford: Stanford University Press, 2001), 101.
16 The data are based on different sources: Artists according to *ArtFacts.Net* (April, 2010), museum directors according to Kunstkompass (2009), gallerists according to *Artinvestor* Galerien Ranking (2008). The directors are categorized into two groups by the editors of the ranking: Rank 1: ten leading museums, Rank 2: all other museums listed. No values exist for the top 50 and top 100 positions. The gallerists and artists show multiple positionings of ranks (e.g. artist duos/groups) and values vary for the different agent categories.

WHY LOVE ENDS

Conversation

Eva Illouz
Barbara Bleisch

"Everything possible, nothing obligatory." This former motto of the swingers scene has completely permeated our romantic relationships. Non-commitment is a popular commodity. But this new freedom comes at a price, according to world-renowned sociologist Eva Illouz. Romantic love is endangered like never before.

With her book "Why Love Hurts", Israeli sociologist Eva Illouz scored a bestselling success in 2012, establishing herself as an interpreter of modern romantic relationships and demonstrating the deficiencies of love in the era of capitalism. One of these deficiencies is that our fear of overlooking a potentially superior partner prevents us from committing to a steady relationship in the first place. In her new book, "Why Love Ends", the sociologist examines how romantic relationships go wrong, resulting in a new "culture of lovelessness." On the following pages Eva Illouz is in conversation with Barbara Bleisch, a philosopher and moderates the program "Sternstunde Philosopie" since many years.

Barbara Bleisch: Your latest book is titled "Why Love Ends". Does every love necessarily have to end?

Eva Illouz: Of course not. Many loves won't. But more and more love does end. It has become a regular feature of our lives, and so the question is, why?

BB: That's it, love is in danger because our circumstances have changed. Maybe we can first address how our romantic relationships have changed when it comes to options of separating. You show how it used to be the economic model which kept partners together, basically exchanging love for money. Men were only able to experience sexuality within a steady relationship, while women needed a steady partner to guarantee economic security. Whereas nowadays, we have love based on romance, with the freedom to leave one another. Is this a progress?

EI: Of course it is a progress. But progress does not mean that things become easier, or that we are necessarily happier. So in previous, let's say "traditional" societies, divorce was much more difficult and there was no choice pursuing such an option, mostly for women, but also for men. So, the capacity to choose a partner has now been coupled with the capacity to "un-choose". Today it's quite simple to back out of a relationship, if one wishes to. So the price we pay for having a greater choice, is that we become the objects of somebody else's un-choice, and that we ourselves exert our ability to un-choose others.

BB: So this means more autonomy doesn't necessarily lead to more happiness?

EI: Yes, that is exactly what I said and I think often people confuse the two. This is the reason why mostly conservative people criticize contemporary society and liberal norms. They do observe that increased freedom does not lead to a greater happiness. But I think we need to make a choice, and we have made it collectively, namely whether we prefer being

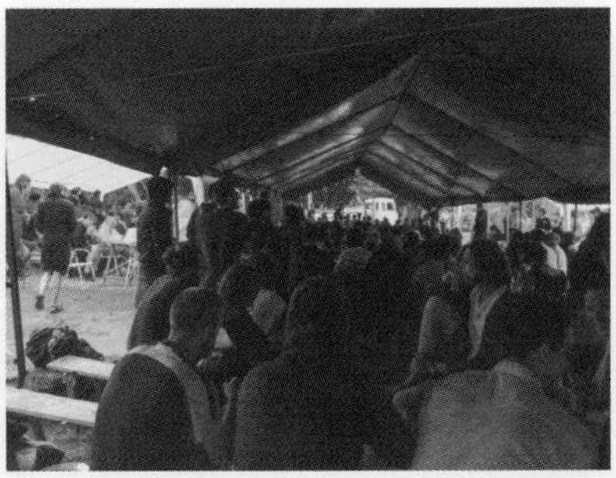

happier or freer. I think that we prefer to be free even if it brings less—I wouldn't say happiness, but a lesser feeling of well-being. I don't think we are well equipped as individuals to live on our own, to live outside strong communities, but I think that communities are yet to prove themselves. Community structures are mostly oppressive of women, they're also fearful of strangers. So, in my opinion, the price to be paid for freedom, is greater morality. That is, more equality between men and women, and more equality between members of and strangers to a community.

I Know What You Did Last Summer (France, 2013), 2013

BB: Which brings us to different separation narratives that you describe (in your book). One of which is what you would call an "epiphany", where someone gets the sudden feeling or states retrospectively: "The scales fell from my eyes." It's like this in life, that we explain things to ourselves in hindsight. Especially when it comes to the breaks in life, we like to retell them with our own narrative in order for them to make sense to us, because we don't want to go through life randomly, but want to make sense of our own actions.

EI: Yes, that would be the epiphany. It's falling in love in reverse. In the same way that some people quite simply fall in love at first sight; they look at someone and know that they are meant to be together. I would call it the narrative of unloving, or "the narrative of falling in love in reverse" one in which you come to the sudden realization that you no longer love your partner.

BB: Which brings us to the term "negative relationship". You show quite clearly that the problem with negative relationships isn't the eventual separation, but the fact that a negative relationship is one that never actually started properly. According to you, we've lost the ability to enter a "proper relationship", meaning there's no need for "proper separation", since said relationship never actually started. Could you explain how you define this understanding of a negative relationship?

EI: The word "negative" has a long philosophical history. I will not go over that history but let me say simply that I use two meanings from the phenomenological traditions; one I would say comes from the Sartrean understanding of consciousness as being indeterminate. That means, in a way, we don't have any attributes. It's why we're free. Indeterminateness actually means that we don't know what we want because we don't know who we are—that is the condition of freedom. It's a condition that is both great and anxiety inducing. The second tradition also stems from phenomenology, but differs slightly. The Heideggerian model concerns what happens when what you normally do breaks down. So when something ceases to function down, you're compelled to pay sudden attention to what it is that you're doing even if a second ago, it was completely routine and you did not give it a second thought. In a way psychology—I mean clinical psychology—compels us to pay attention to the lurking, constant risk of our relationships breaking down, and to the reasons as to why our relationships have broken down. These are the two meanings of "negative" I used in the book. As you rightly suggested, one of the book's main claims is that the forces making it difficult to enter into relationships are the same forces at work when long-term relationships crumble.

BB: The interconnection of emotional worlds and market relationships as part of a large-scale project you've established. You've analysed this connection for 20 years. In your dissertation "Consuming the Romantic Utopia", you already looked at Romanticism and capitalism, love and commodity, how they interact with each other and how they corrupt each other. Then came "Why love Hurts" and now "When Love Ends". You keep coming back to this connection. What makes you, as a sociologist, focus on the world of love in relation to the world of capitalism?

EI: I would say that the questions of the nature of modernity—what does it mean to be modern, what does it mean to have a capitalist economy and what does it mean to live in societies where individuals are separated—are the main sociological questions. I focus on love because traditionally speaking, love is associated with a woman's fear, and because sociologists, until quite recently when the sociological canon was still mostly masculine, thought love didn't belong to sociology. The point of my research agenda is to show that this feeling that is seemingly universal, personal and individual actually undergoes constant change and transformation, particularly under the influence of capitalism. The worlds of feeling and economics are traditionally thought of as being opposing, but I think this is more a question of ideological belief than of empirical fact.

So, for example, women and men have always considered finance when deliberating a prospective relationship. Whether or not it is actively acknowledged, money, status and education play very significant roles in determining who we choose to fall in love with and share our lives with. For me, the question is about what

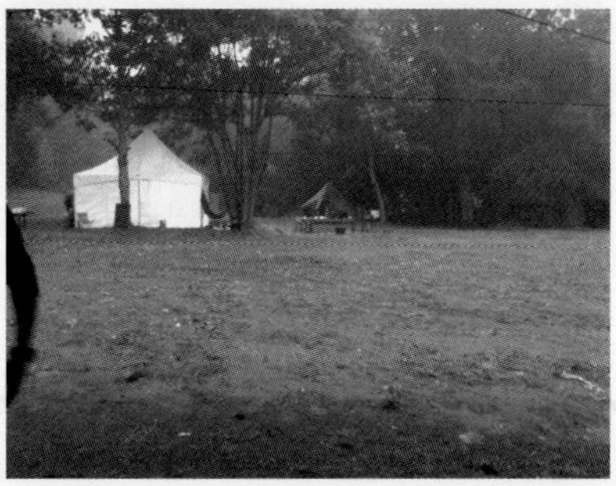

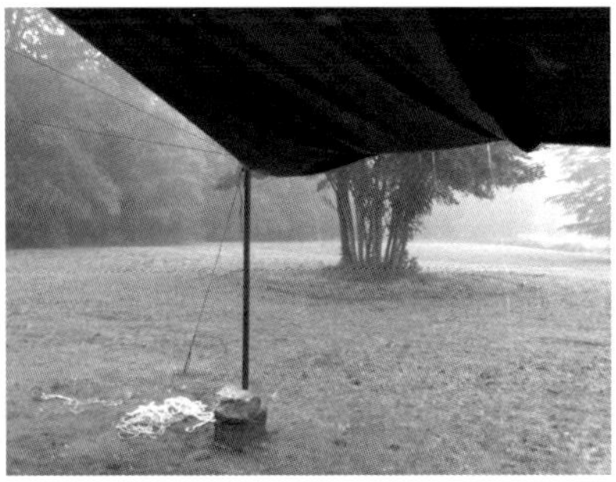

happens now that families are no longer responsible for matchmaking. What happens now that the family unit is no longer a person's primary economic concern, since we now work in a capitalist market? What happens to romantic sentiments, now that romantic love is the main object, theme and target of vast consumer markets, as it has been since the early twentieth century?

BB: On the one hand, our romantic relationships have changed to the extent that the majority of them are negative ones, relationships that don't even start properly, a multitude of very fleeting relationships, based largely on hedonism. It's all about getting what yourself are hoping for, as opposed to opening up to the other person. But at the same time, we're still hoping for the great, one and only love?

EI: We have different tendencies in our culture. Modern cultures are supremely contradictory; I would say that it is in fact these contradictions that define what it means to be a modern human being. We aspire for security and stability, whilst simultaneously seeking excitement, a sense of freedom and autonomy. This dichotomy keeps us moving and in a way, I would also argue that its what keeps the economy moving too. We're attempting to reconcile this contradiction so that romantic, utopic love does not disappear from contemporary culture. On the contrary. I think our culture has never been as obsessed with romantic love as it is presently. The couple is a substitute for community and family. It's because today, once individuals reach adulthood, they are thrown into a highly competitive society in which the future is highly uncertain. Not to mention the economy, which hardly accommodates young, single adults trying to make ends meet. So, really there are many good reasons—psychological, emotional and economic —to make the couple the necessary unit to allow people to lead a life of stability, to have an emotional basis for recognition, and for the validation of oneself. But at the same time, there are many factors working to undermine the ideal of the finding your "one-and-only". This is why we go visit psychologists. This is why we consume self-help books. This is why we watch pornography. All of these tensions and contradictions are the gateway to enormous consumption.

BB: I love listening to you because, unlike most other people, you force me to accept that things are complex. You keep saying, "on the one hand... on the other hand..." "There are pros and cons, we must observe before we judge." I find this both incredibly challenging and also fascinating. Listening to you, I wonder if there is an aspect among these matters of love where you would say you've exhausted applying a complex balanced view, and it's clear beyond any doubt that something's very wrong there?

EI: I think that what is wrong is that there are two imperatives. There is one of production, economic production, and one of reproduction. Reproduction means biological reproduction. Societies need to reproduce. Capitalism undermines reproduction, and this is what we need to understand. I think many people understand that a contradiction between production and reproduction exists. Increasing amounts of people are living alone, and less people are having children. This has created a so-called "reproduction crisis". This isn't a crisis provoked of women's movements, feminism or freedom as such; it's provoked by the conditions of life in late capitalism.

BB: Another aspect you point out is that the old feminist proposition actually holds true, which is that the personal is political. Our matters of love are deeply permeated by economic and political circumstances. This begs the question what happened to the feminist movement when the female image perpetuated by the advertising and porn industries is this sexist. Did the feminist movement, the female revolution, come unstuck about half way through or what happened there?

EI: I think that what has happened is that, when you own almost all the infrastructure of society, the economy, the military, the culture, now I'm talking about men, it is almost impossible to really change the structure of domination. So let's not forget that despite the considerable gains and advances that women have made and they have made these advances only thanks to feminists to struggle for them, for all of women; despite this, most of the social infrastructure in politics, the military, the economics, the religion and the courts has remained in the hands of men. If that is the case, I think even when you put out there an emancipatory ideology, and an emancipatory idea, it is very easily recuperated by forces that are more powerful than you. This is what happened I think to the idea of sexual freedom for example, feminism has been hijacked by capitalist industries.

BB: In closing, I'd like to talk about a more recent phenomenon, which is that men also suffer from this new kind of romantic relationship. There are men organising themselves online as so-called "incels", which is short for "involuntary celibates". They're a group

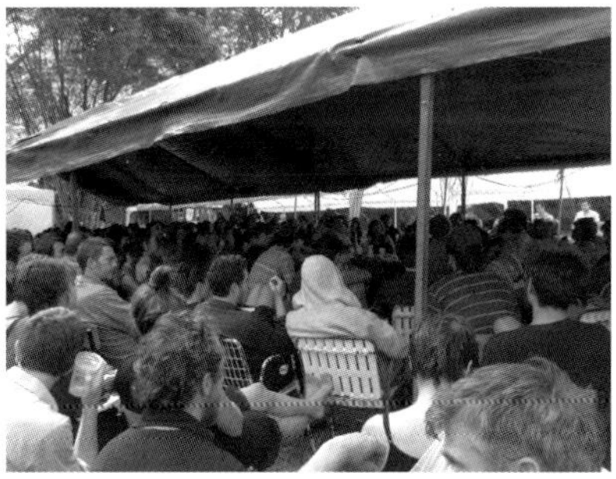

of men probably first highlighted by Michel Houellebecq, men in a hyper- sexualised world who feel they're losing out by not finding a partner. They organise themselves online in an aggressively sexist manner, demanding that women should be forced into monogamy so that there's one woman for each man. Are these men also a result of capitalism?

EI: Well, first of all they are an effect of the change of patriarchal structure. So we have now different 'if you want' modes of domination that are competing with each other. Their patriarchy is contested by women and whereas most men in the past could have an easy access to the body of women, I think that access is much more scrutinized and regulated. So, what they are reacting to is a slight change to males privilege and easy and unproblematic access to women. But also what capitalism has changed is that men and women heterosexuals now meet each other as if on a market, it has marketized heterosexual relationships. That is: a market is governed by the law of supply and demand, it's not regulated by families or by communities which try to match up couples. In the sexual new liberalism, the market has the effect of making some people less successful, less in demand and therefore they are left out, they are left out of the competition and so they do react to this marketization of heterosexual relationships and the loss of male privilege.

BB: Market mechanisms will always create losers, and this is one of the effects. If we could finally get back to the subject of romantic love, as someone who's researched love for 20 years. Why would you say it's still worth searching for the one partner or at least a stable relationship, if love hurts and if love ends?

EI: Well, first of all I never said that it's worthwhile. I think it is worthwhile developing meaningful relationships but meaningful relationships are not necessarily romantic relationships or sexual relationships. So if there is one thing I would like to do in my studies, it is to definitely enlarge our field of vision and have a much broader conception of what a meaningful relationship is which can be inspired by friendship, it can be inspired by the care for others, it can be inspired by the love of children. I would want us to widen our imagination and to see our lives as having many more possibilities of extremely meaningful bonds than the idea of romantic love. The idea of romantic love creates very narrow paths for human development and human fraternity in brotherhood or sorority and sisterhood.

BB: Is this also why you dedicated this book to your family members? It's dedicated to "siblings, mother and children".

EI: I think the family today is the only non-capitalist institution in the sense that it is the only institution you do not really choose, and so that's why, for me, the family has become so interesting. In a world in which one chooses how to present oneself, the haircut, what to eat, et cetera, we don't make autonomous choices regarding our families. It means the family becomes a unit of enormous learning and growing. It's a place where we quite simply have to live with what's been given to us. That's why I find it so interesting, and why I call it a non-capitalist, non-modern place. The family is the sole remnant of traditional society in modern times.

The conversation "Why Love Ends" is an abridged transcript of Barbara Bleisch's conversation with sociologist Eva Illouz from the television programme "Sternstunde Philosophie" which aired on March 17, 2019. The programme is broadcasted each Sunday morning at 11a.m. on SRF 1 and is also available online on https://www.srf.ch/play/tv/sendung/sternstunde-philosophie?id=b7705a5d-4b68-4cb1-9404-03932cd8d569

Notes

WHY LOVE HURTS

Letter to

Eva Illouz

Dear Eva,

I just listened to the conversation between yourself and Barbara Bleisch, and it prompted me to write you this letter. I'm sure you won't have time to answer the questions I'm trying to formulate here, but anyway, I wanted to send you this letter—even if only for the sake of writing.

We met and spoke—briefly—a few years ago following a talk of yours in a small, rural village in France. The name of the village started with a "T", and it was host to the three-day camp where you spoke. That was in 2013. I took note of the fact that many of the audience's questions about your book, *Why Love Hurts* (2012), aimed to reveal the formula as to how to love in the twenty-first century. You were surrounded by a group of young, hungry and willing twenty-somethings, eager to change both themselves and the society we live in. You're a sociologist —you observe and analyse—but you clearly aren't writing self-help books. How do you feel about this desperate situation?

When viewed from certain perspectives, philosophy, sociology, and the fine arts are areas of interest pursued without necessarily tangible goals— aside of those that are self-determined. Yet, much like love, art has become instrumentalized by capitalism. In your opinion, what social developments have had an impact upon your field of research and work? I'm not talking about changes in academia, but more about the duty we have to accommodate and transform the "weapons" of science.

During your conversation with Bleisch, you mentioned that the traditional family is one of the last zones yet to be capitalized upon. Though children cannot choose their parents, parents can choose their children, and are doing so increasingly. In queer circles, concepts of kinship and family are being redefined—think of the 'houses' in Ballroom culture. Why? Is this restricted to people falling out of the nuclear family canon, or creating new models out of desire and necessity? But according to your comment, it makes these people out to be forerunners of a neoliberal family model based on choice. I have no direct "question" regarding this topic, rather thoughts. I see your point regarding the traditional family as an escape from capitalism and a society based on making "choices", but then again this is exactly the heteronormative model based on all possible forms of reproduction.

I guess none of these issues can be solved; that is, as you say, how our times are defined in this state of constant flux and contradiction. The contemporary human is a living contradiction. Rainer Werner Fassbinder featured the following quote in the prelude of his 1974 film, *Effi Briest*, "Many people are aware of their own capabilities and needs, yet acquiesce to the prevailing system in their thoughts and deeds, thereby confirming and reinforcing the system."

Nuns and sex workers separate love and sex. Nuns are required by the church to abstain, whilst at the same time loving unconditionally. We understand, on the other hand, that sex workers needn't have a loving connection with their clients in order to work. At what point in the history of Western society were love and sex intrinsically linked? Do you know?

Here is something from my side, something you might like. Are you aware of Swiss feminist, activist, writer, and sex-worker Grisélidis Réal (1929–2005)? She studied art in her youth and is buried in Geneva. Besides being a sex worker, she was also a feminist and activist who published her own books. At one point she published "The Little Black Book"—an index of her clients, their sexual preferences, and her rates. This black book, initially written to help her to remember her clients needs and details, created a small scandal when published. The power of publishing and fiction! Is imagination what we are missing?

All the best,

PROVENCE
April 2019

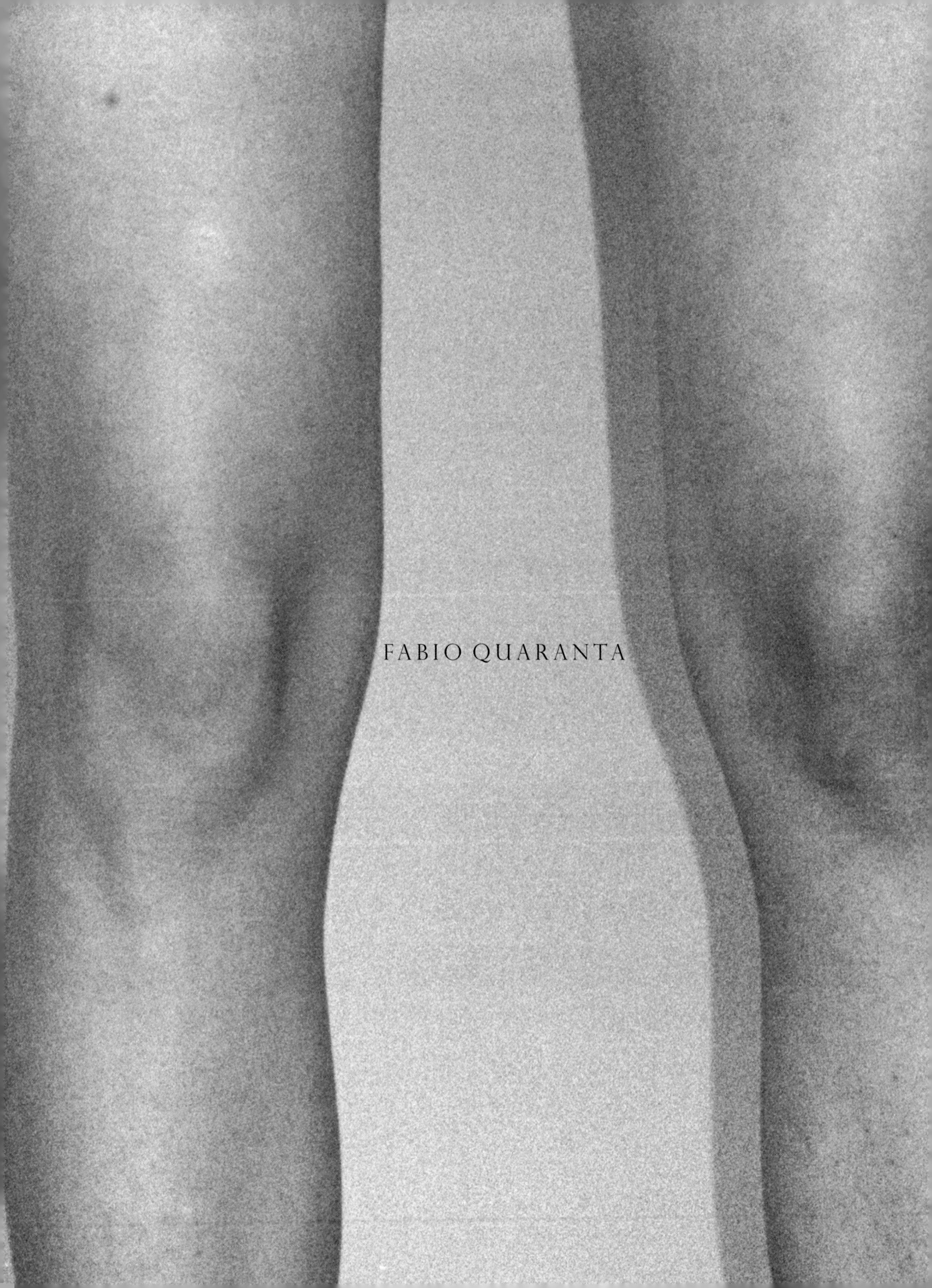
FABIO QUARANTA

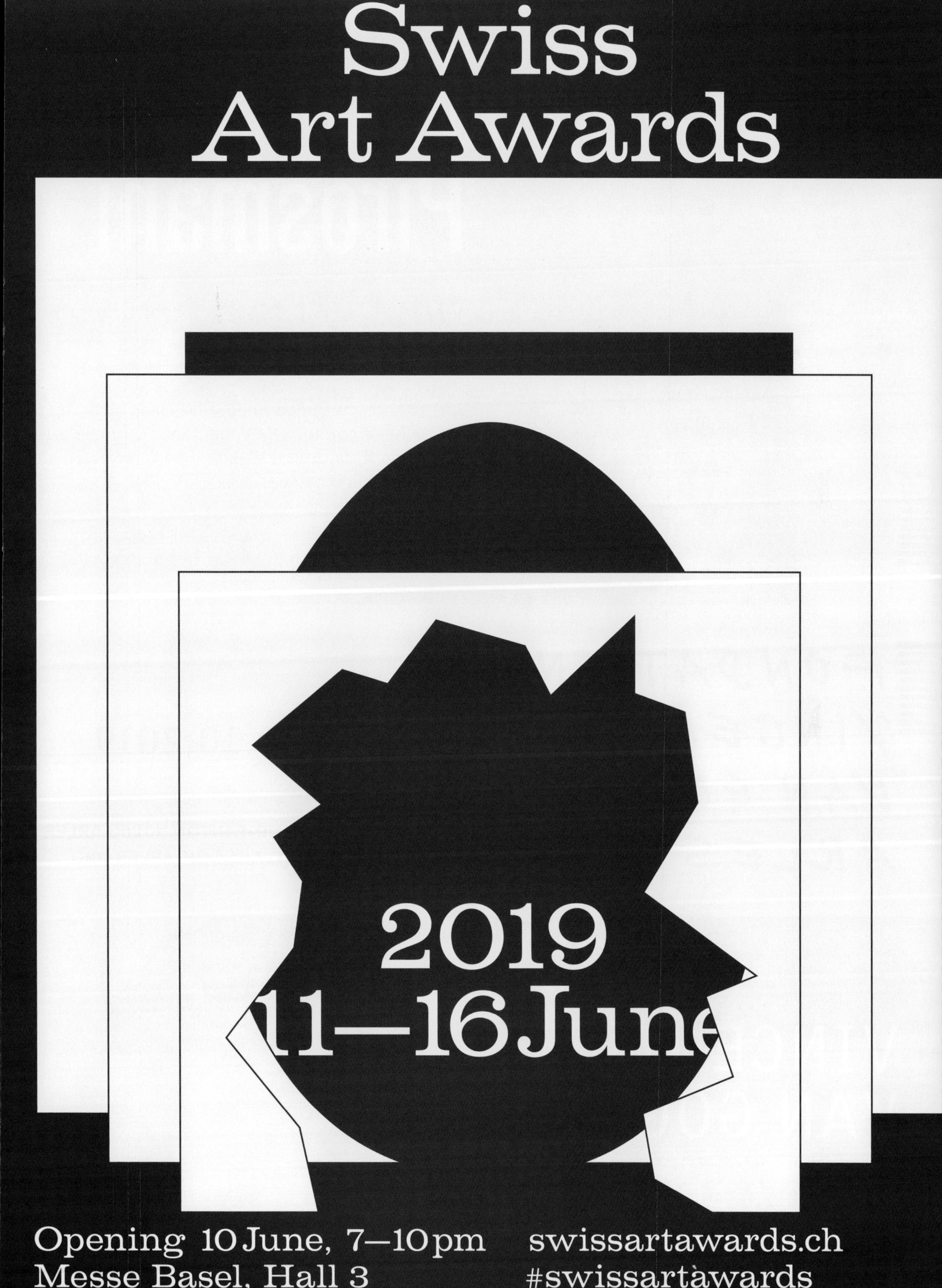
Swiss
Art Awards
2019
11—16 June
Opening 10 June, 7—10 pm
Messe Basel, Hall 3
swissartawards.ch
#swissartawards

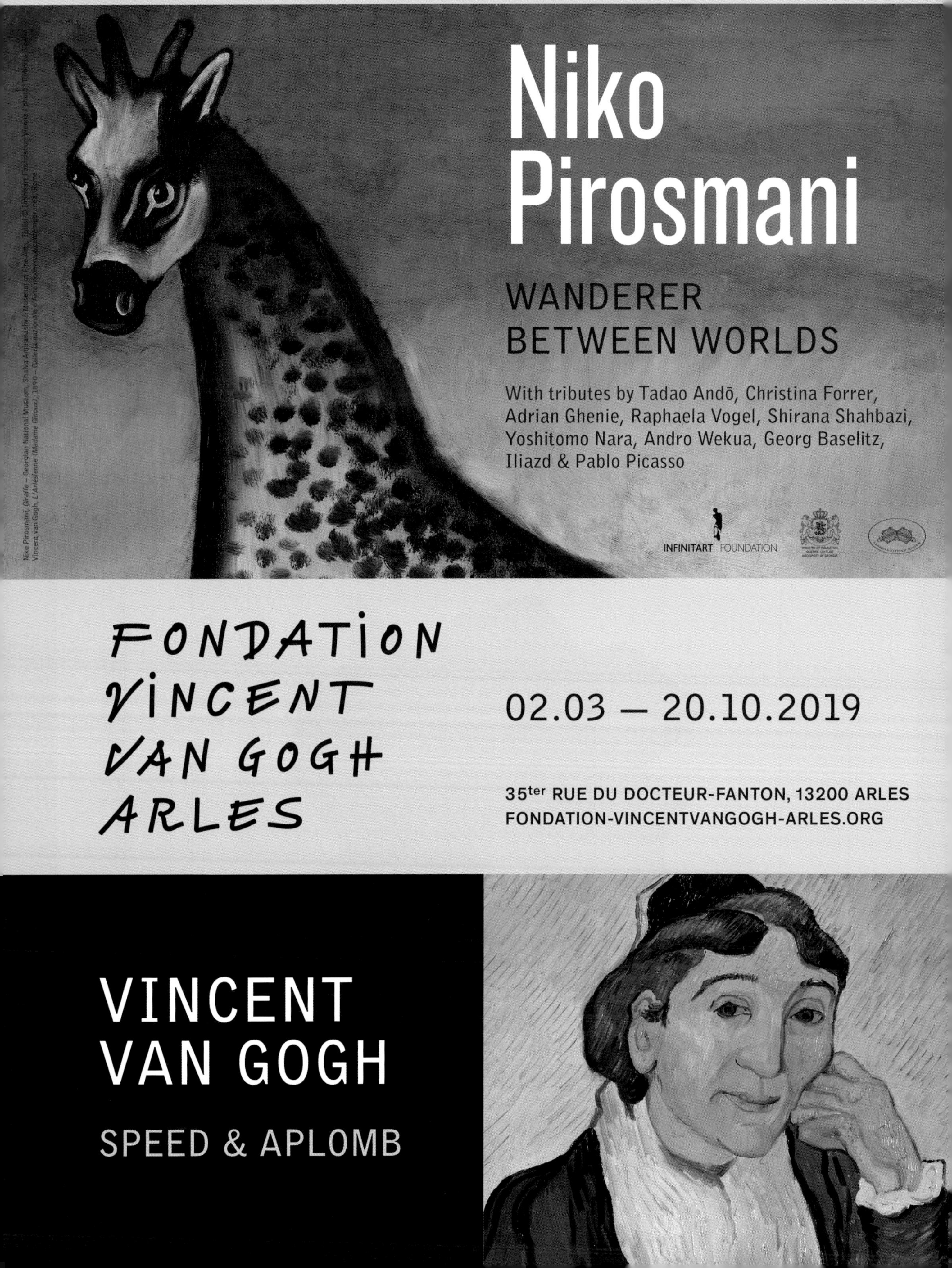
Niko
Pirosmani
WANDERER
BETWEEN WORLDS
With tributes by Tadao Andō, Christina Forrer, Adrian Ghenie, Raphaela Vogel, Shirana Shahbazi, Yoshitomo Nara, Andro Wekua, Georg Baselitz, Iliazd & Pablo Picasso
INFINITART FOUNDATION
FONDATION
VINCENT
VAN GOGH
ARLES
02.03 – 20.10.2019
35ter RUE DU DOCTEUR-FANTON, 13200 ARLES
FONDATION-VINCENTVANGOGH-ARLES.ORG
VINCENT
VAN GOGH
SPEED & APLOMB
Niko Pirosmani, Giraffe – Georgian National Museum, Shalva Amiranashvili Museum of Fine Arts, Tbilisi © Infinitart Foundation Vienna | photo: Roberto Rinaldi
Vincent van Gogh, L'Arlésienne (Madame Ginoux), 1890 – Galleria nazionale d'Arte moderna e contemporanea, Rome

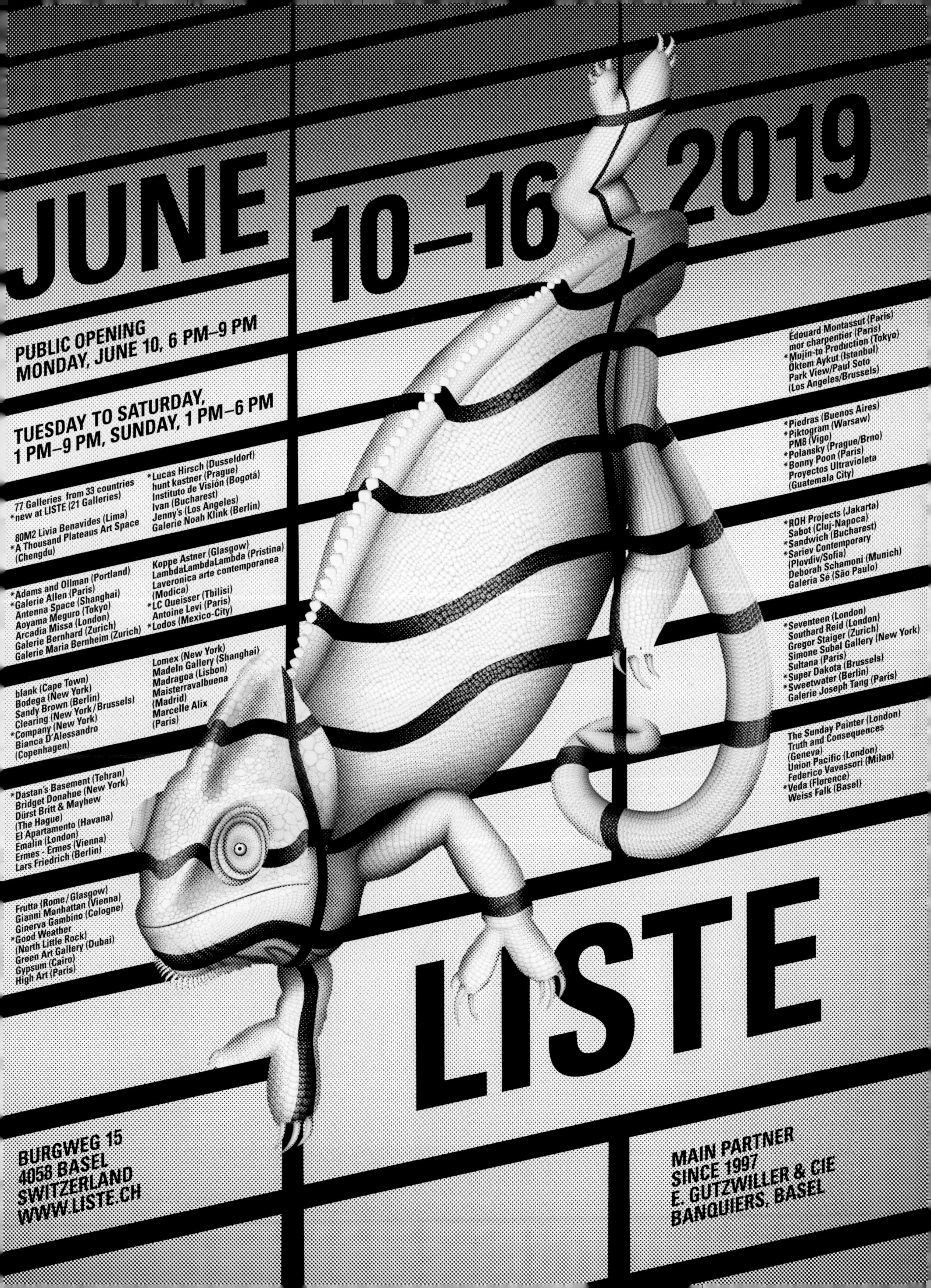
JUNE 10–16 2019
PUBLIC OPENING
MONDAY, JUNE 10, 6 PM–9 PM
TUESDAY TO SATURDAY,
1 PM–9 PM, SUNDAY, 1 PM–6 PM
77 Galleries from 33 countries
*new at LISTE (21 Galleries)
80M2 Livia Benavides (Lima)
*A Thousand Plateaus Art Space (Chengdu)
*Adams and Ollman (Portland)
*Galerie Allen (Paris)
Antenna Space (Shanghai)
Aoyama Meguro (Tokyo)
Arcadia Missa (London)
Galerie Bernhard (Zurich)
Galerie Maria Bernheim (Zurich)
blank (Cape Town)
Bodega (New York)
Sandy Brown (Berlin)
Clearing (New York/Brussels)
*Company (New York)
Bianca D'Alessandro (Copenhagen)
*Dastan's Basement (Tehran)
Bridget Donahue (New York)
Dürst Britt & Mayhew (The Hague)
El Apartamento (Havana)
Emalin (London)
Ermes - Ermes (Vienna)
Lars Friedrich (Berlin)
Frutta (Rome/Glasgow)
Gianni Manhattan (Vienna)
Ginerva Gambino (Cologne)
*Good Weather (North Little Rock)
Green Art Gallery (Dubai)
Gypsum (Cairo)
High Art (Paris)
*Lucas Hirsch (Dusseldorf)
hunt kastner (Prague)
Instituto de Visión (Bogotá)
Ivan (Bucharest)
Jenny's (Los Angeles)
Galerie Noah Klink (Berlin)
Koppe Astner (Glasgow)
LambdaLambdaLambda (Pristina)
Laveronica arte contemporanea (Modica)
*LC Queisser (Tbilisi)
Antoine Levi (Paris)
*Lodos (Mexico-City)
Lomex (New York)
Madeln Gallery (Shanghai)
Madragoa (Lisbon)
Maisterravalbuena (Madrid)
Marcelle Alix (Paris)
Édouard Montassut (Paris)
mor charpentier (Paris)
*Mujin-to Production (Tokyo)
Öktem Aykut (Istanbul)
Park View/Paul Soto (Los Angeles/Brussels)
*Piedras (Buenos Aires)
*Piktogram (Warsaw)
PM8 (Vigo)
*Polansky (Prague/Brno)
*Bonny Poon (Paris)
Proyectos Ultravioleta (Guatemala City)
*ROH Projects (Jakarta)
Sabot (Cluj-Napoca)
*Sandwich (Bucharest)
*Sariev Contemporary (Plovdiv/Sofia)
Deborah Schamoni (Munich)
Galeria Sé (São Paulo)
*Seventeen (London)
Southard Reid (London)
Gregor Staiger (Zurich)
Simone Subal Gallery (New York)
Sultana (Paris)
*Super Dakota (Brussels)
*Sweetwater (Berlin)
Galerie Joseph Tang (Paris)
The Sunday Painter (London)
Truth and Consequences (Geneva)
Union Pacific (London)
Federico Vavassori (Milan)
*Veda (Florence)
Weiss Falk (Basel)
LISTE
BURGWEG 15
4058 BASEL
SWITZERLAND
WWW.LISTE.CH
MAIN PARTNER
SINCE 1997
E. GUTZWILLER & CIE
BANQUIERS, BASEL

ラ・メゾン・デ・ランデブー

ラムダラムダラムダ
ルル
ミサコアンドローゼン
パーク・ビュー・ポール・ソト

http://www.lamaisonderendezvous.com

30.06.–30.11.2019
PAX
Bea Schlingelhoff

Off Kunsthaus Glarus
Museum des Landes Glarus Freulerpalast
www.kunsthausglarus.ch

Midway
Contemporary
Art

Loretta Fahrenholz
Hans-Christian Lotz

June
Basel, Switzerland
June 10–14, 2019

www.midwayart.org

BERGEN KUNSTHALL

THE FESTIVAL EXHIBITION
MARI SLAATTELID
KYSTVERKET
23. 5. – 11. 8. 2019

JILL JOHNSTON, THE DISINTEGRATION OF A CRITIC
23. 5. – 11. 8. 2019

WWW.KUNSTHALL.NO

Christian Andersen, Bispevej 29, 2400, Copenhagen NV, +45 25374101, info@christianandersen.net
Lina Viste Grønli, Julia Haller, Lasse Schmidt Hansen, Benjamin Hirte, Tom Humphreys, Hans-Christian Lotz, Sven Loven, Morten Skrøder Lund, Carl Mannov, Till Megerle, Shelly Nadashi, Rolf Nowotny, Astrid Svangren

June, Basel, 10–14 June: Hans-Christian Lotz

Jenny's

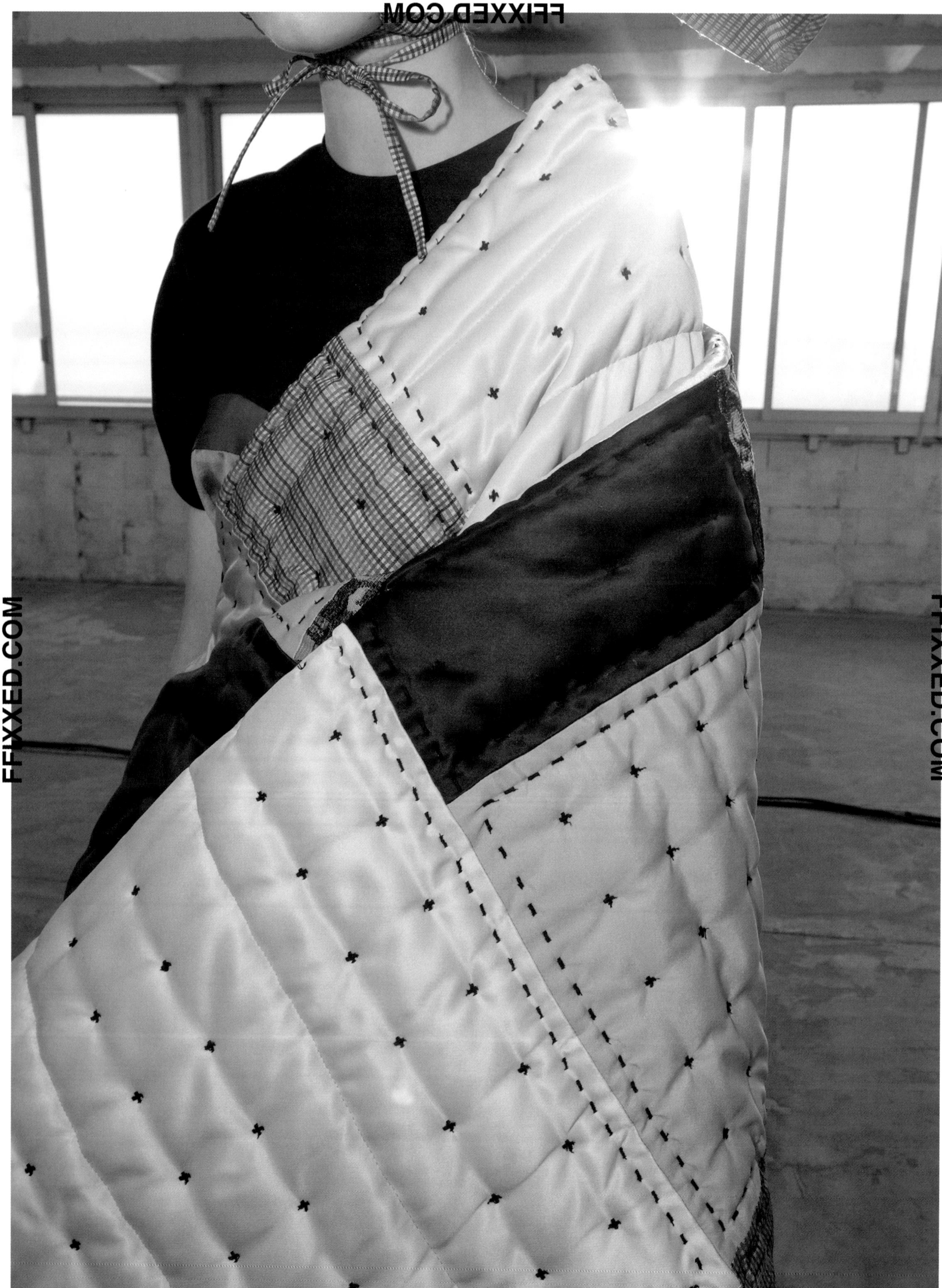

FFIXXED.COM
FFIXXED.COM
FFIXXED.COM
FFIXXED.COM

FASHION

FASHION NOVA

Photography	Marc Asekhame
Styling	Ursina Gysi
Model	Karina Zharmukhambetova

Marc and Ursina produced an editorial exclusively using clothes from the fashion entity famous for manufacturing replicas at incredible speed, Fashion Nova. The brand produces counterfeit designer outfits, growing through social media with the garnered support of influencers such as Kylie Jenner, Cardi B, and Amber Rose, by issuing cheap copies of their looks. They operate with the understanding that iconic influencers function like institutions—anything you put them in becomes fashionable. Both highly valuable and universally affordable, Fashion Nova sell a meagre taste of fame along with their wares. Fashion Nova capitalised upon the quality of big fashion houses and the creative value they retain, whilst relying on image-making and online viral culture to launch said replicas to stardom. Somehow, it's wildly ironic. By appropriating the creative value of the biggest fashion houses and cross-curating this with savvy communication strategies, Fashion Nova has managed to build a reputation that rivals some of the major fashion houses themselves, becoming one of the most searched fashion brands alongside Gucci, Louis Vuitton, Supreme and Chanel.

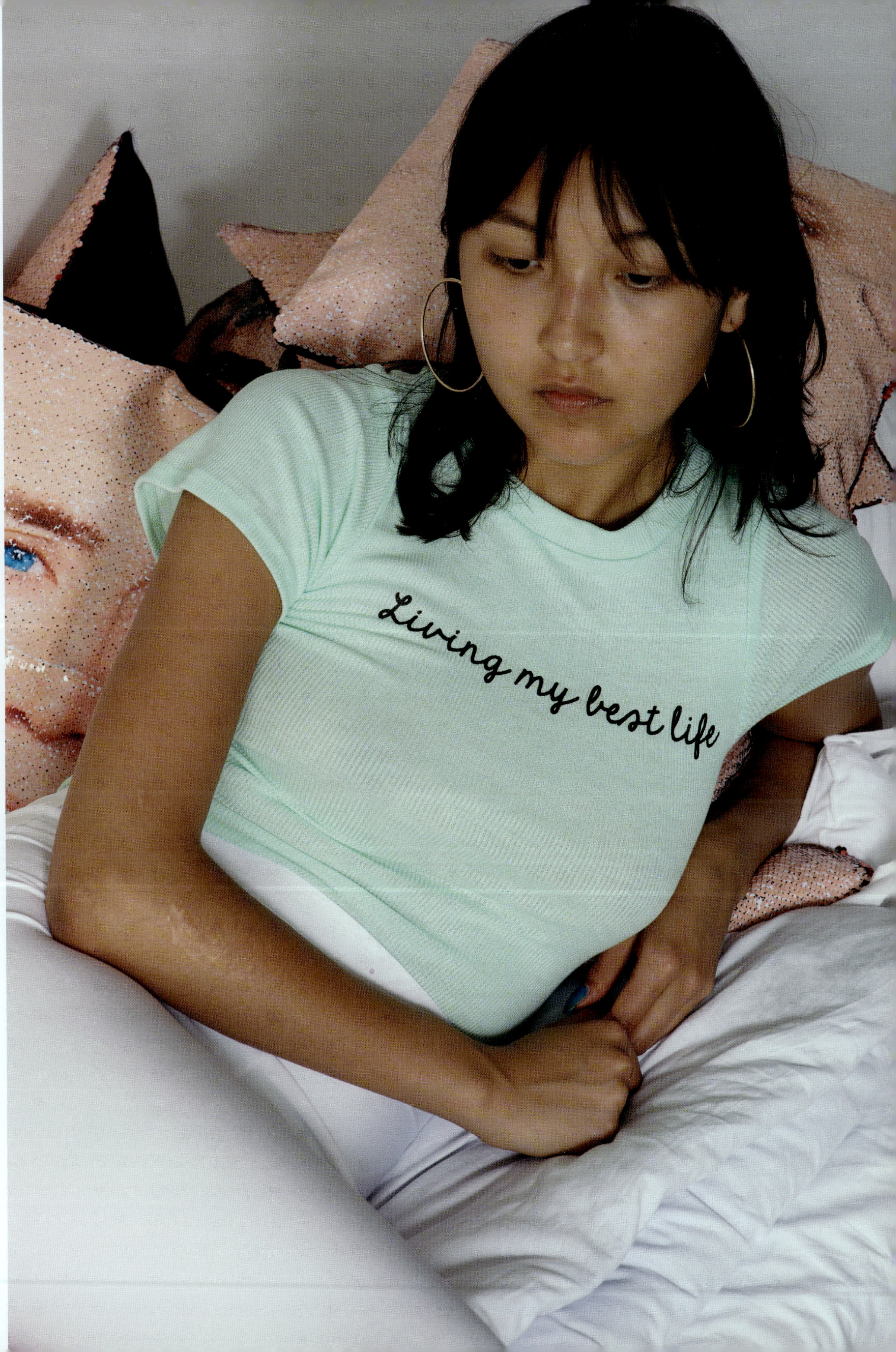

Living my best life bodysuit, Fashion Nova exclusive legging

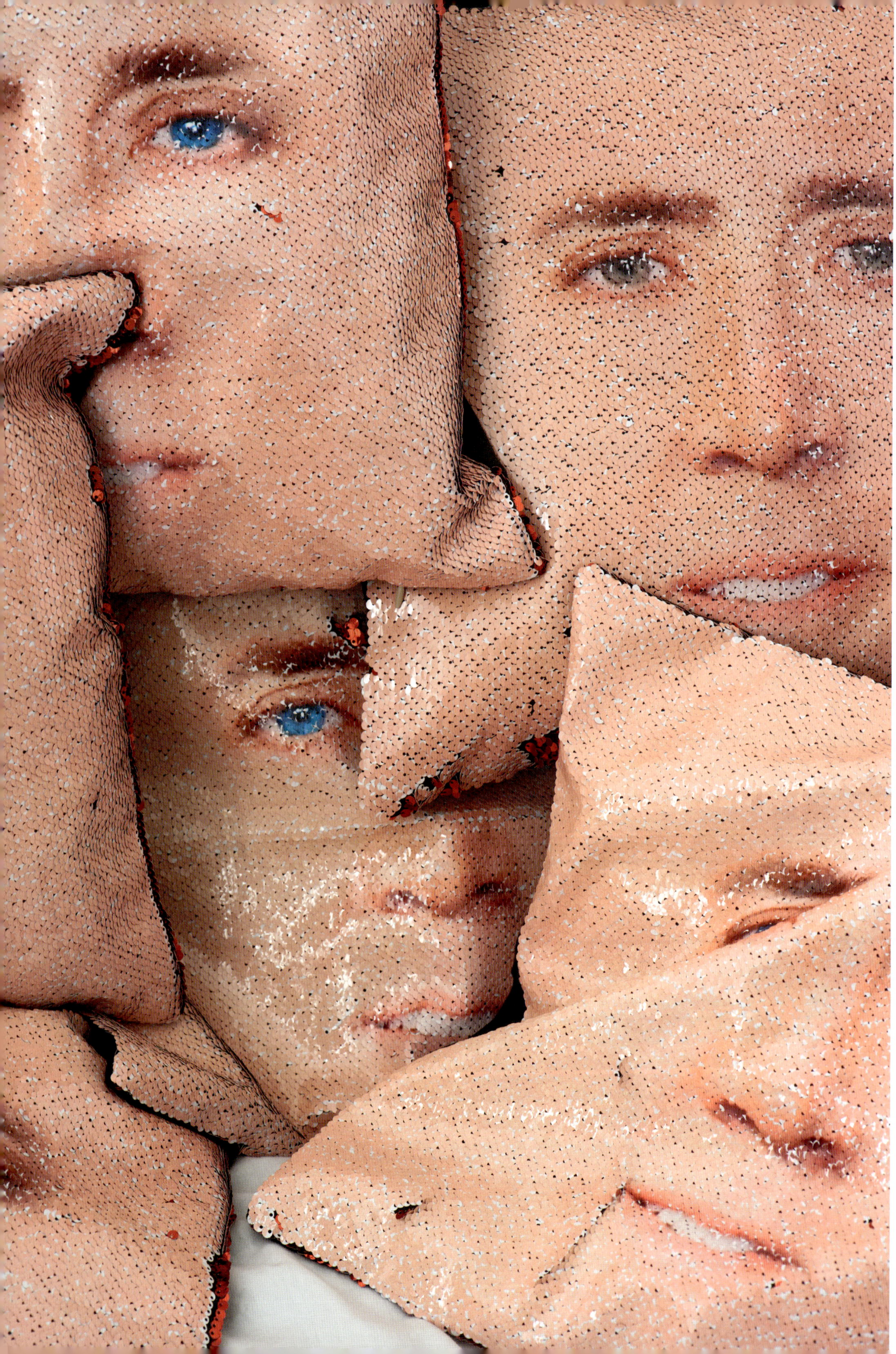

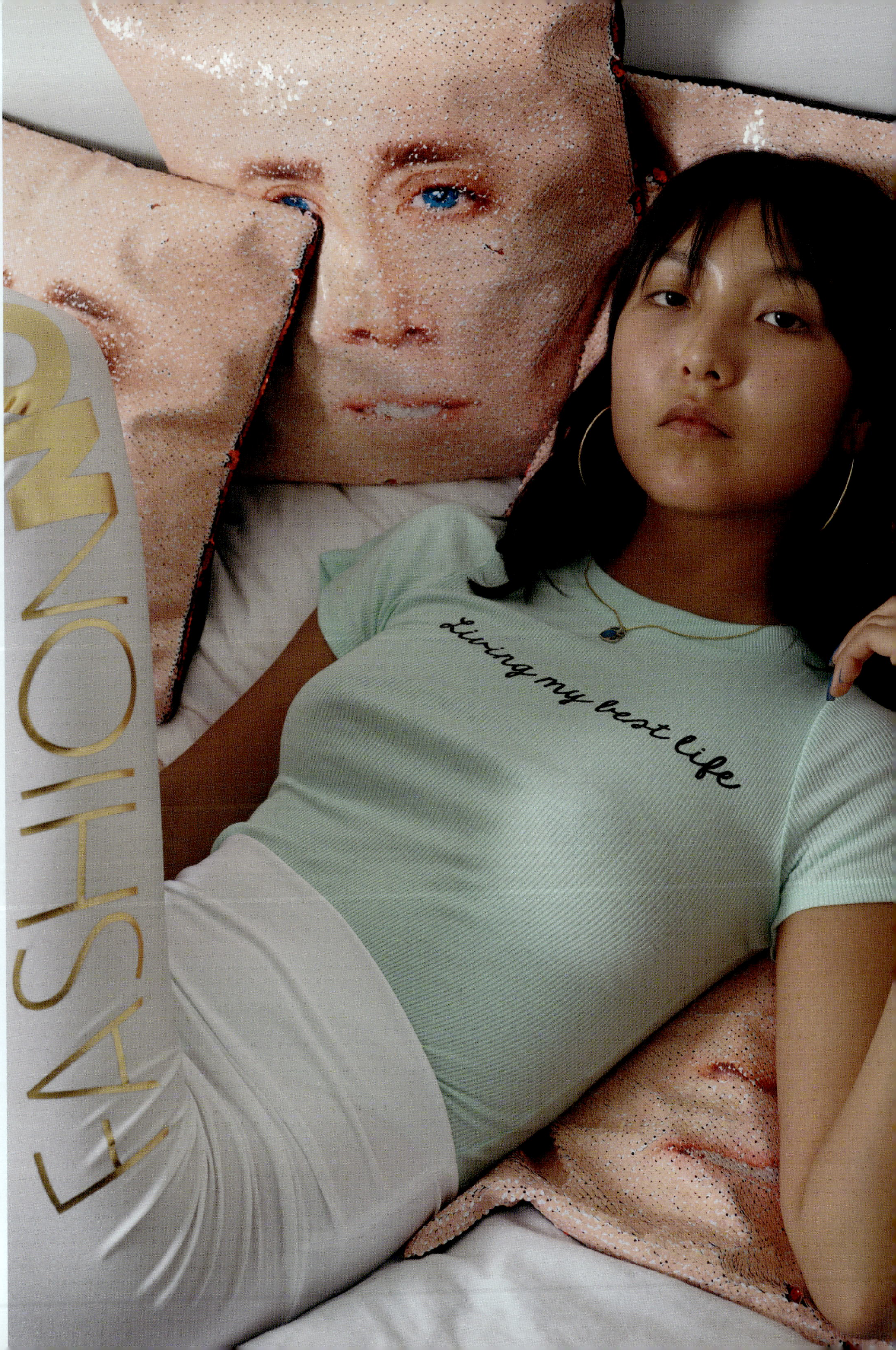

Living my best life bodysuit, Fashion Nova exclusive legging
Overleaf: *Brush your shoulders off* velvet Capri set

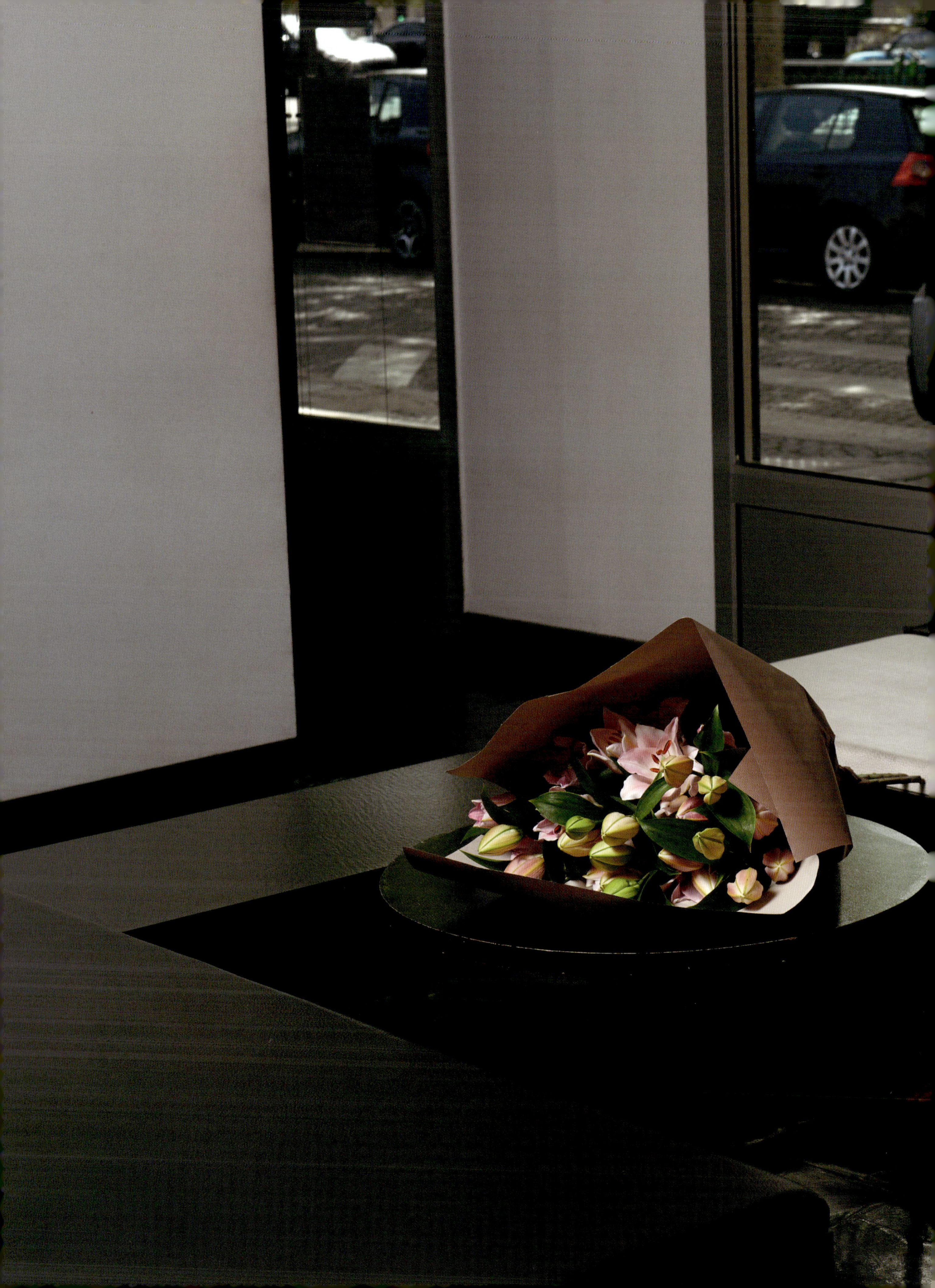

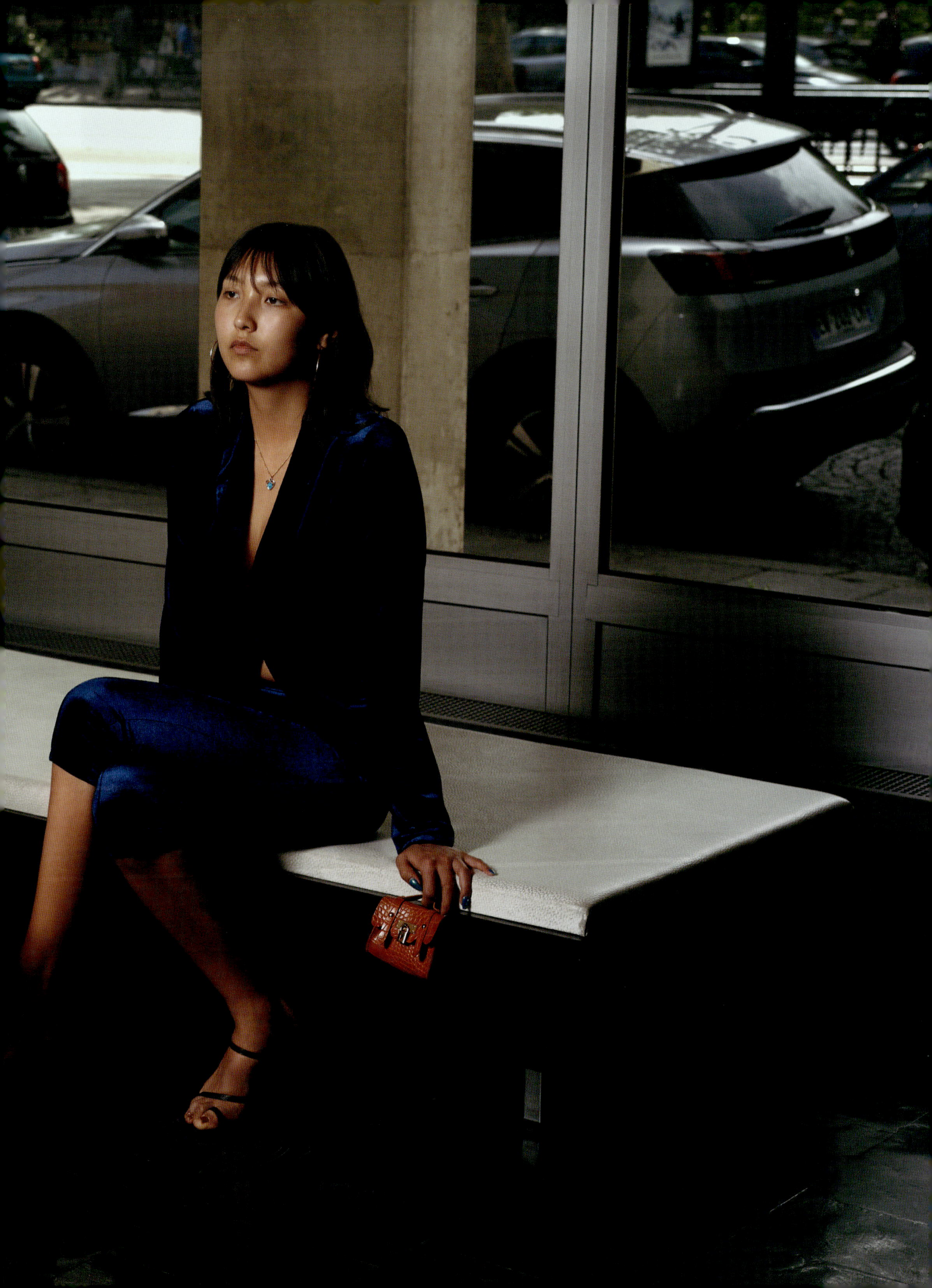

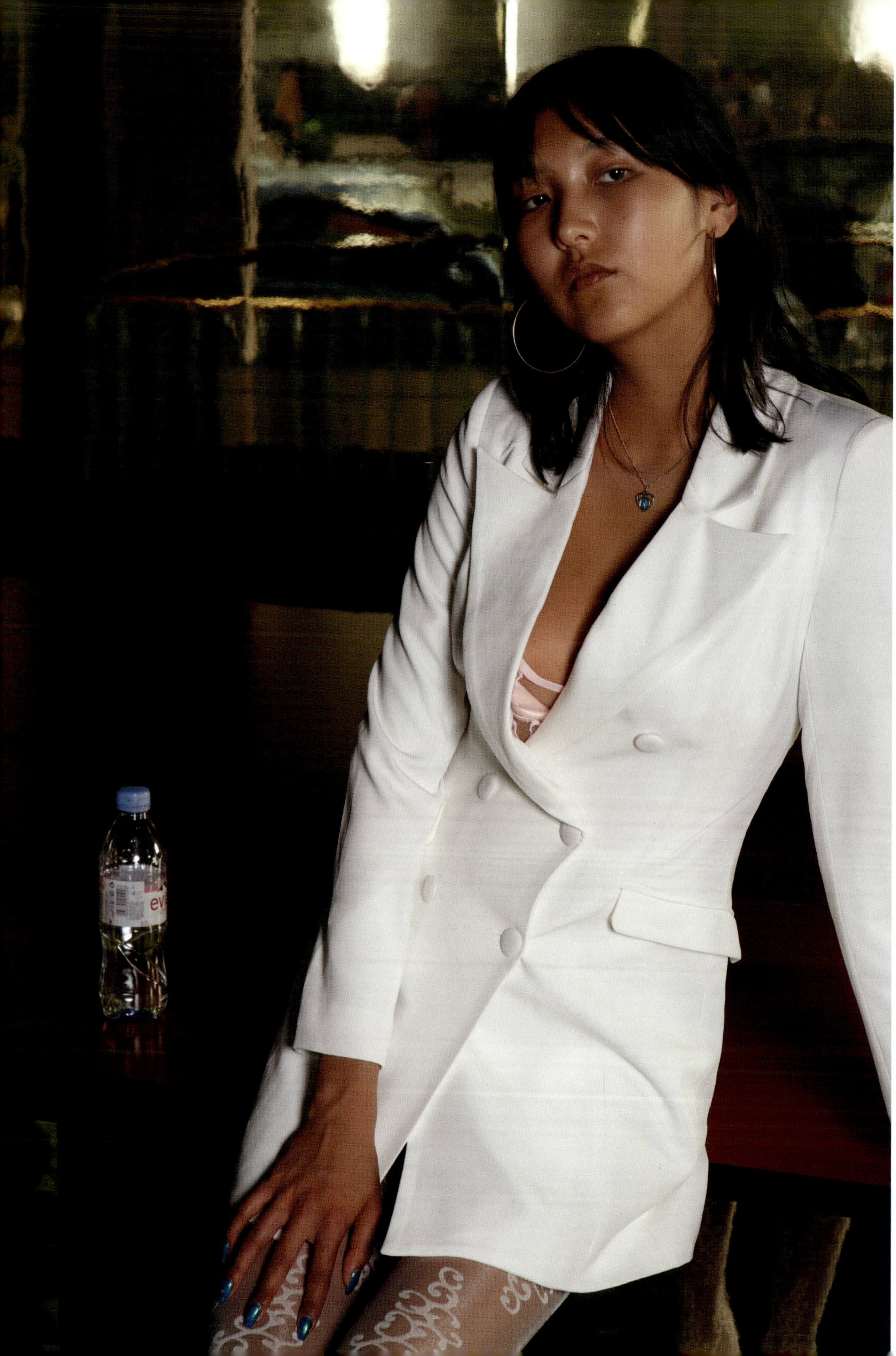

Sophisticated women blazer dress

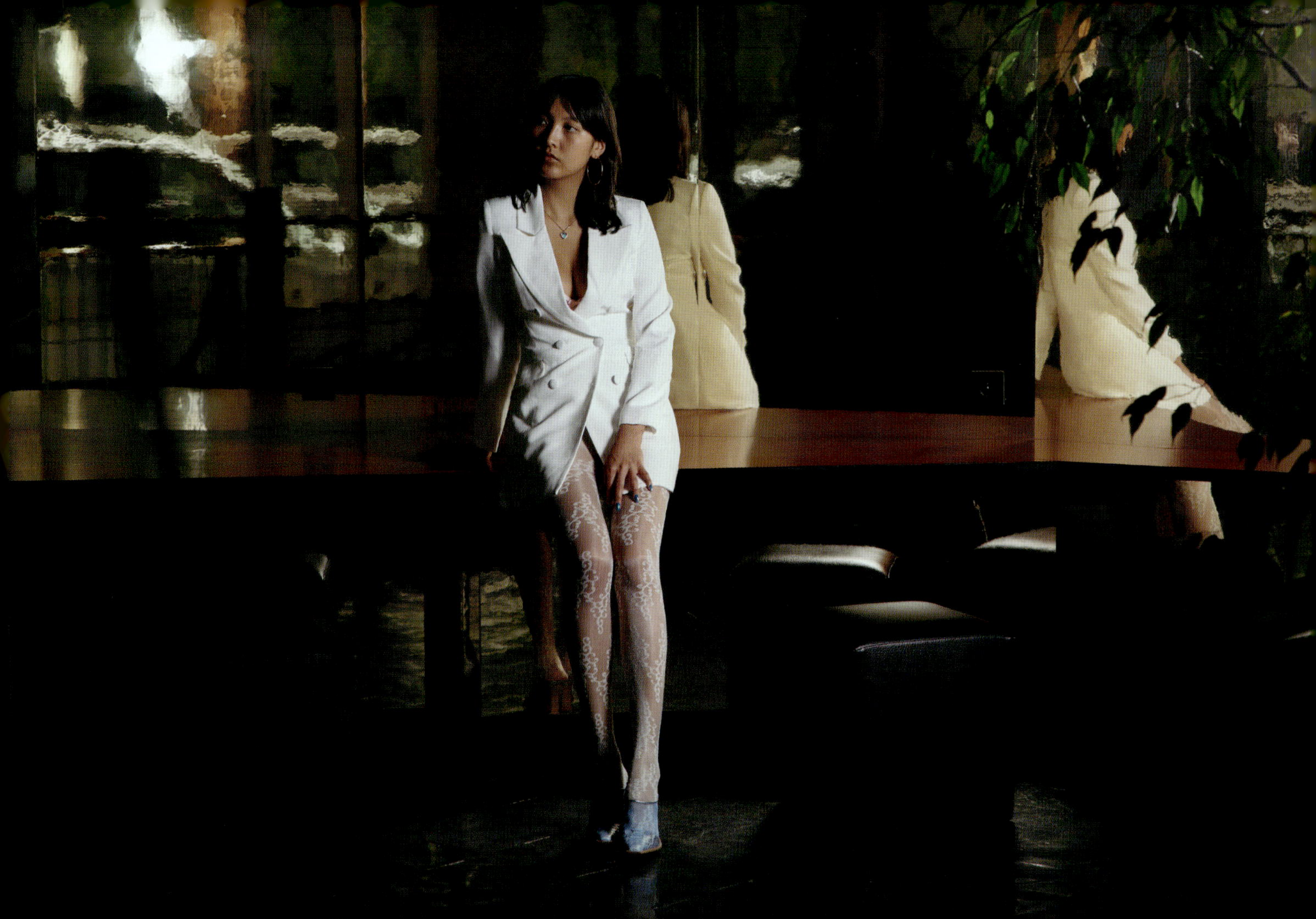

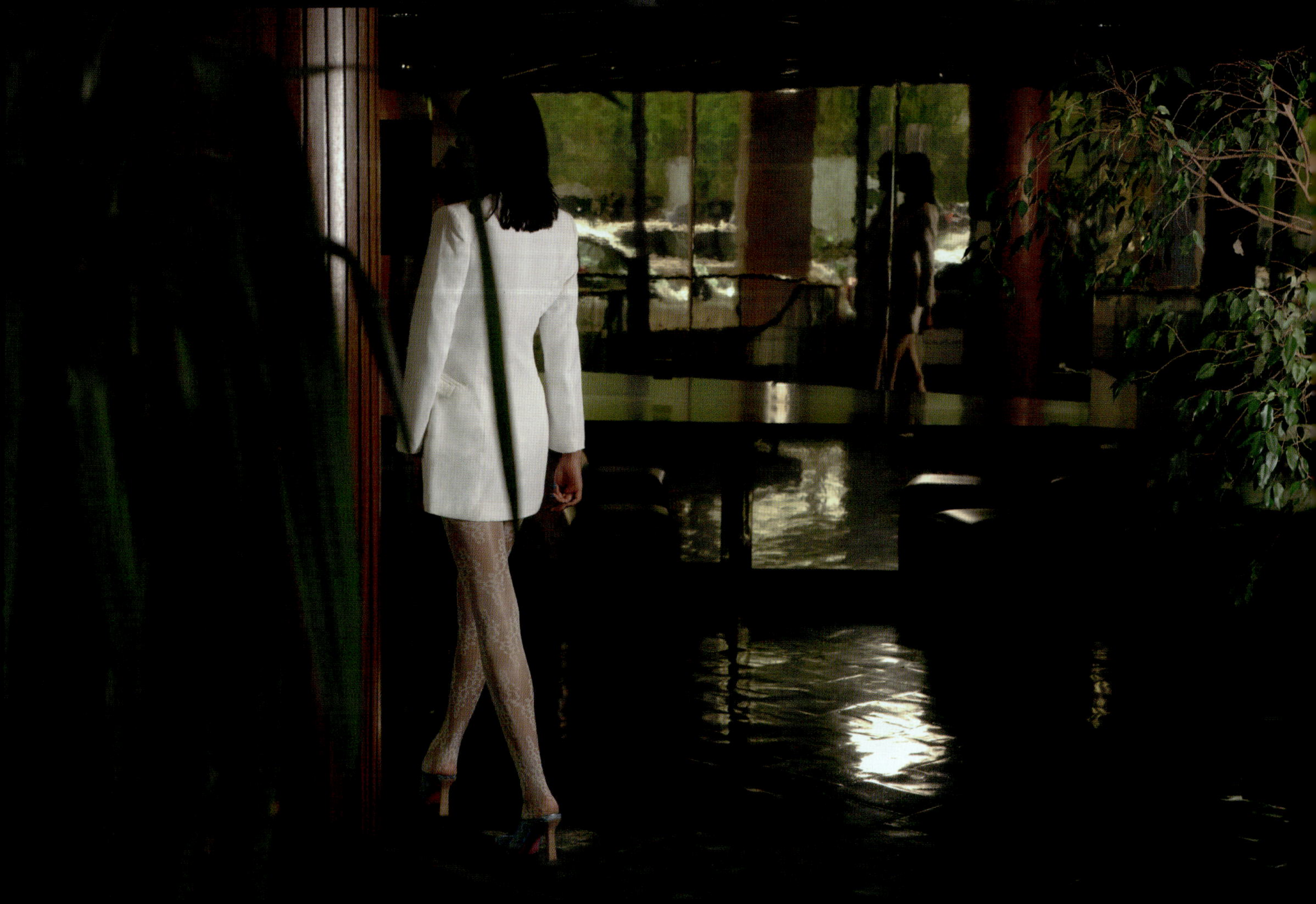

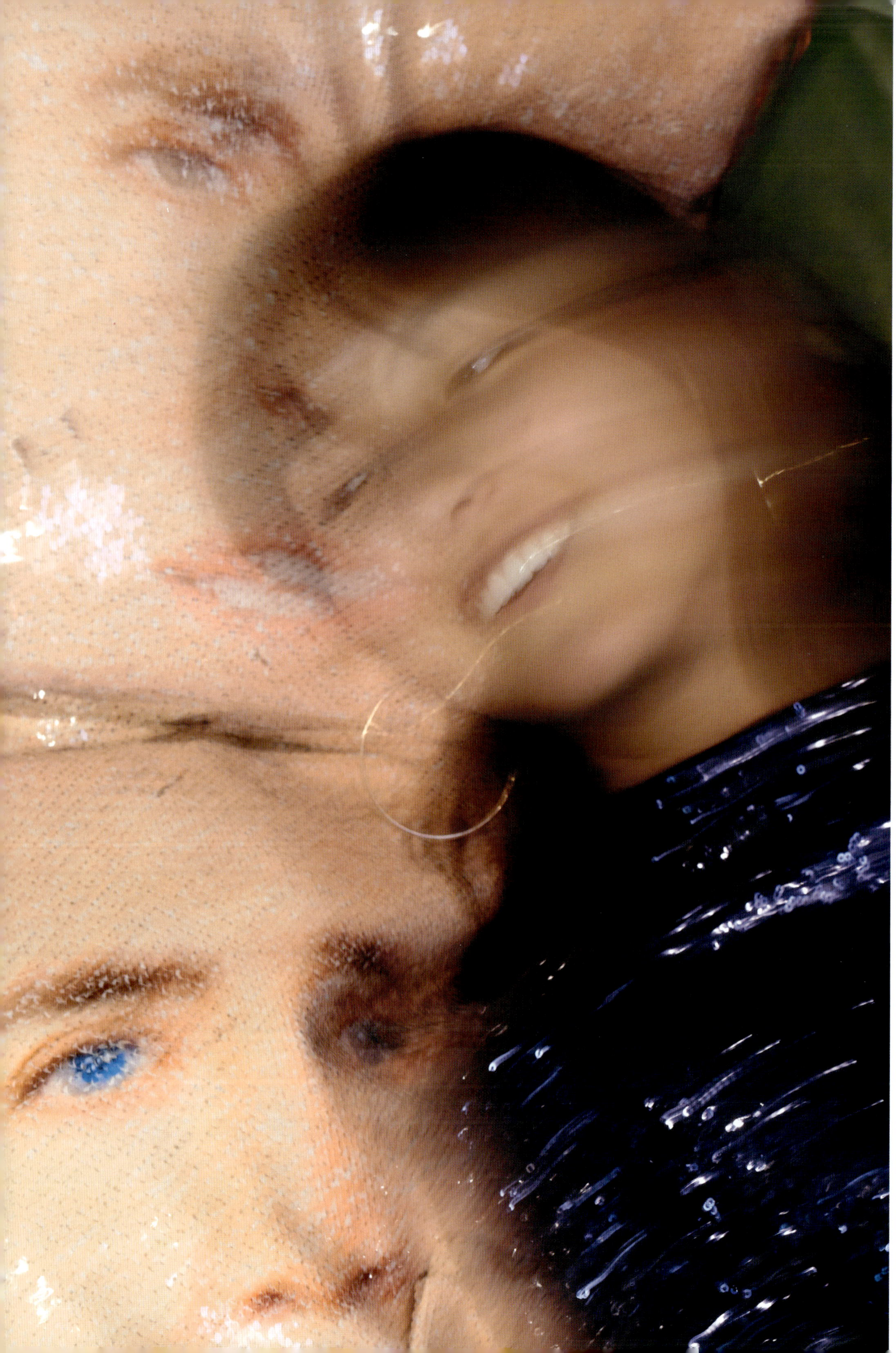

Dimmed with smoke mini dress

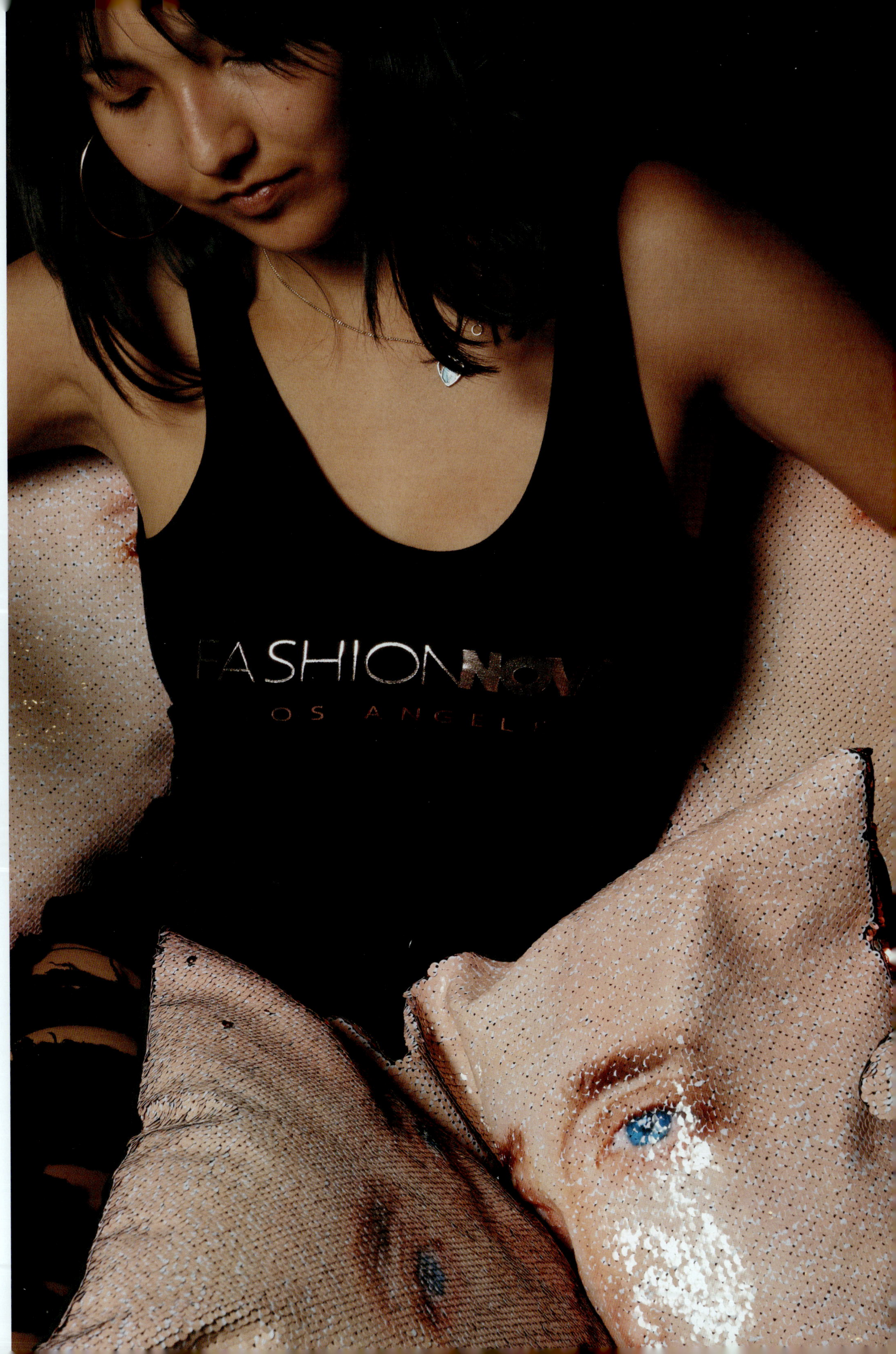

Fashion Nova exclusive bodysuit, *Things are looking up* distressed jeans

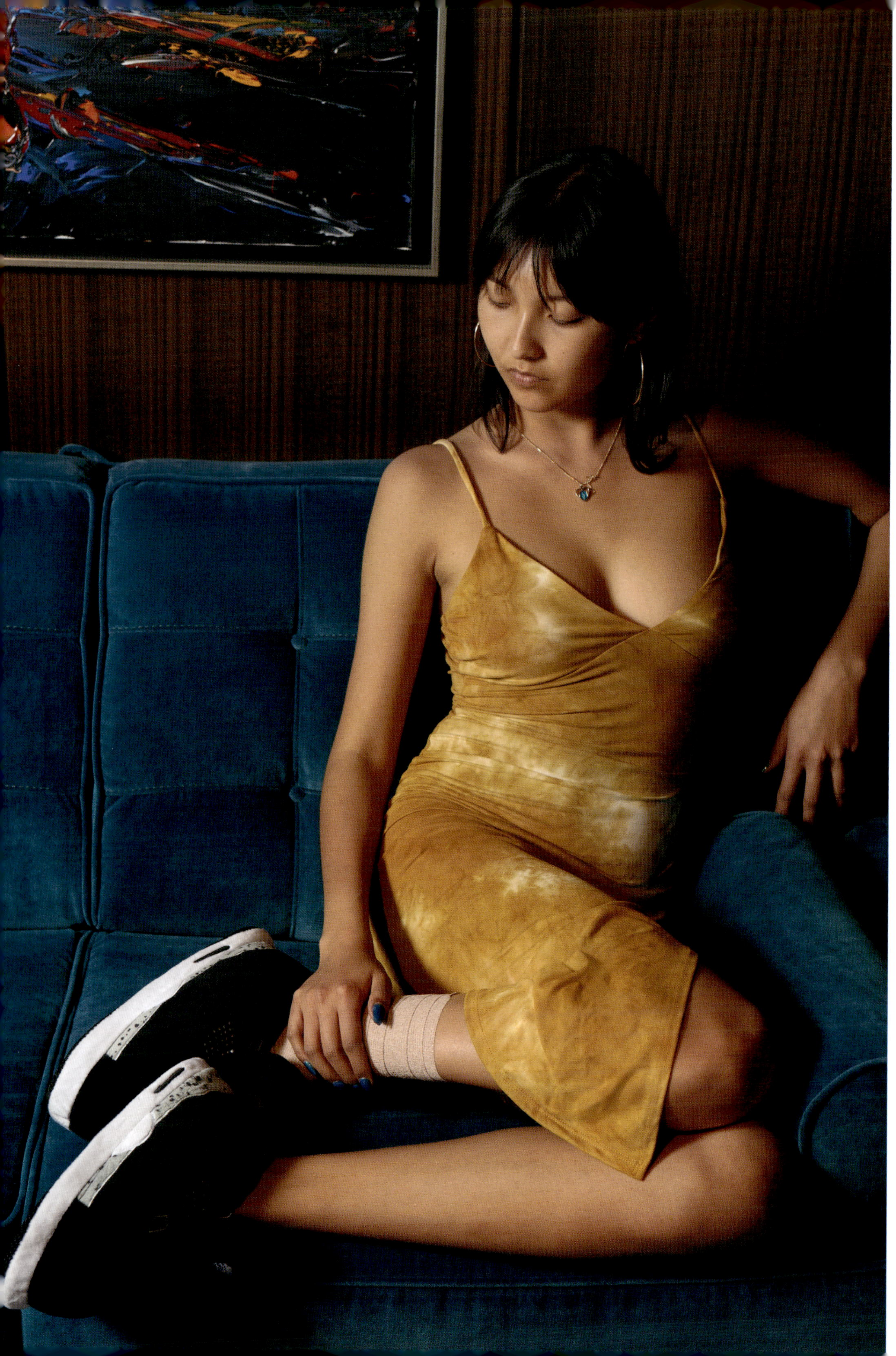

Keep your groove on *midi* dress

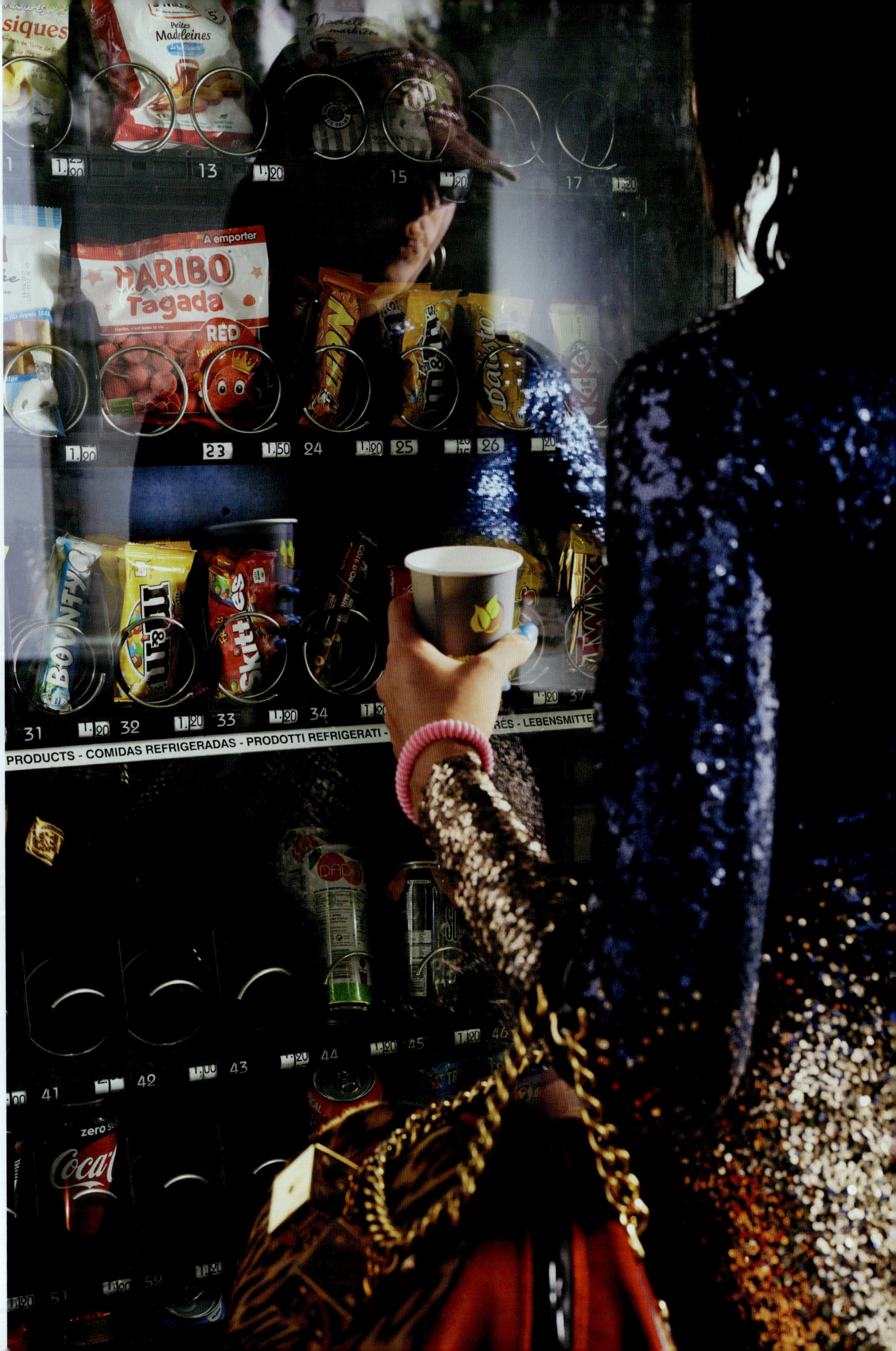

Dimmed with smoke mini dress

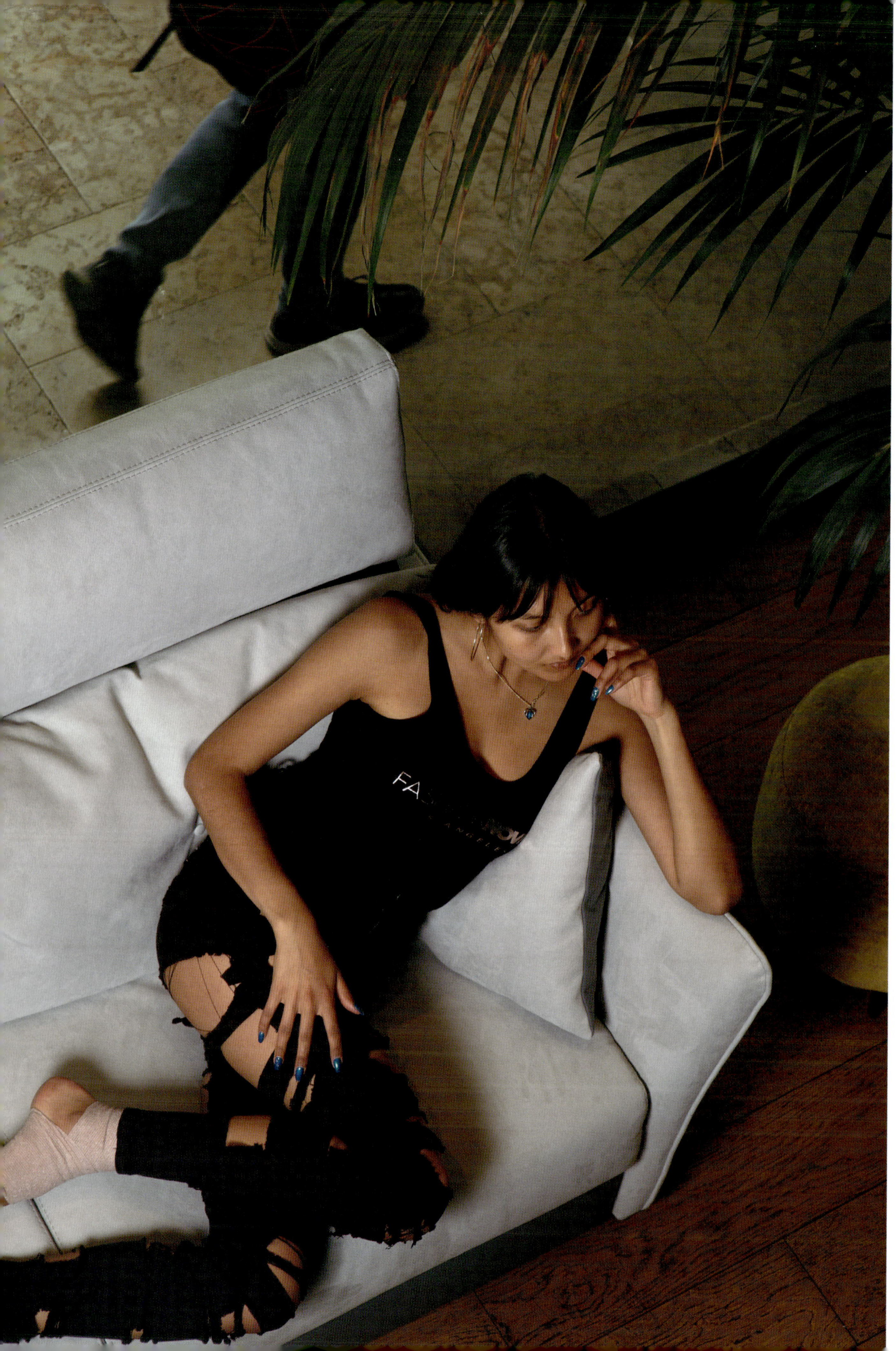

Fashion Nova exclusive bodysuit, *Things are looking up* distressed jeans

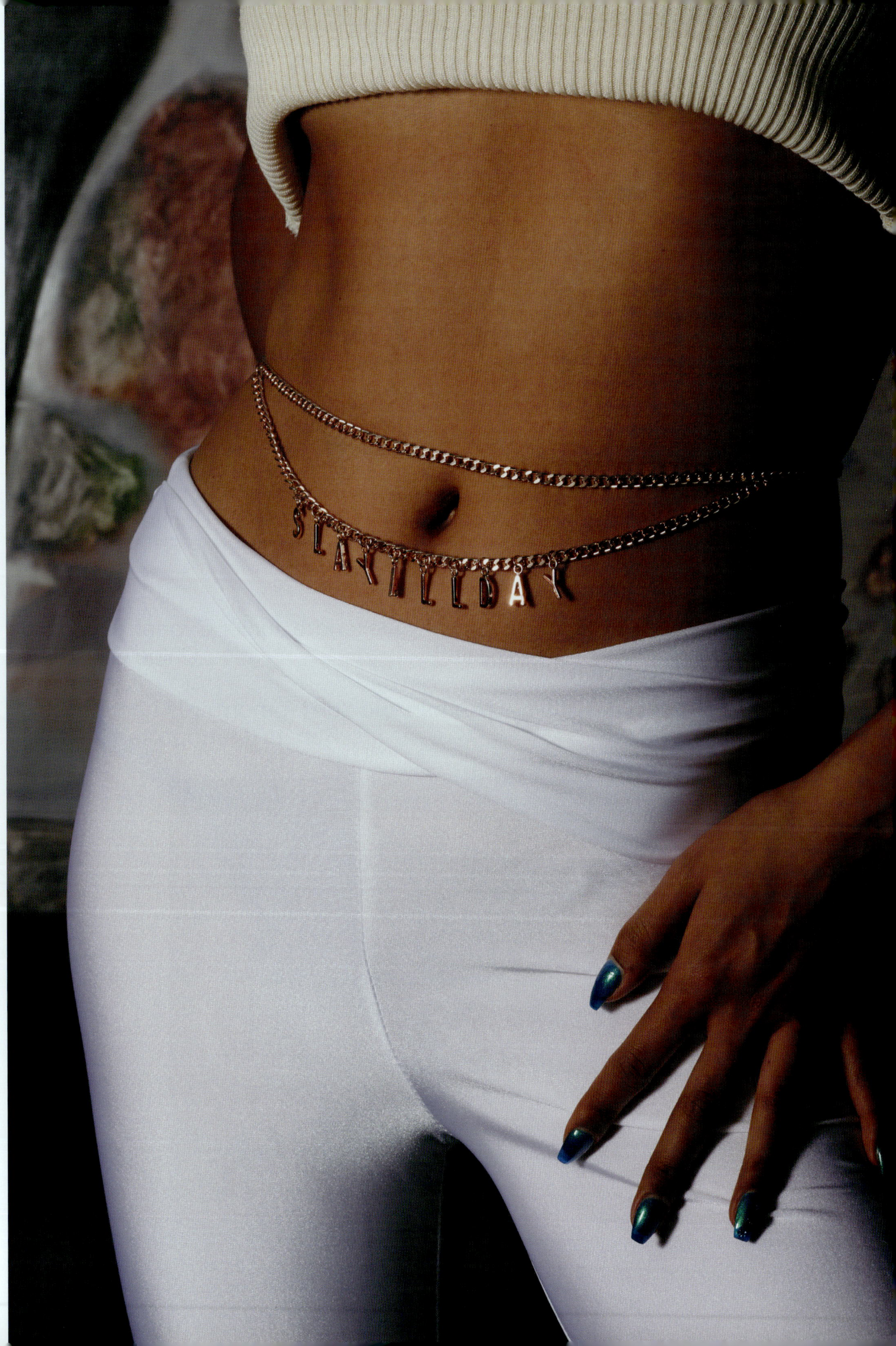

No stylist top, *Slay all day* belly chain, Fashion Nova exclusive legging

INNUMERABLE CIRCUMSTANCES CAN TRIGGER THIS PROCESS

Photographer	Boris Ovini
Fashion editor	Nina Hollensteiner
Hair	Dushan Petrovich
Makeup	Vanessa Bellini (Agence Saint Germain)
Set Designer	A+V Studios
Nail Designer	Jinyoung Chun
Casting Director	Alexandre Junior Cyprien (Creartvt)
Fashion assistant	Chloe Girardeau
Photo assistant	Julia Vadée
Models	Norman and Yuri (Tomorrow is Another Day)
	Renata (Metropolitan Models)

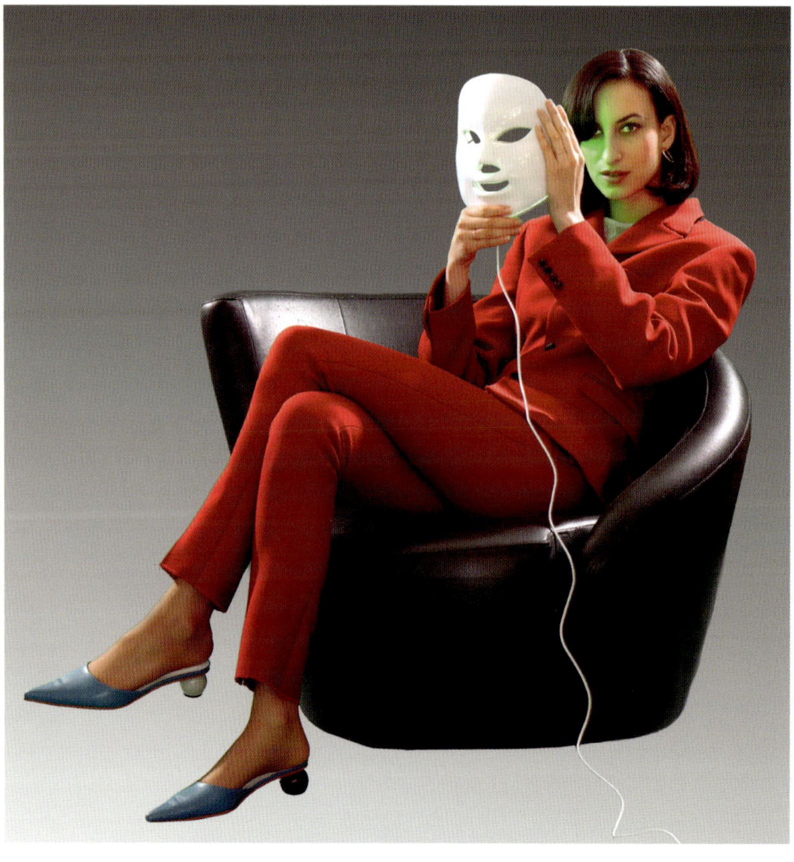

(Renata wears) Suit: GmbH / Body: Drag & Drop / Earring in hand: Diana Law / Earrings: D'heygere / Shoes: Flat Apartment

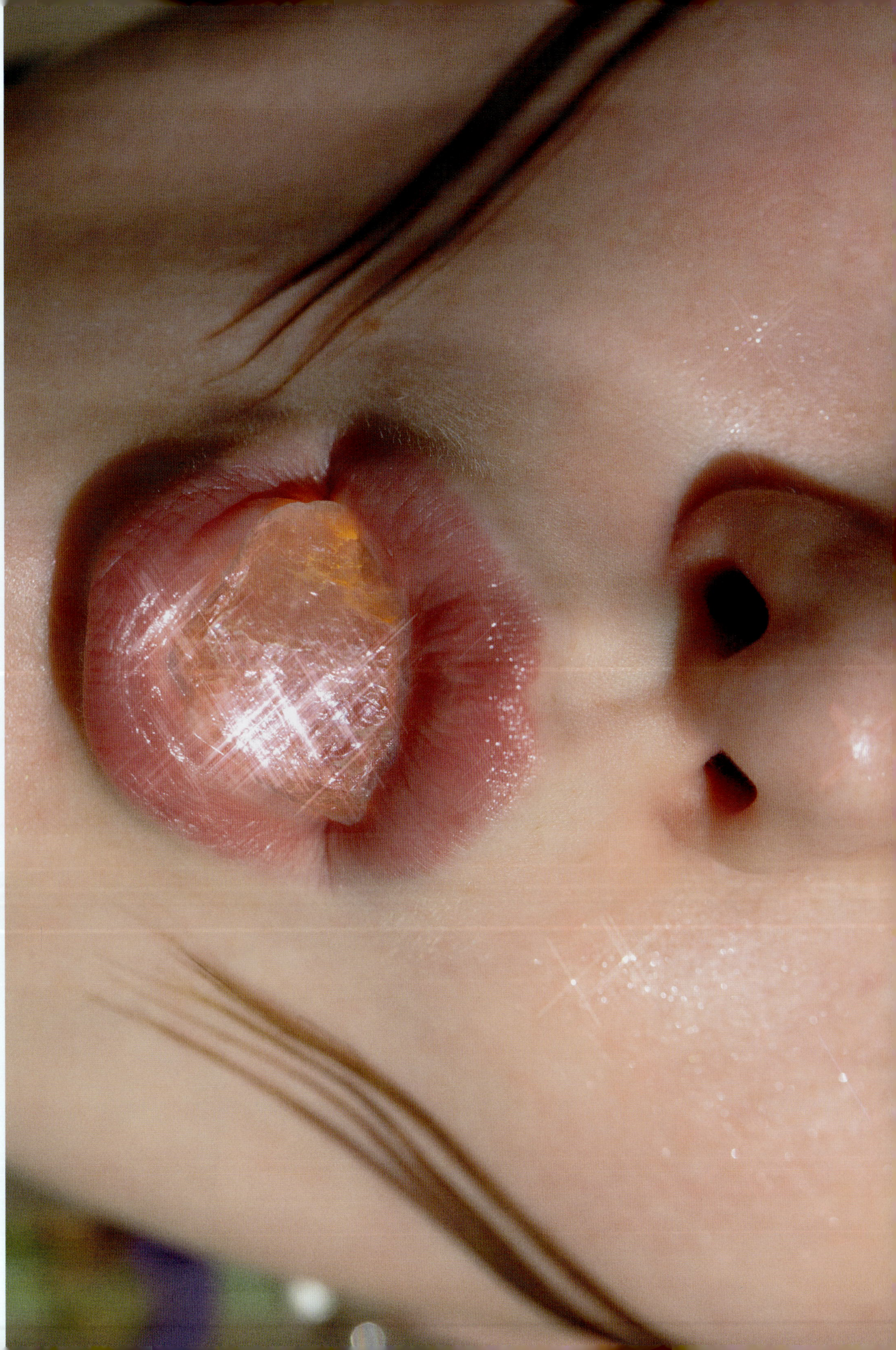

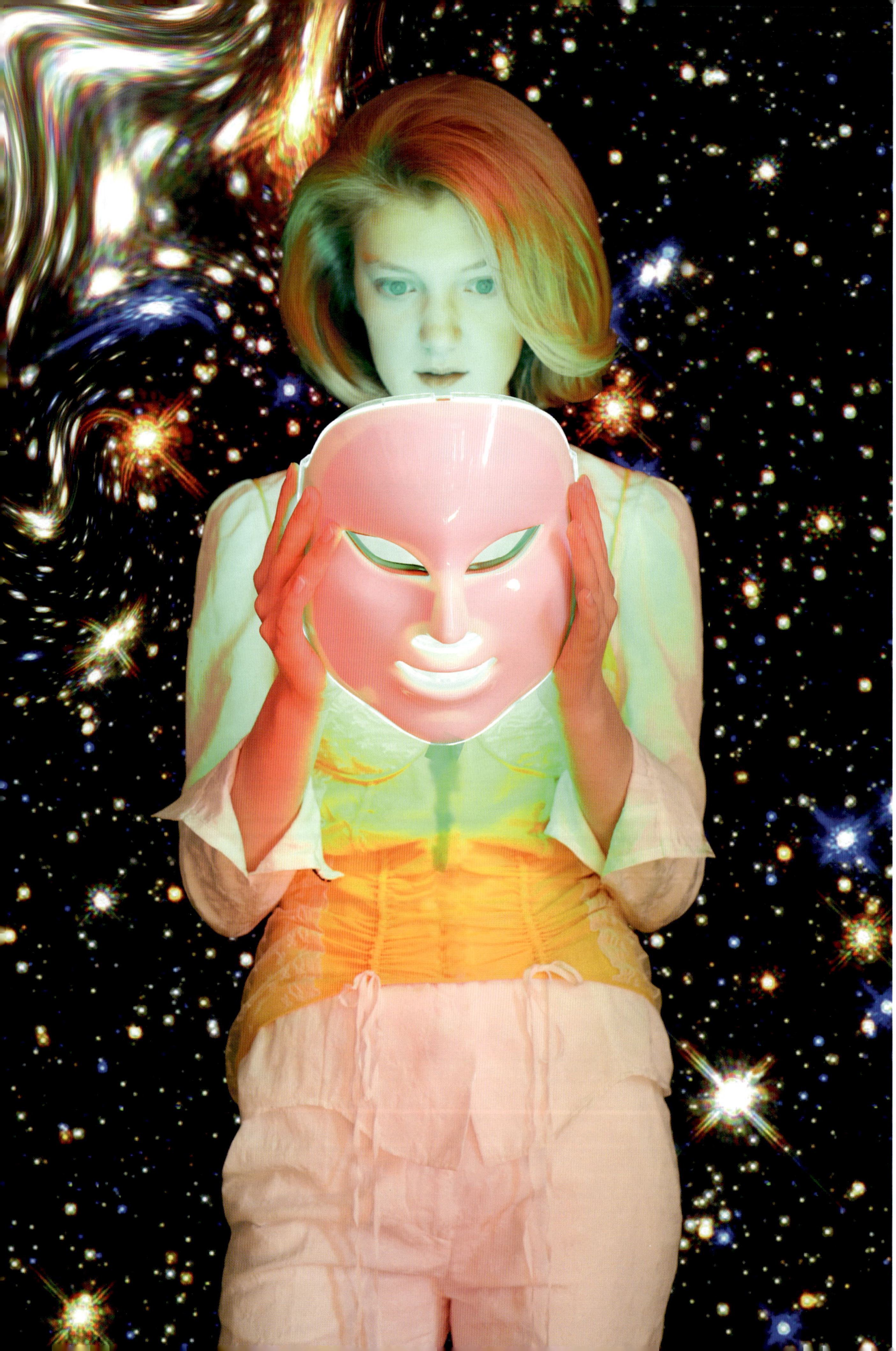

(Yuri wears) Blouse, Top and Pants: Olivier Theyskens

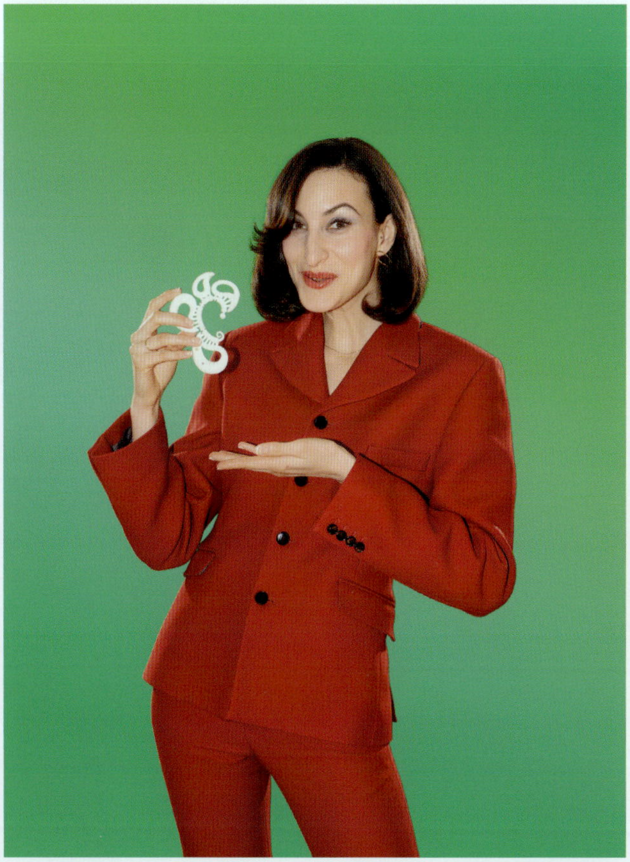

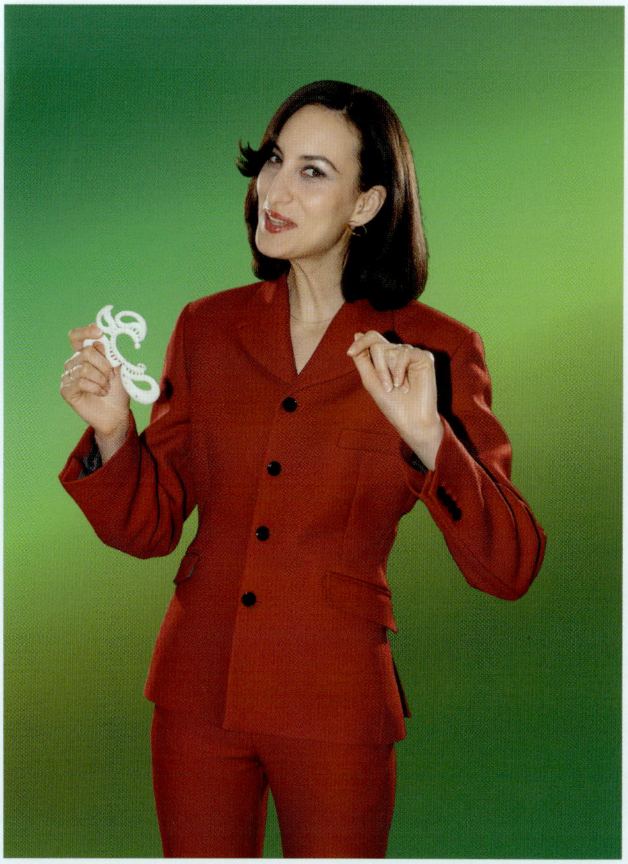

THE SECRET THE MEDICAL INDUSTRY DOESN'T WANT YOU TO KNOW

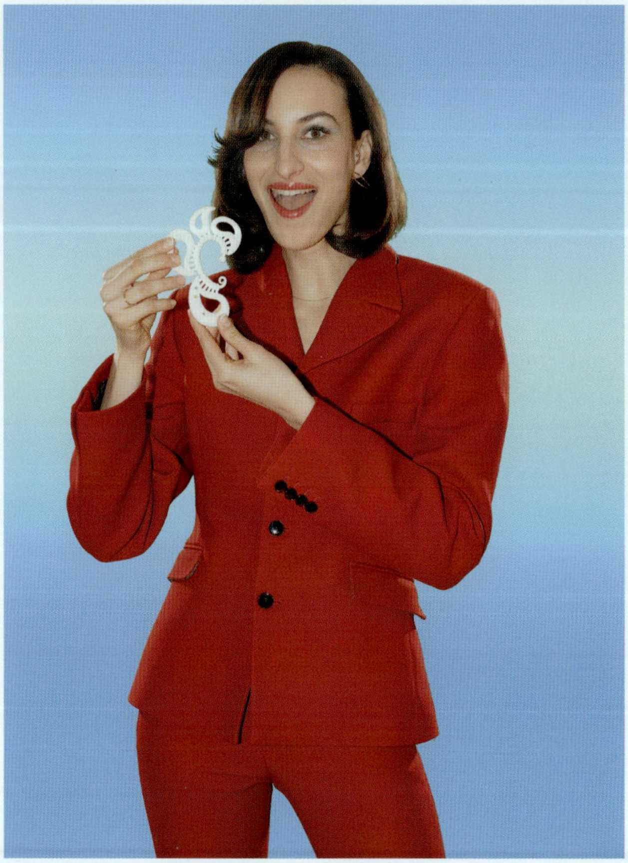

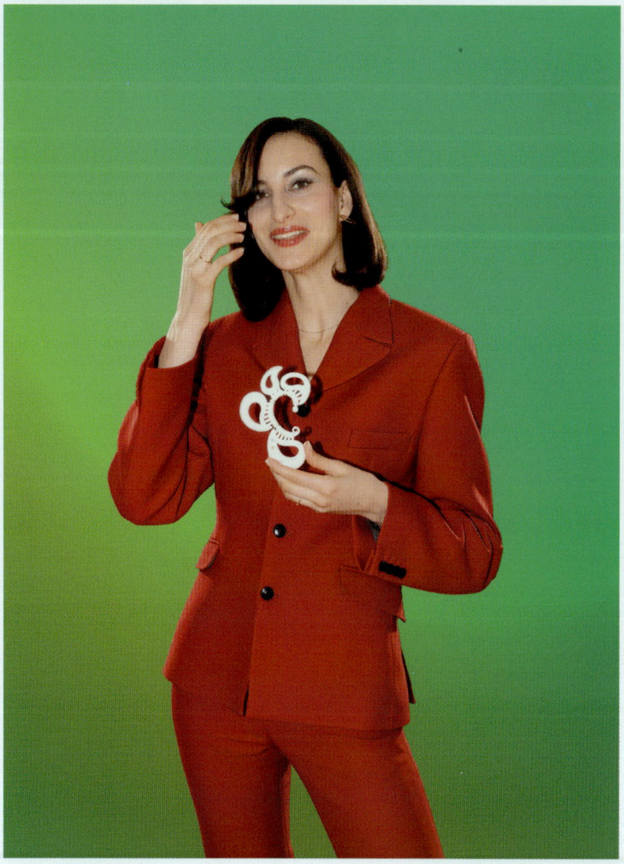

(Renata wears) Suit: GmbH / Earring in hand: Diana Law / Earrings: D'heygere
Overleaf: (Norman wears) Pullover: 032c / Pants: Our Legacy / Necklace: Regina Dabdab

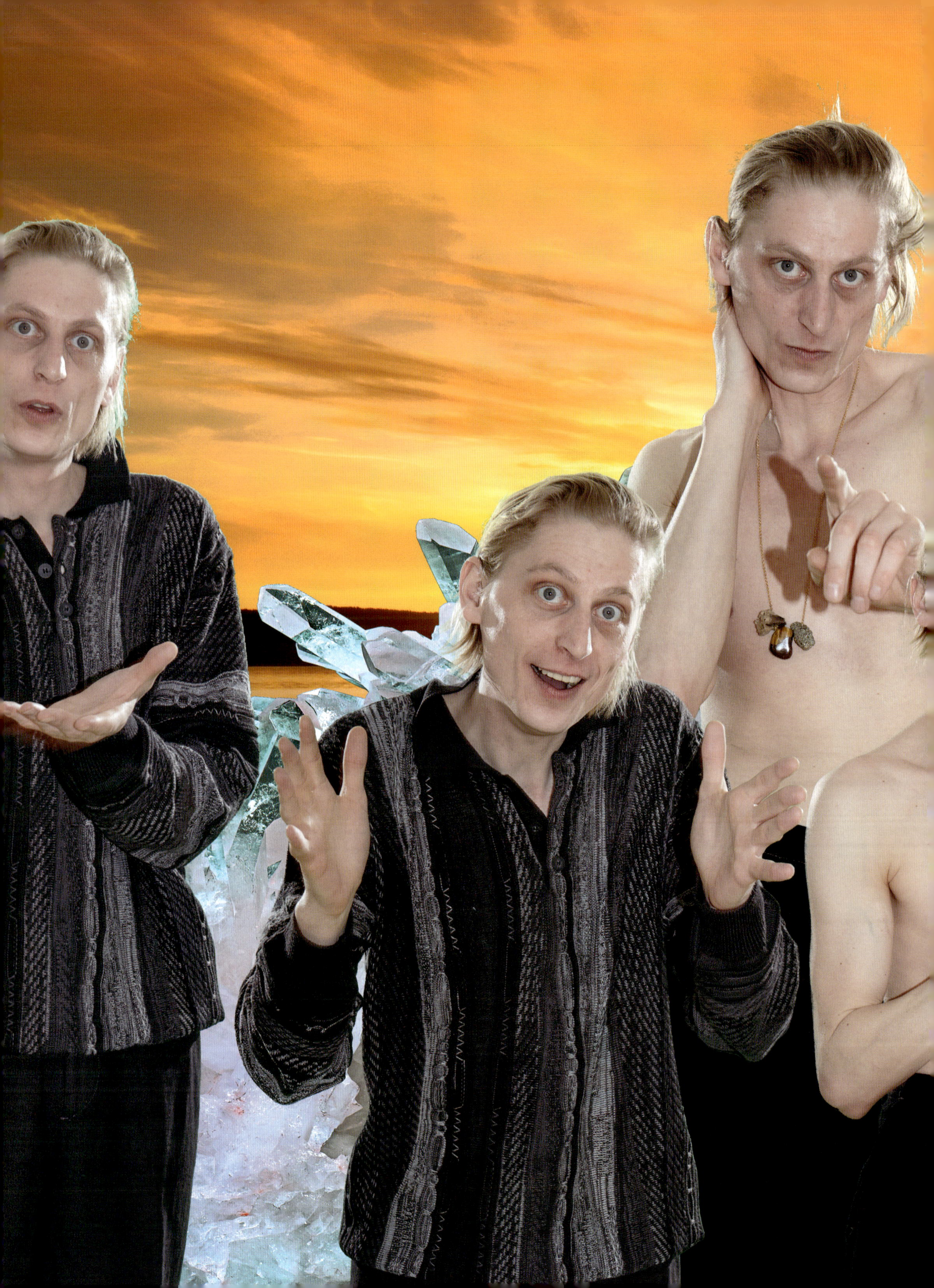

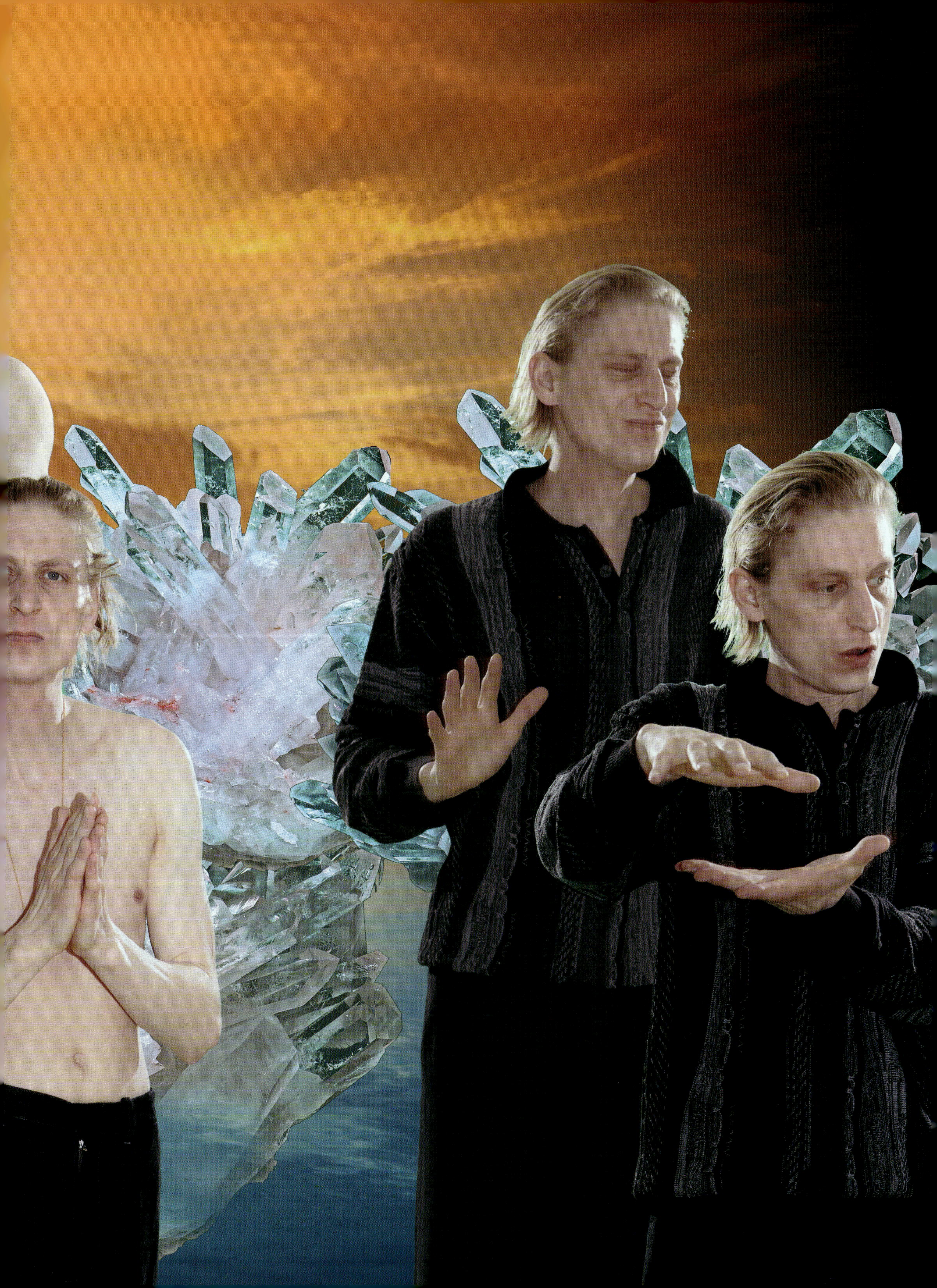

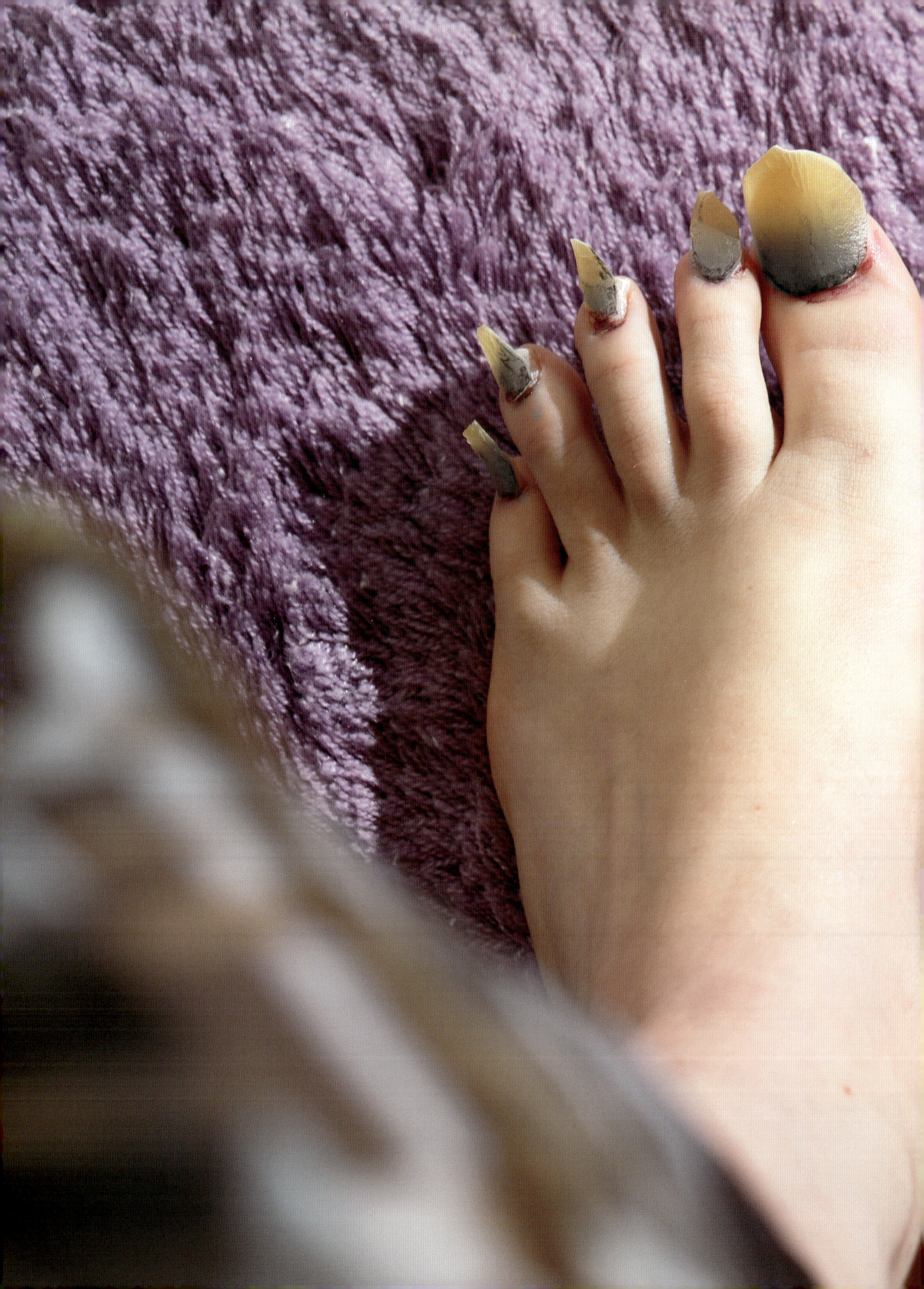

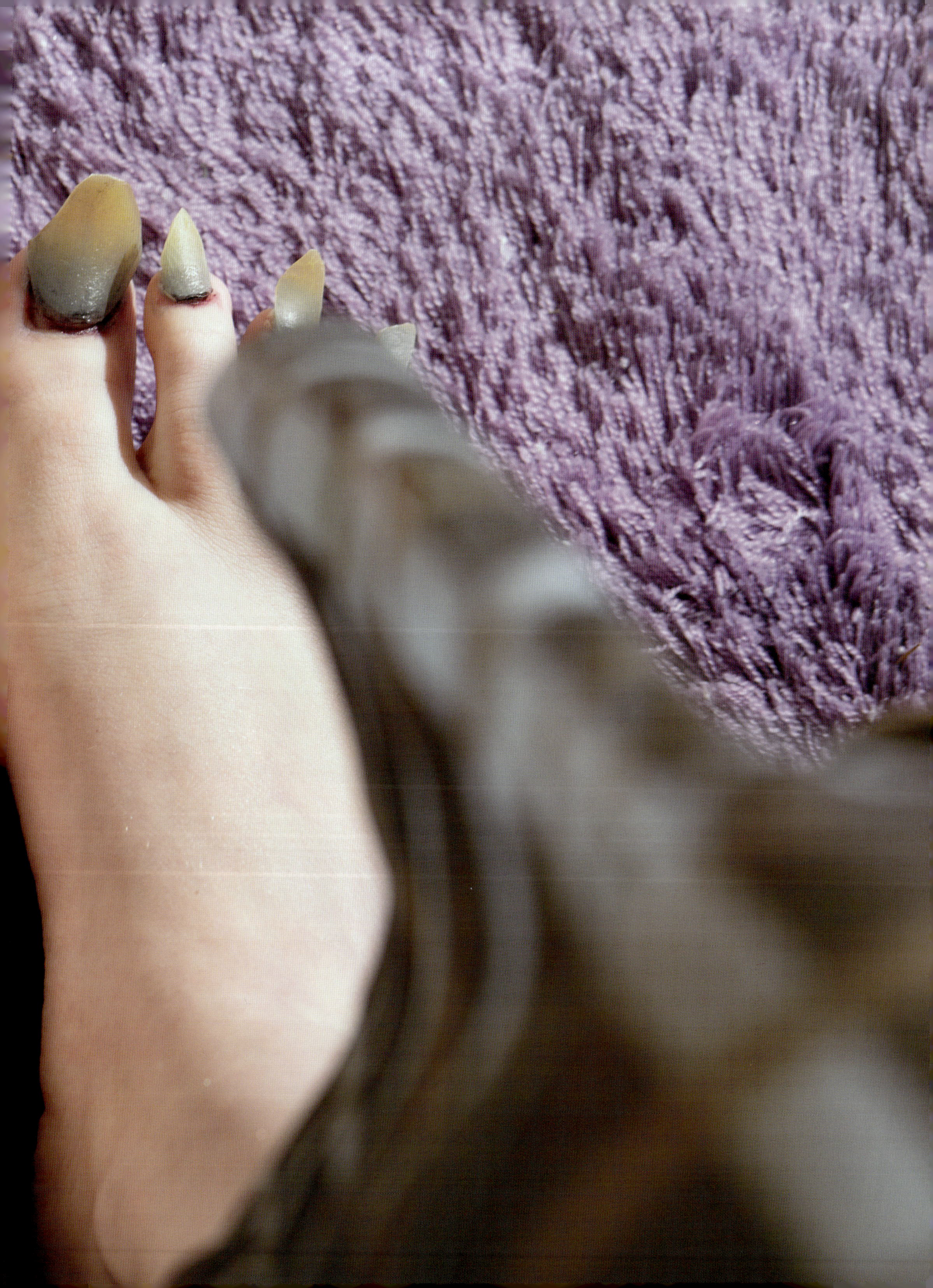

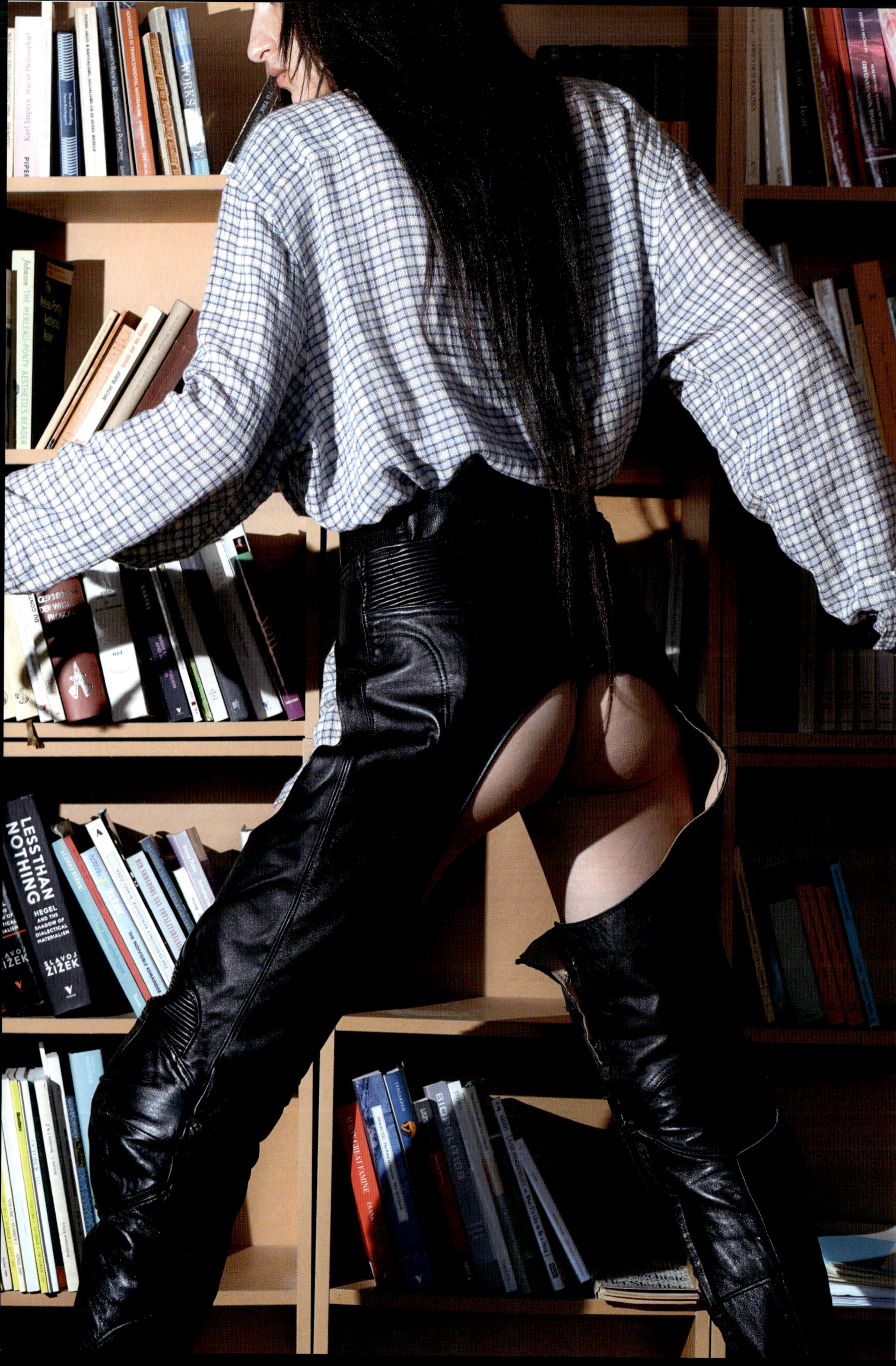

(Renata wears) Shirt: Our Legacy / Pants: Nina Mounah

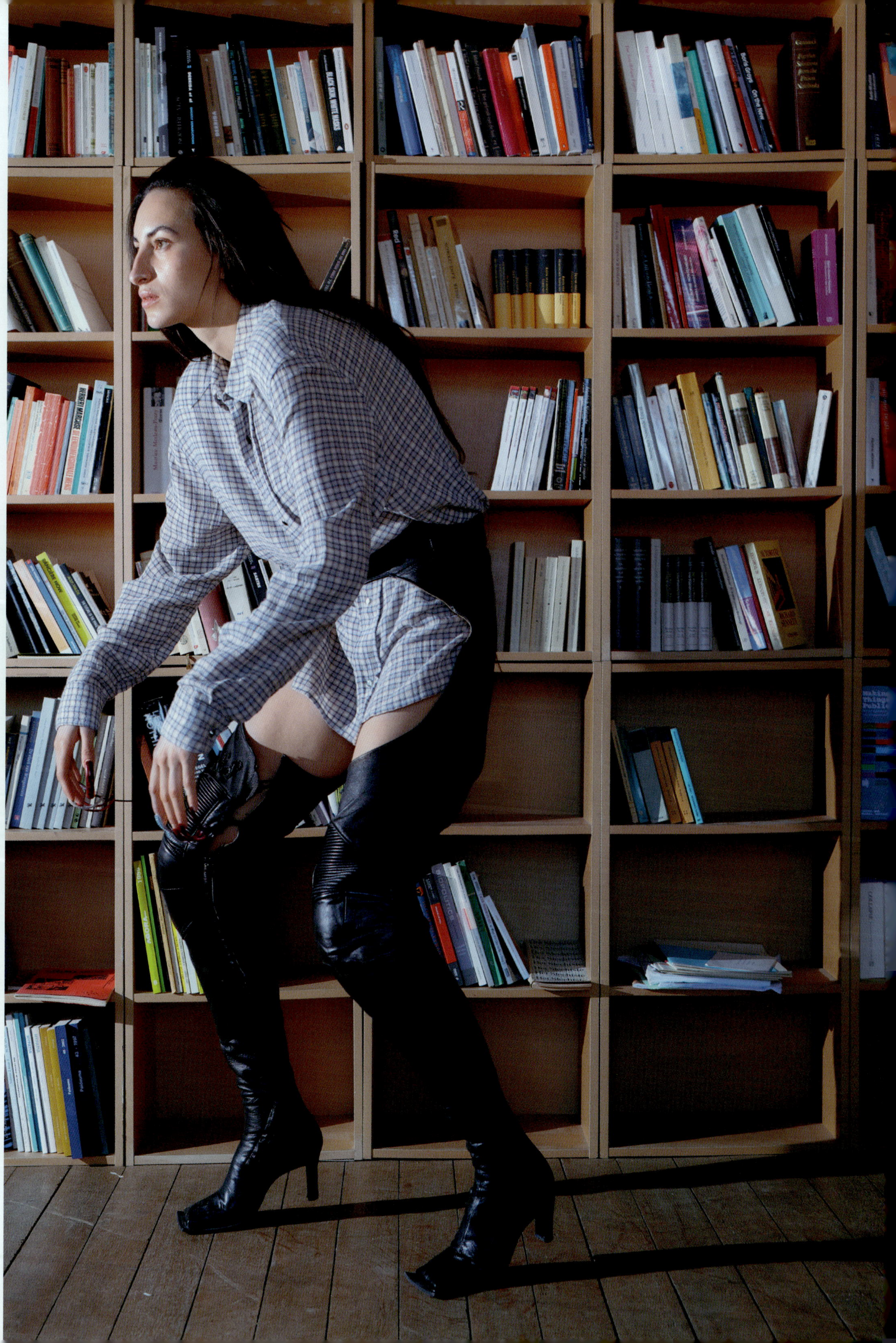

Overleaf: (Norman wears) Shirt and Tie: Vintage / Pants: Bless / Bracelet: Regina Dabdab / Shoes: Camper / (Yuri wears) Dress: Léa Peckre / Necklace: D'heygere / Shoes: Flat Apartment

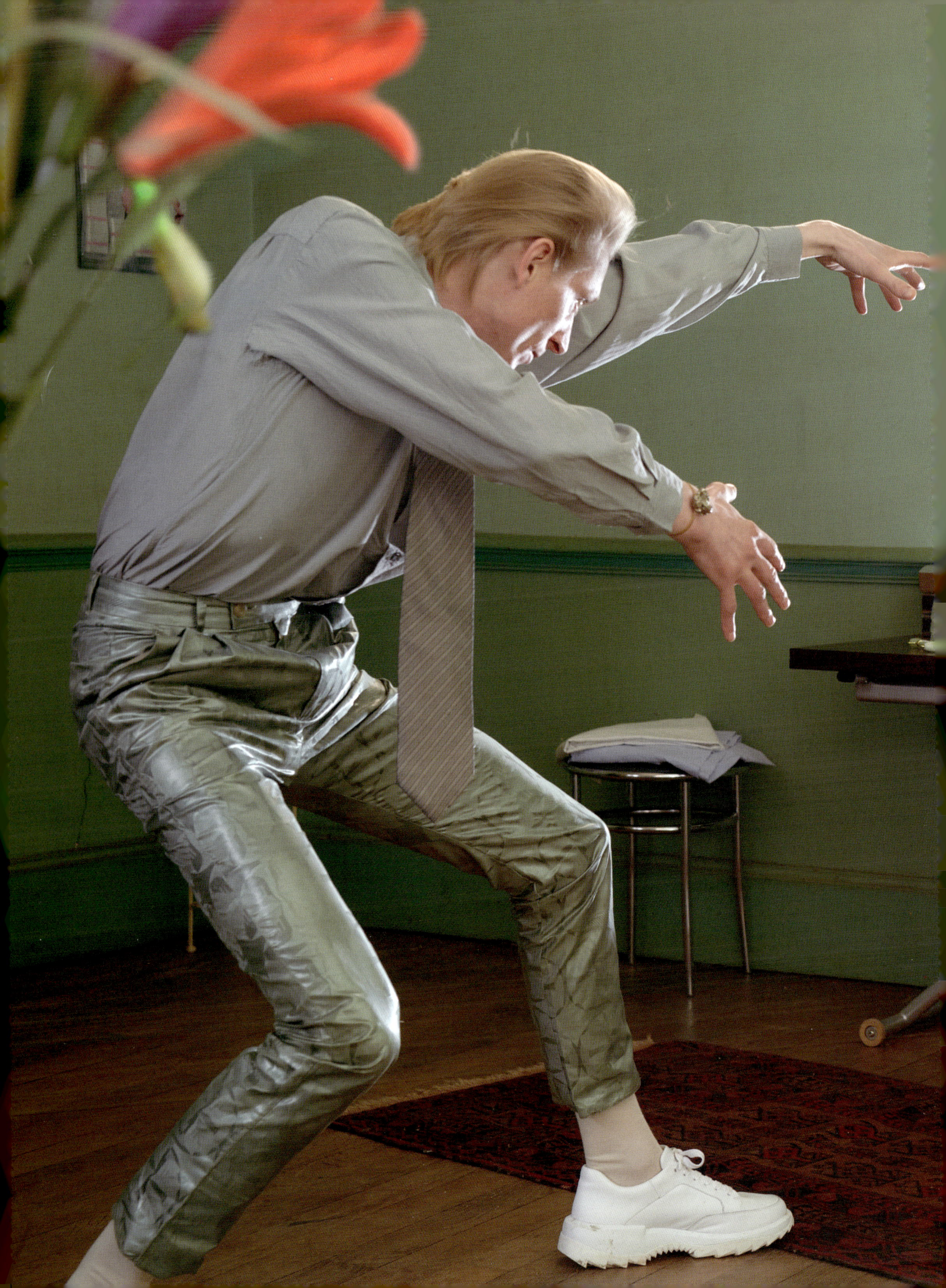

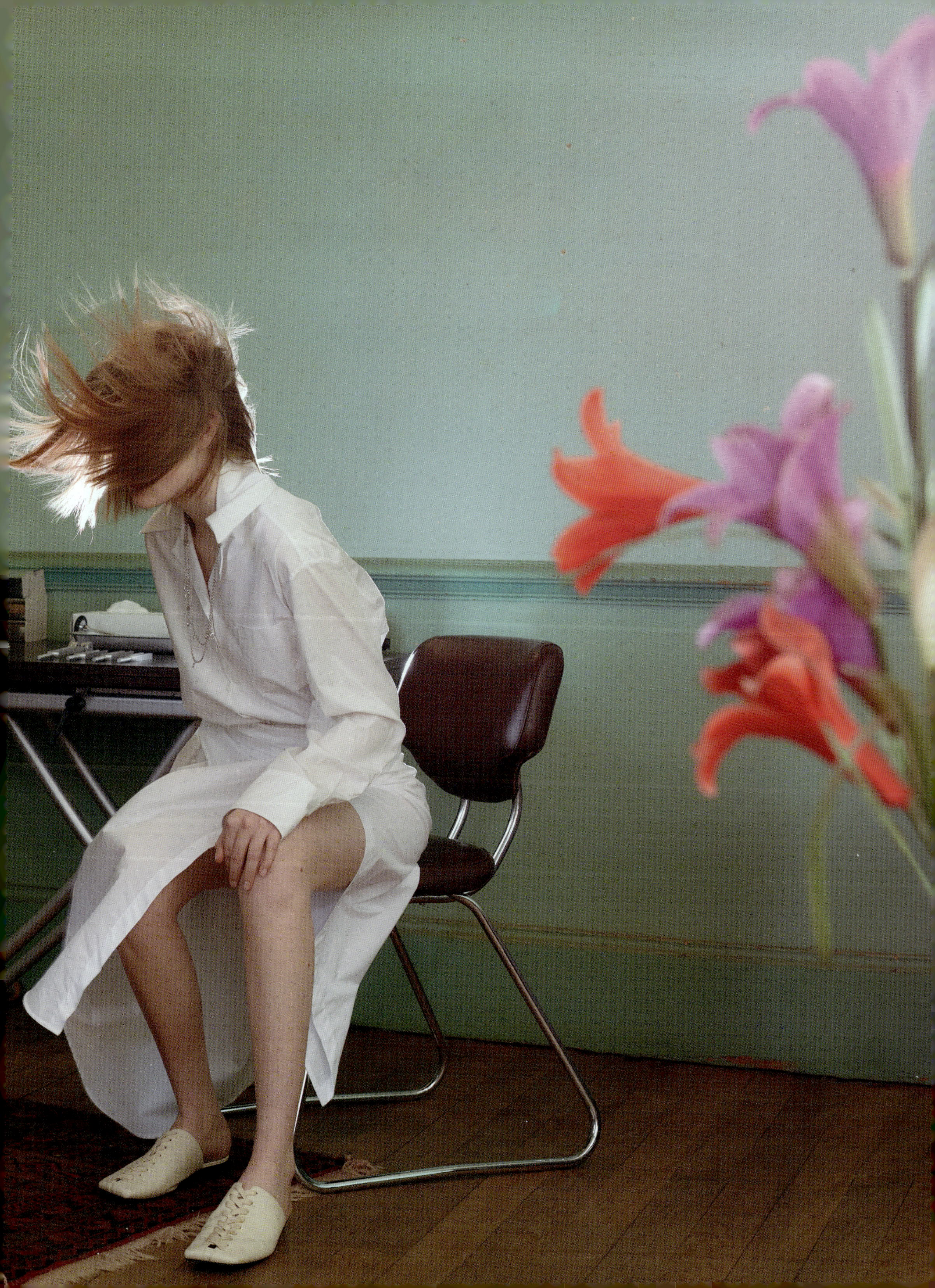

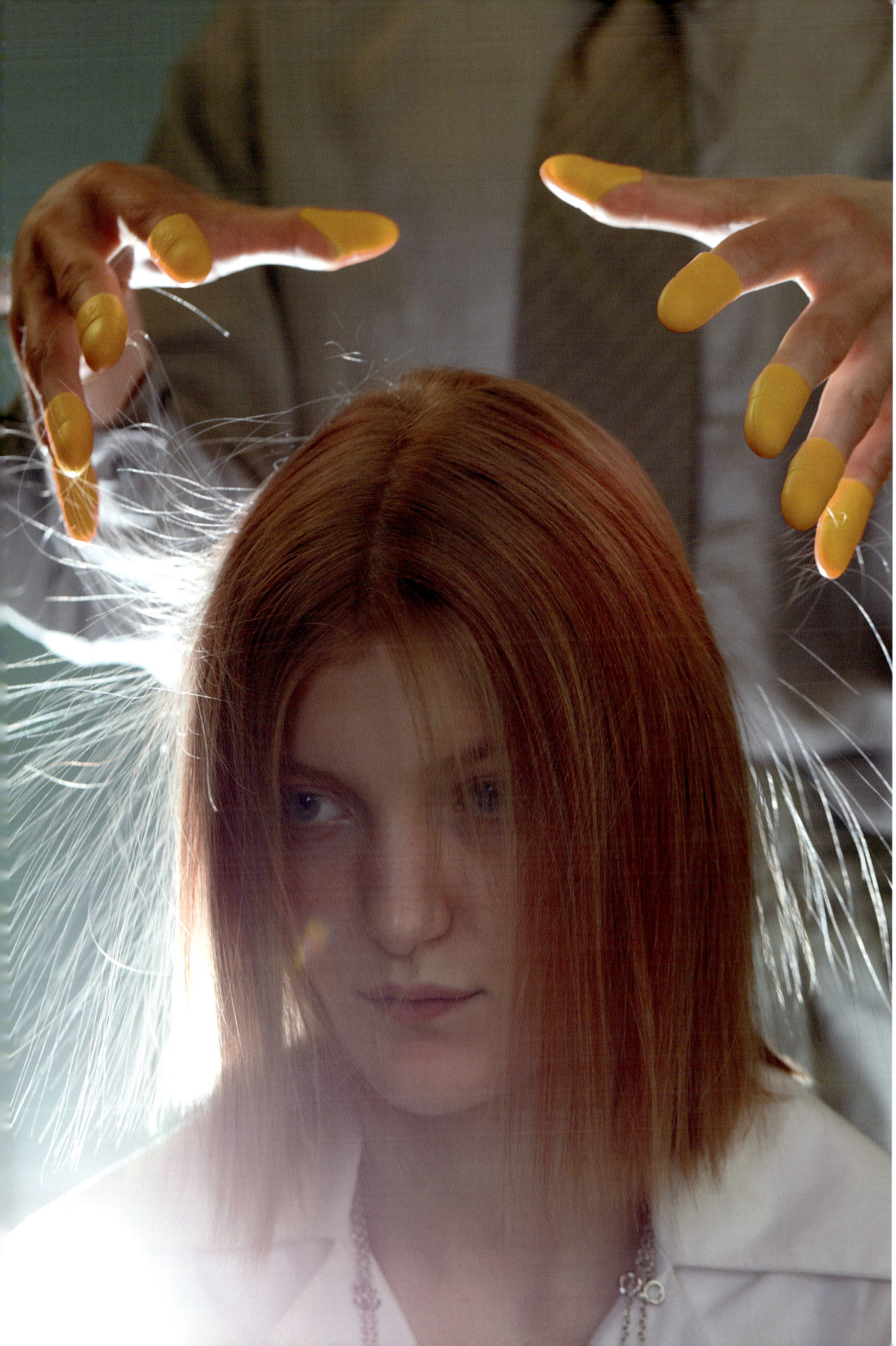

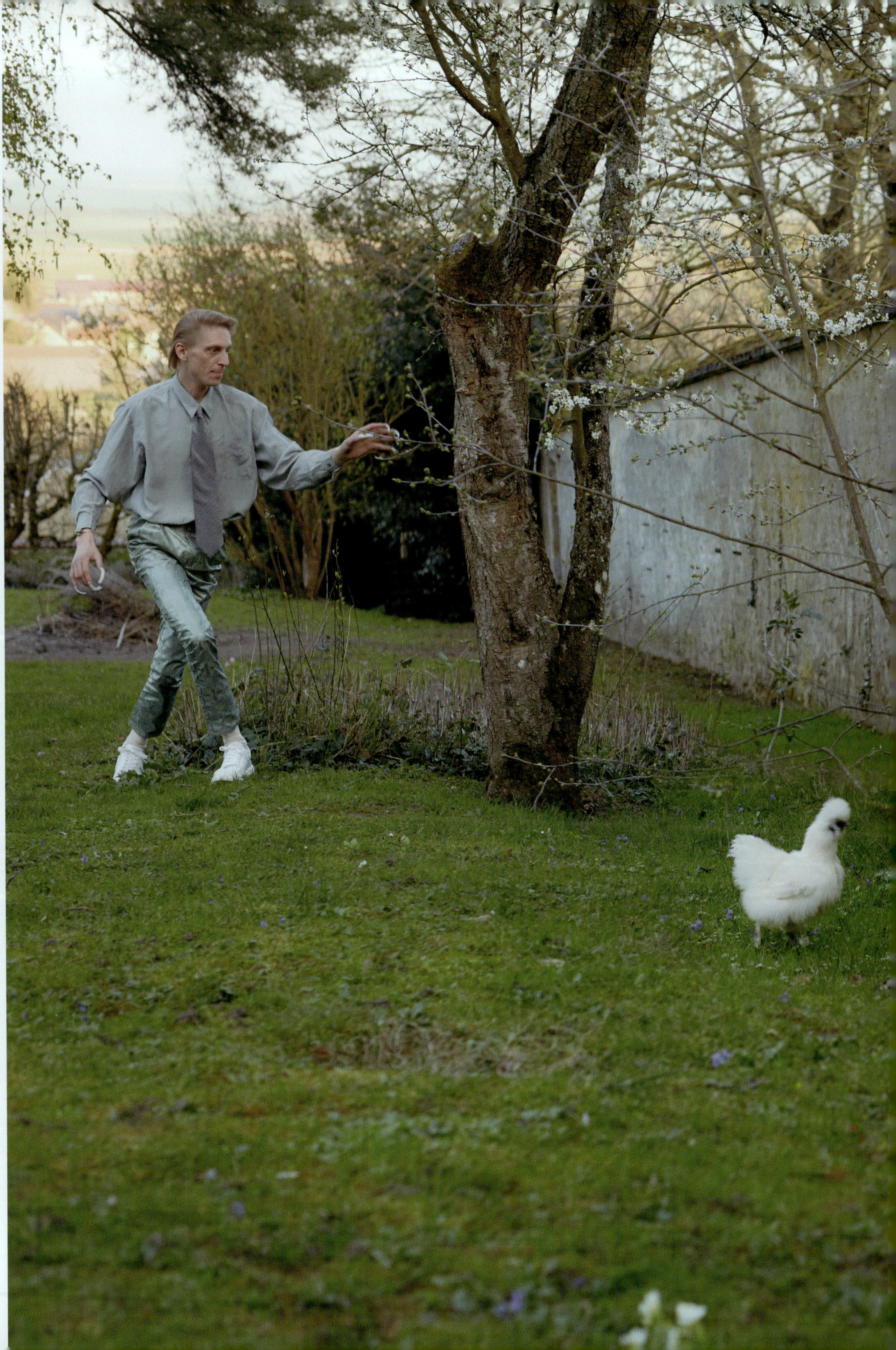

(Norman wears) Shirt and Tie: Vintage / Pants: Bless / Bracelet: Regina Dabdab / Shoes: Camper
Overleaf: (Norman wears) Dress: Louis-Gabriel Nouchi / Shoes: Camper / Necklace: D'heygere / Scarfs folded on bench: labrume / (Yuri wears) Dress and Body: Léa Peckre / Earrings: Anatheine Studio

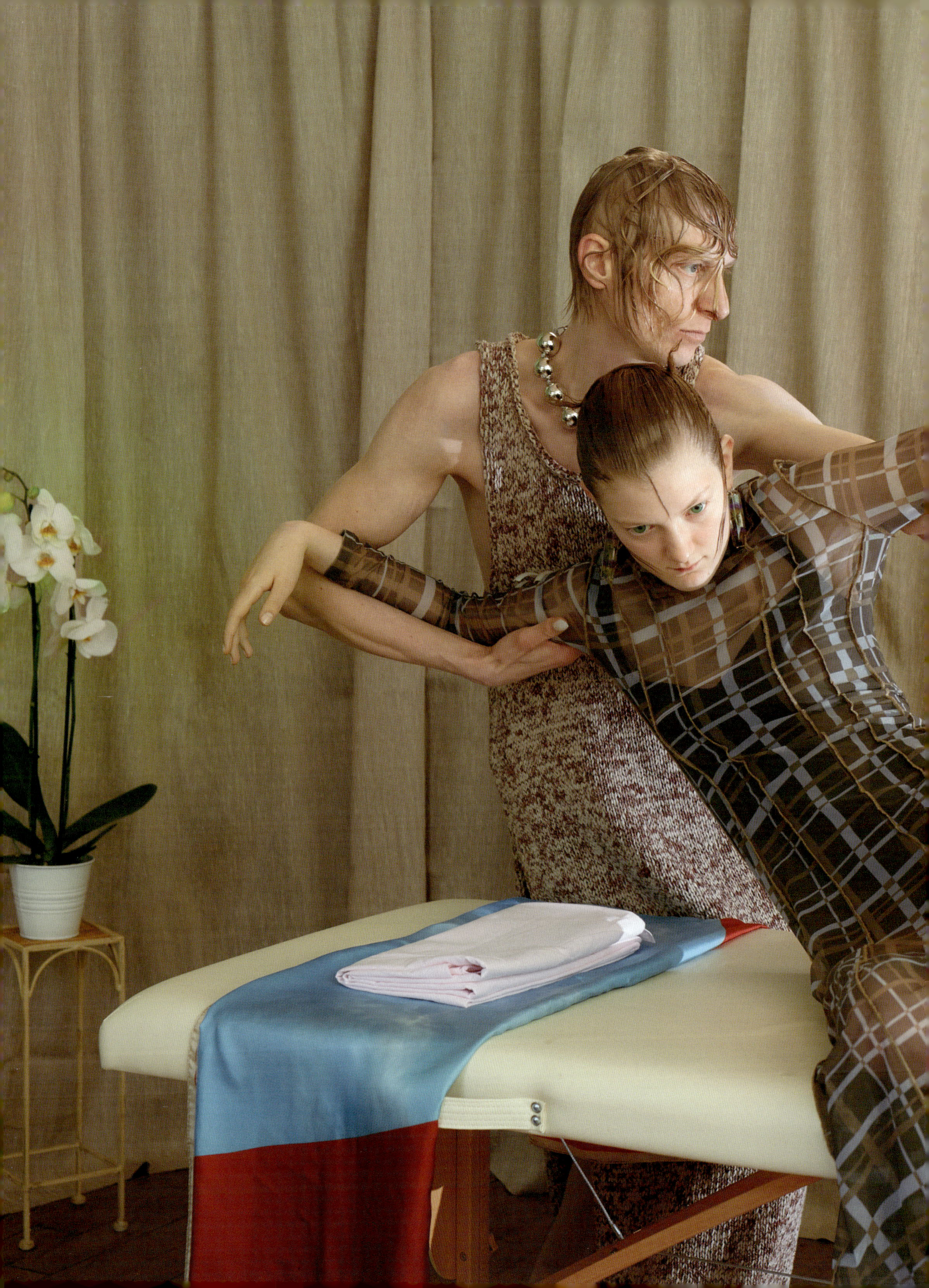

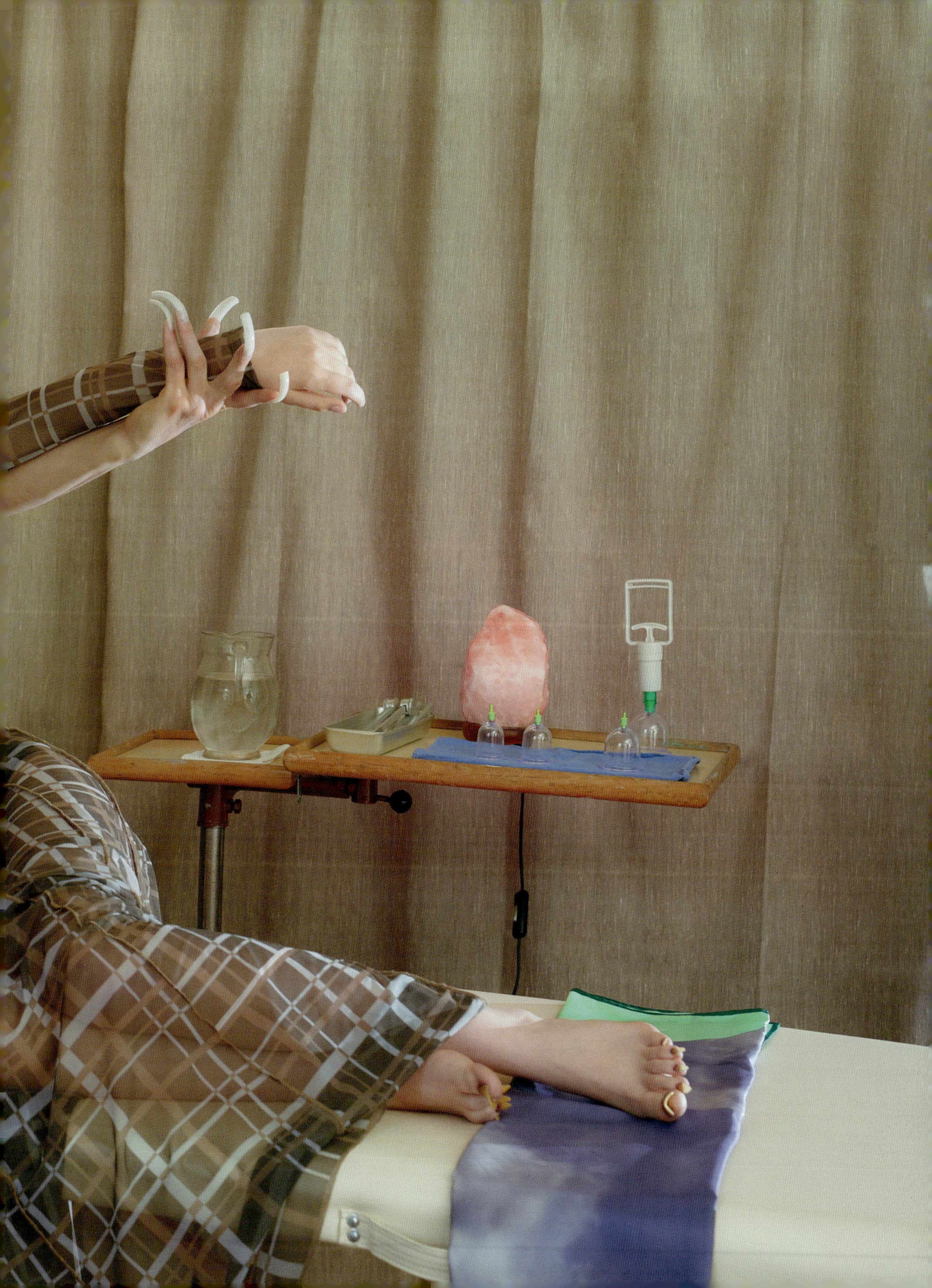

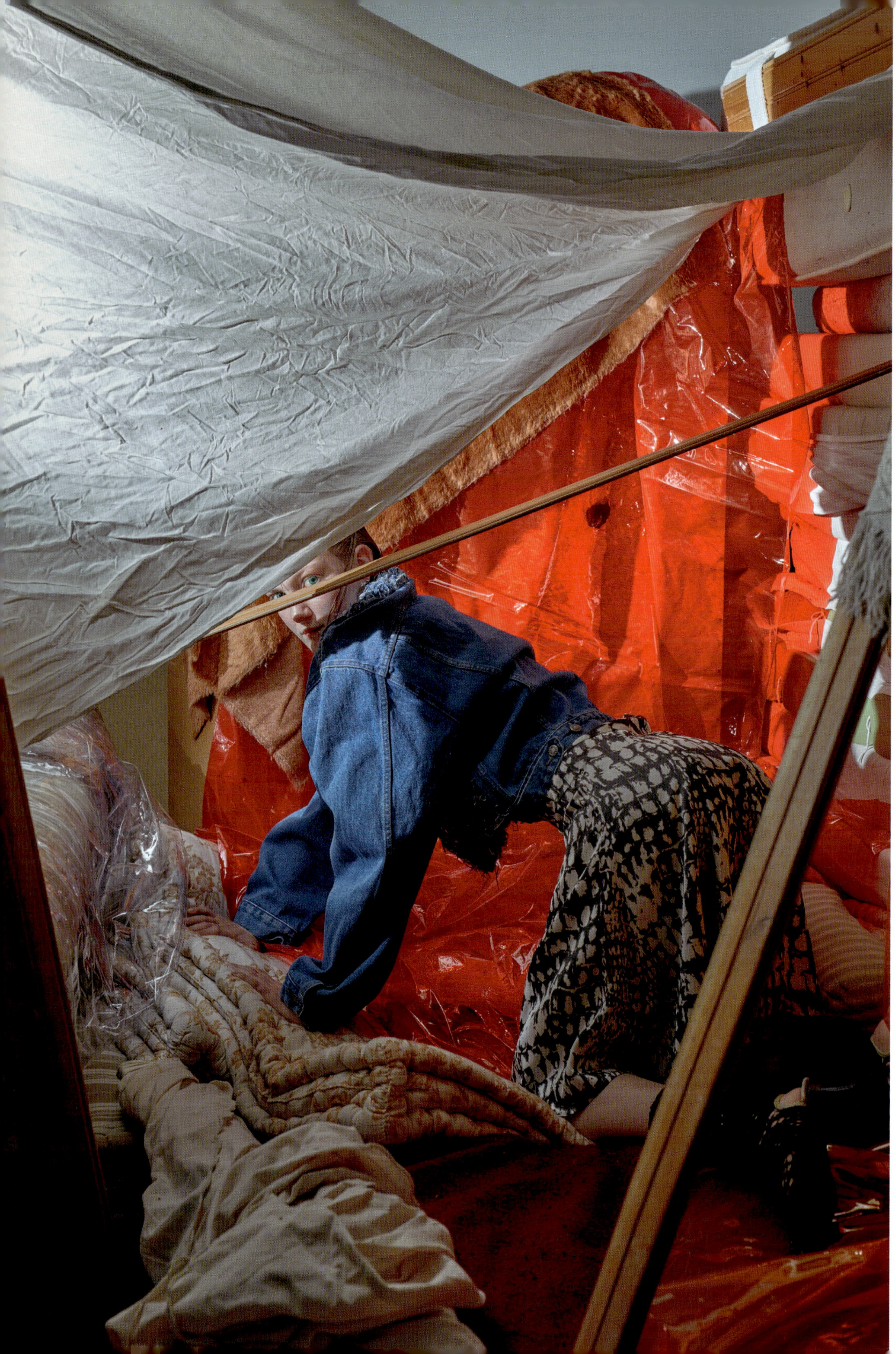

(Yuri wears) Jeans Pullover: Bless / Skirt: Lutz Huelle / Shoes: Véronique Leroy / Earrings: D'heygere

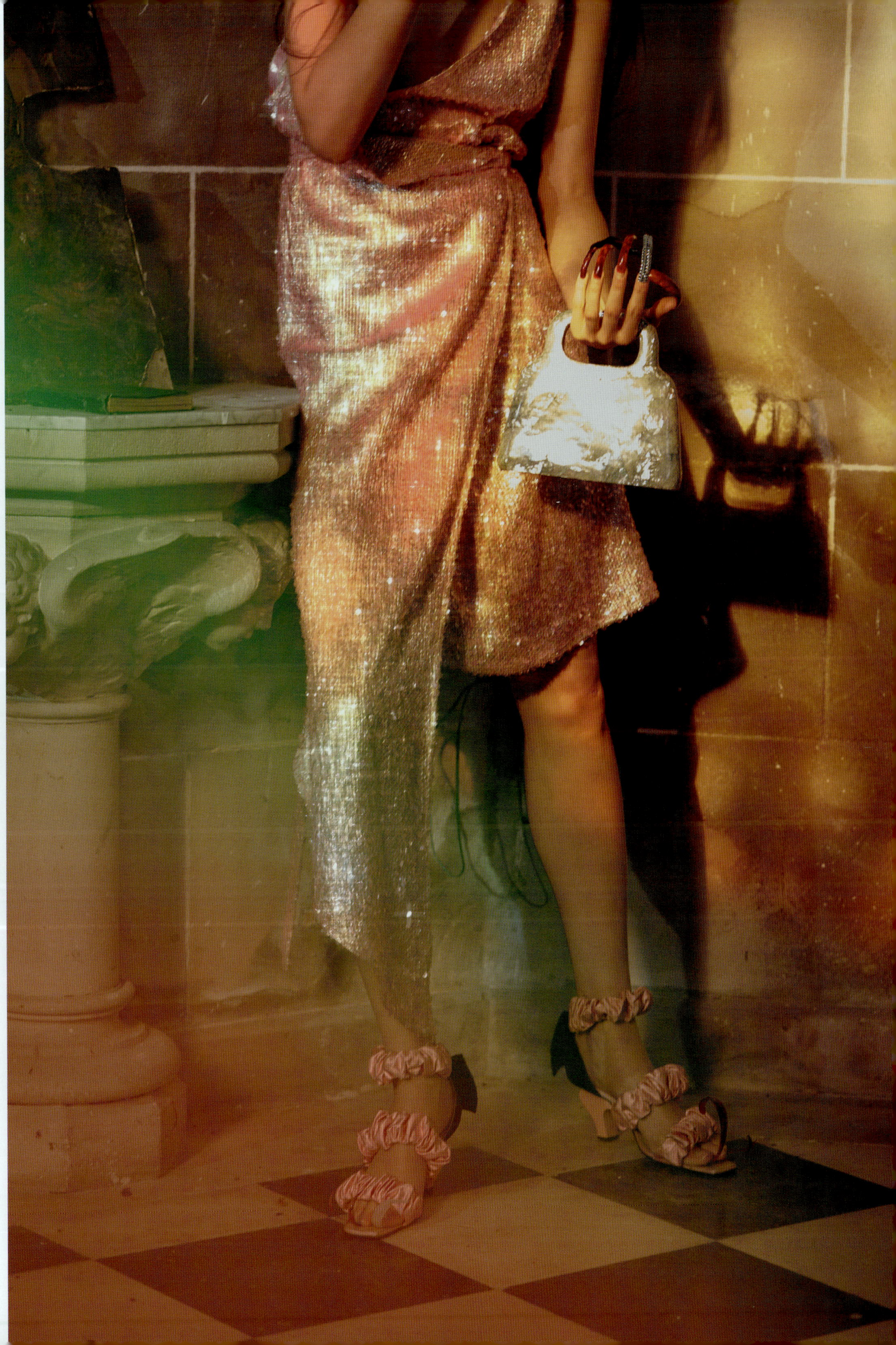

(Renata wears) Dress and Shoes: Neith Nyer / Bag: Mele+Marie

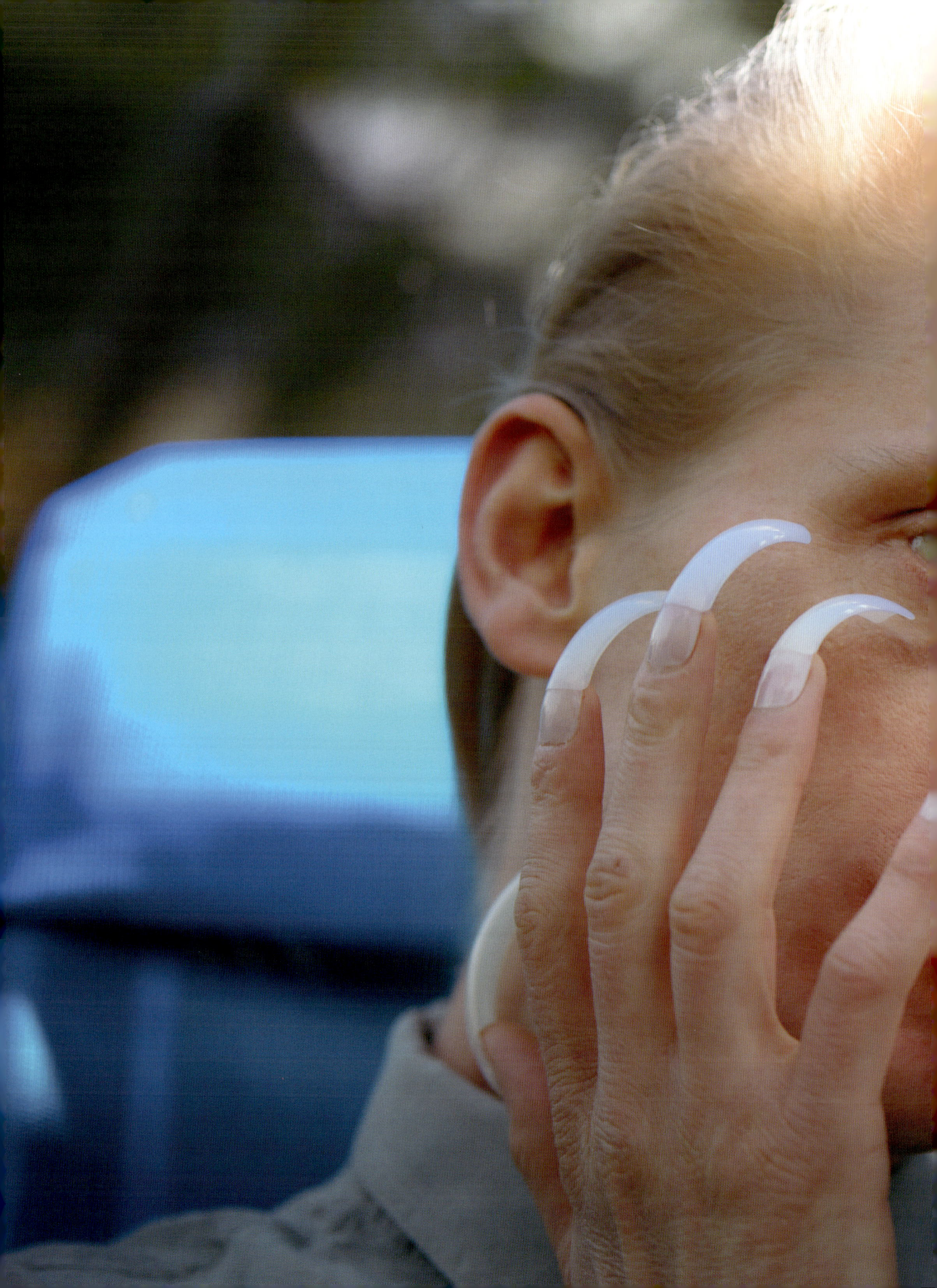

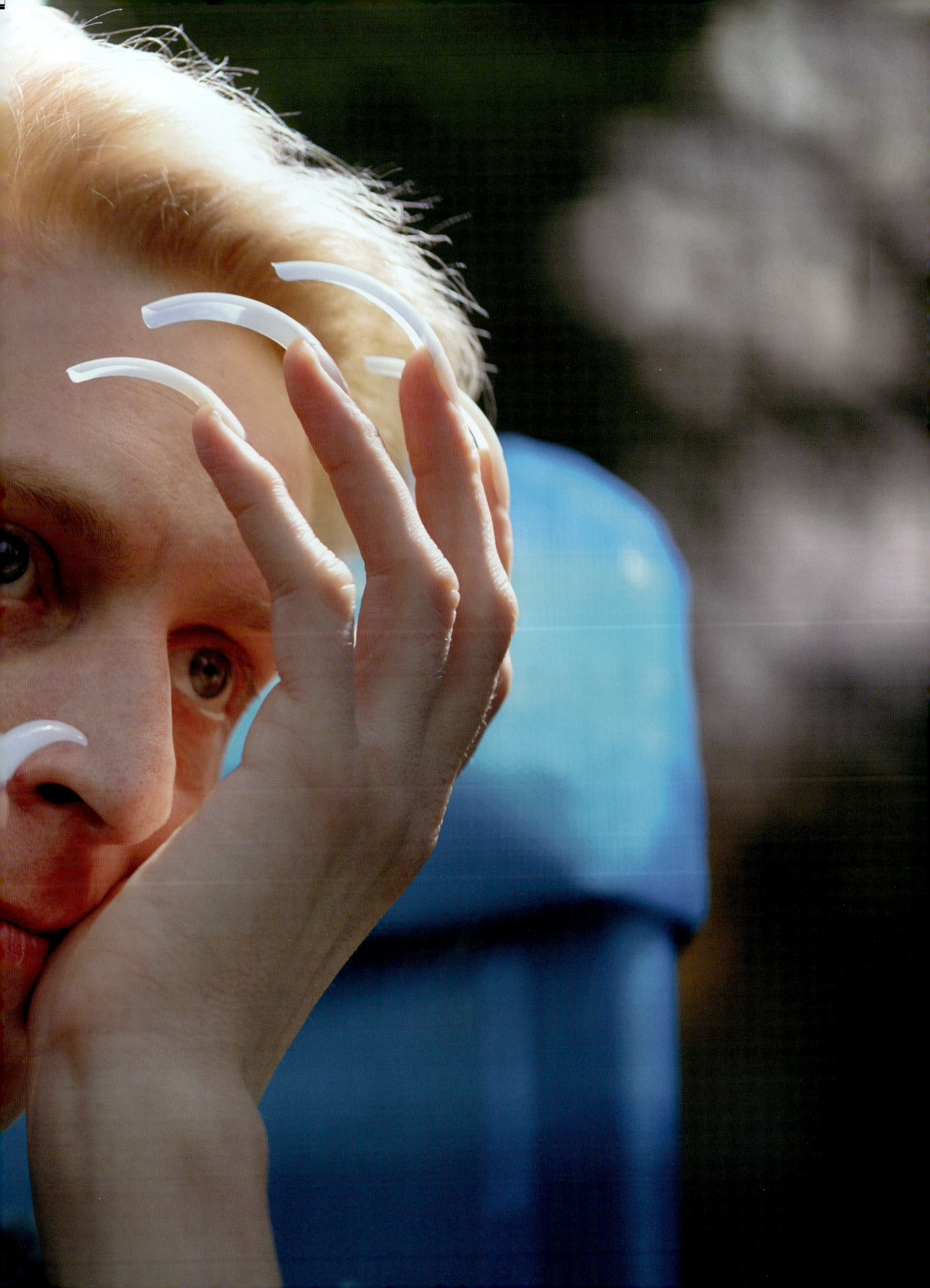

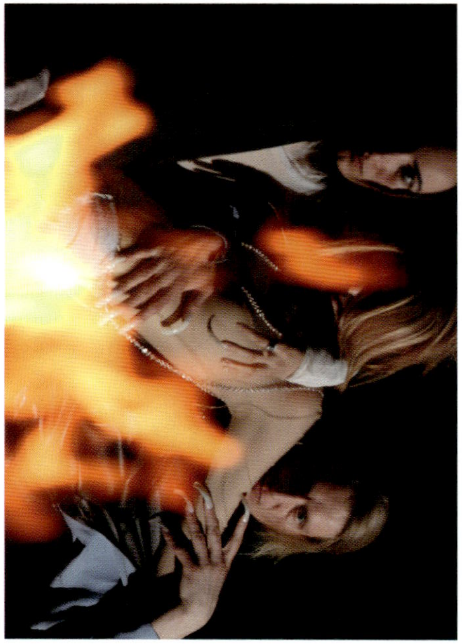
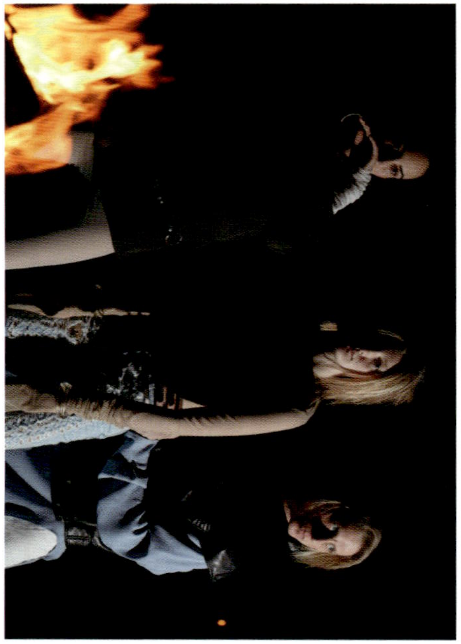
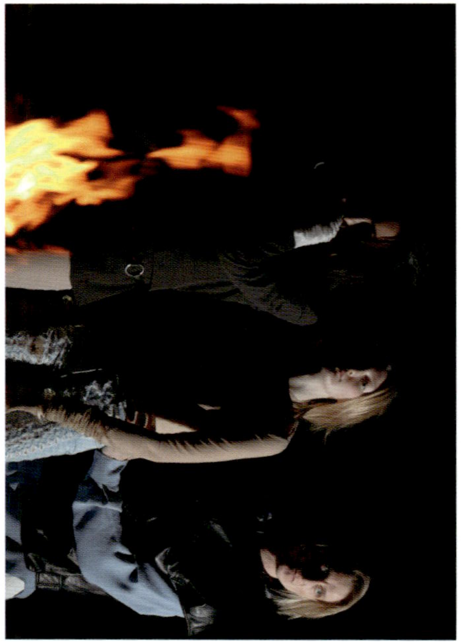
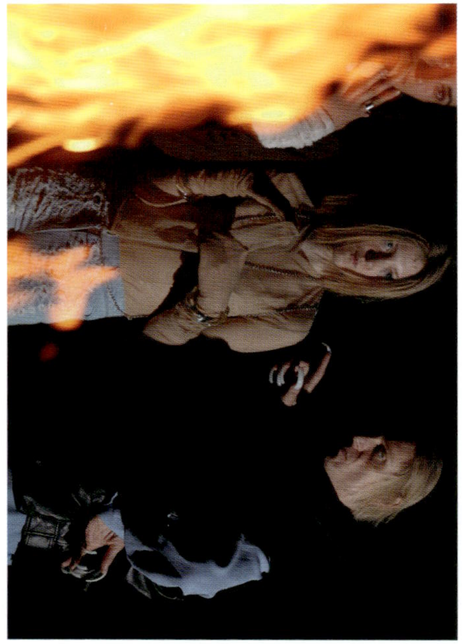
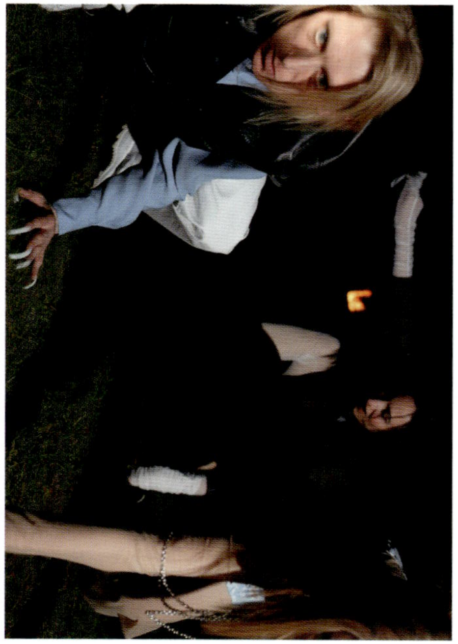
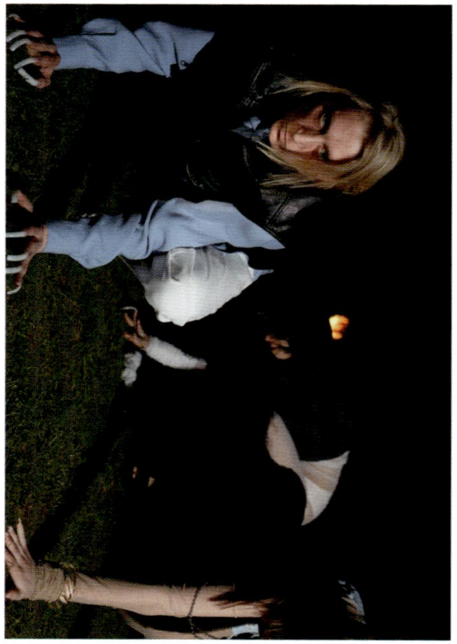
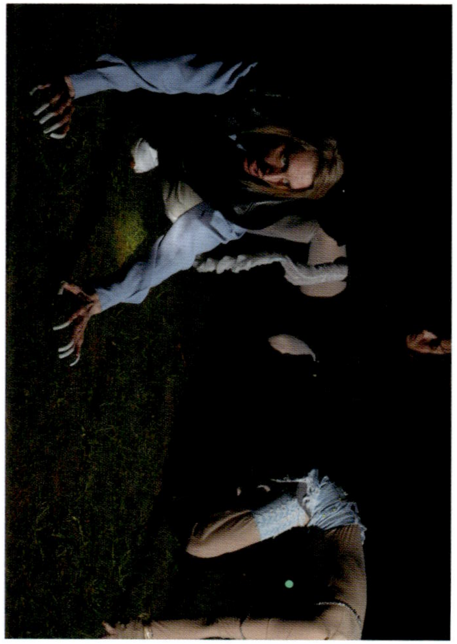
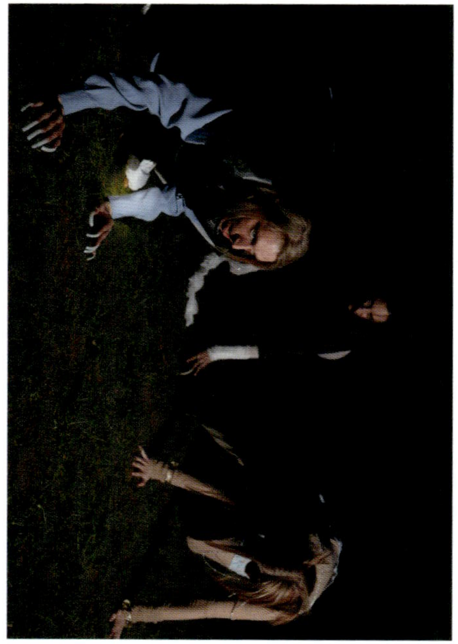

(Renata wears) Top: Léa Peckre / Pants: Marta Martino / Jacket: Our Legacy / Shoes: Flat Apartment / (Norman wears) Shirt: Louis Gabriel Nouchi / Leather vest: A.A. Spectrum / Pants: 032c / Shoes: Camper / (Yuri wears) Combi: Léa Peckre / Shorts: Drag & Drop / Body jewellery: D'heygere / Shoes: Rombaut / Bracelet: Anatheine Studio

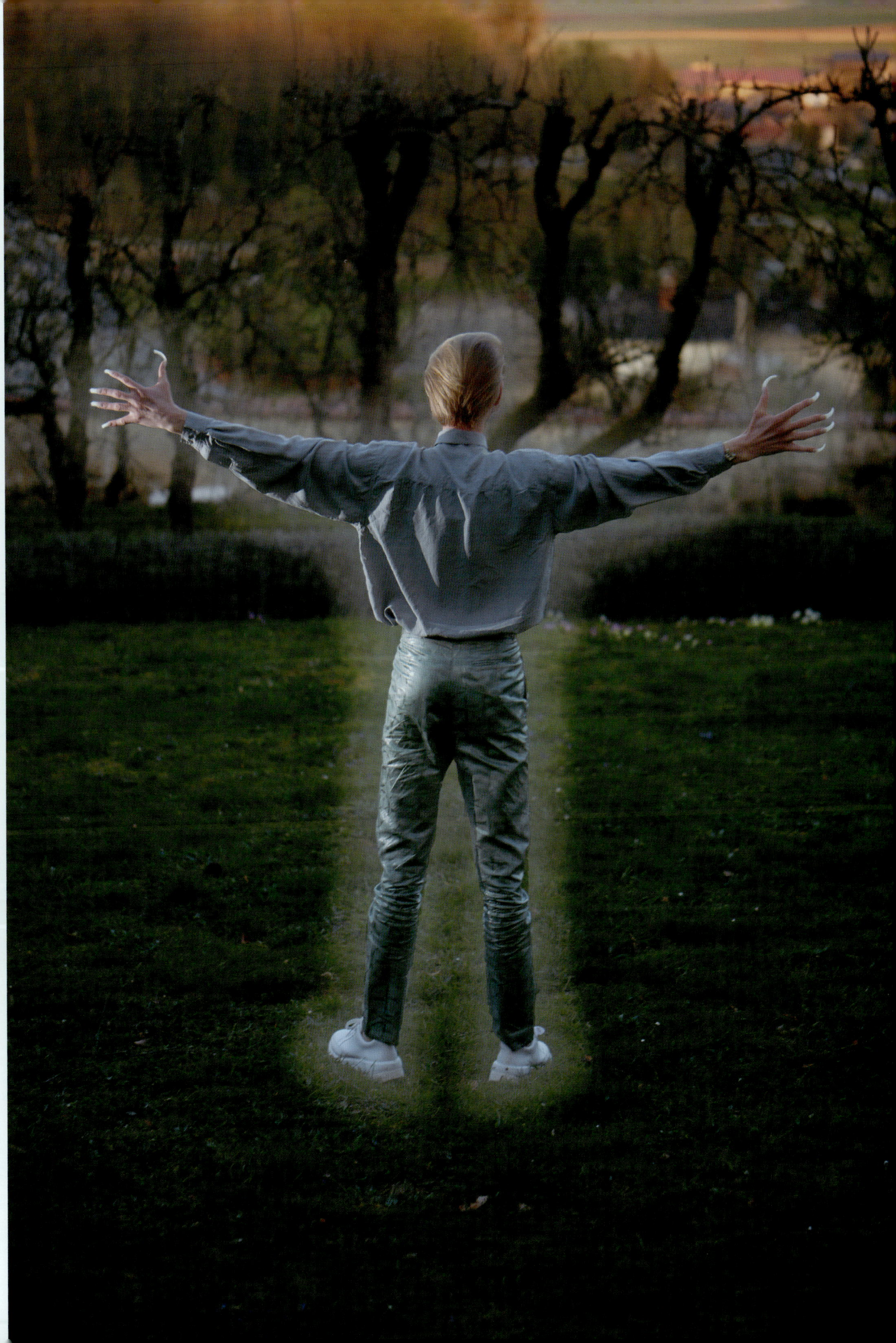

(Norman wears) Shirt and Tie: Vintage / Pants: Bless / Bracelet: Regina Dabdab / Shoes: Camper
Overleaf: (Renata wears) Dress and Shoes: Neith Nyer / Earrings: Lutz Huelle / Bag: Mele+Marie / (Norman wears) Top: Wendy Jim / Jacket: A.A. Spectrum / Shoes: Rombaut / Rings: Léa Peckre

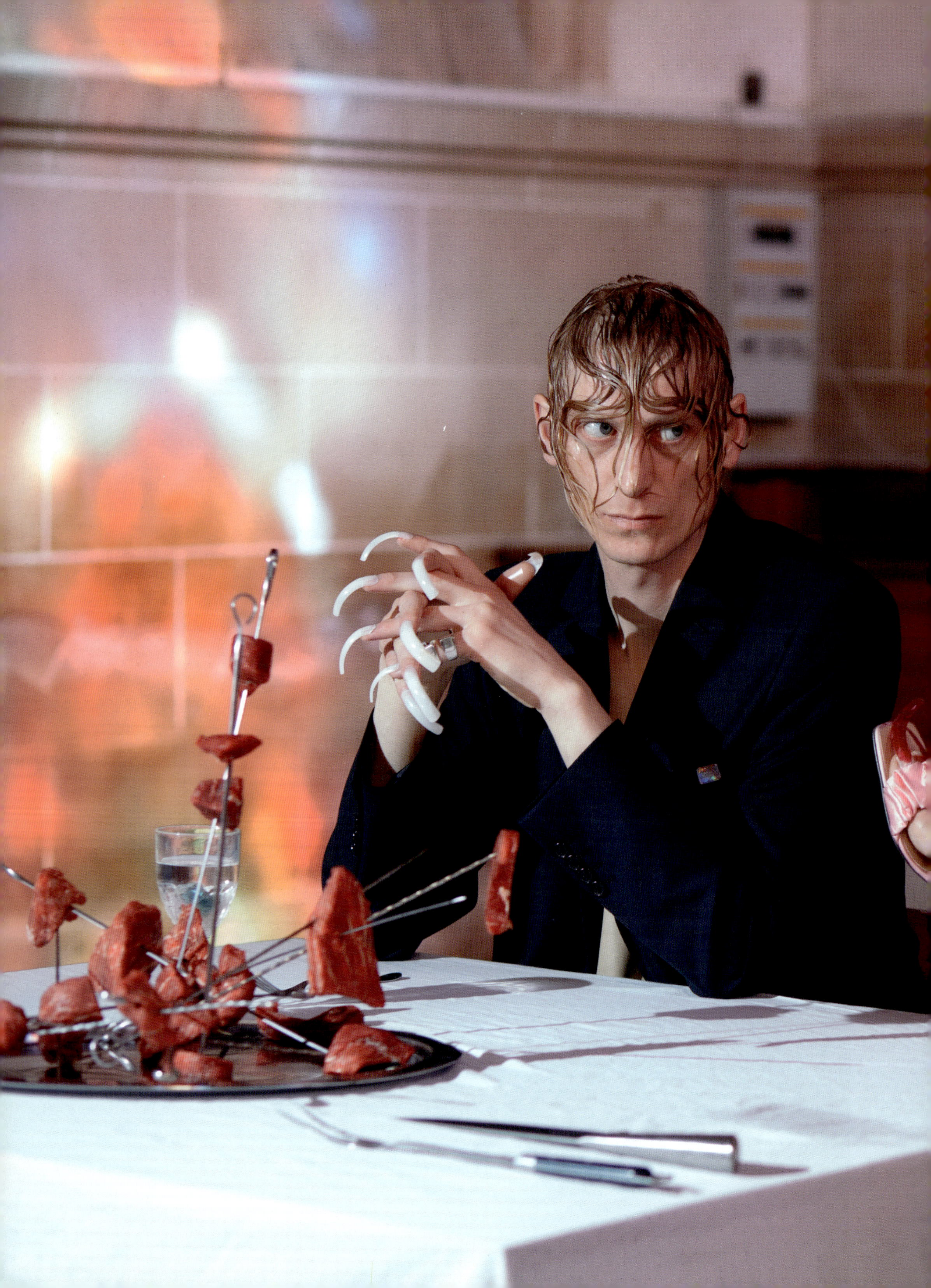

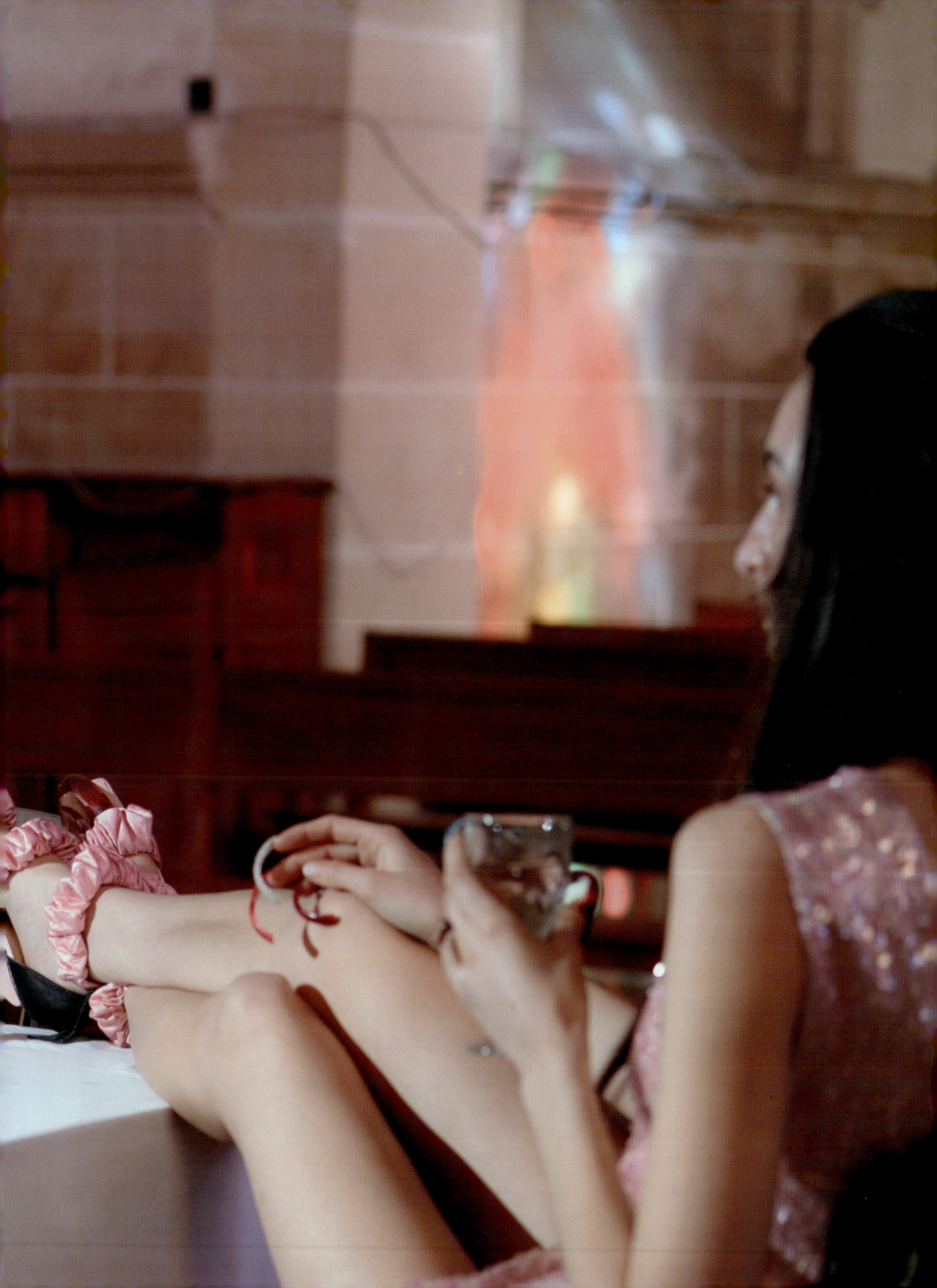

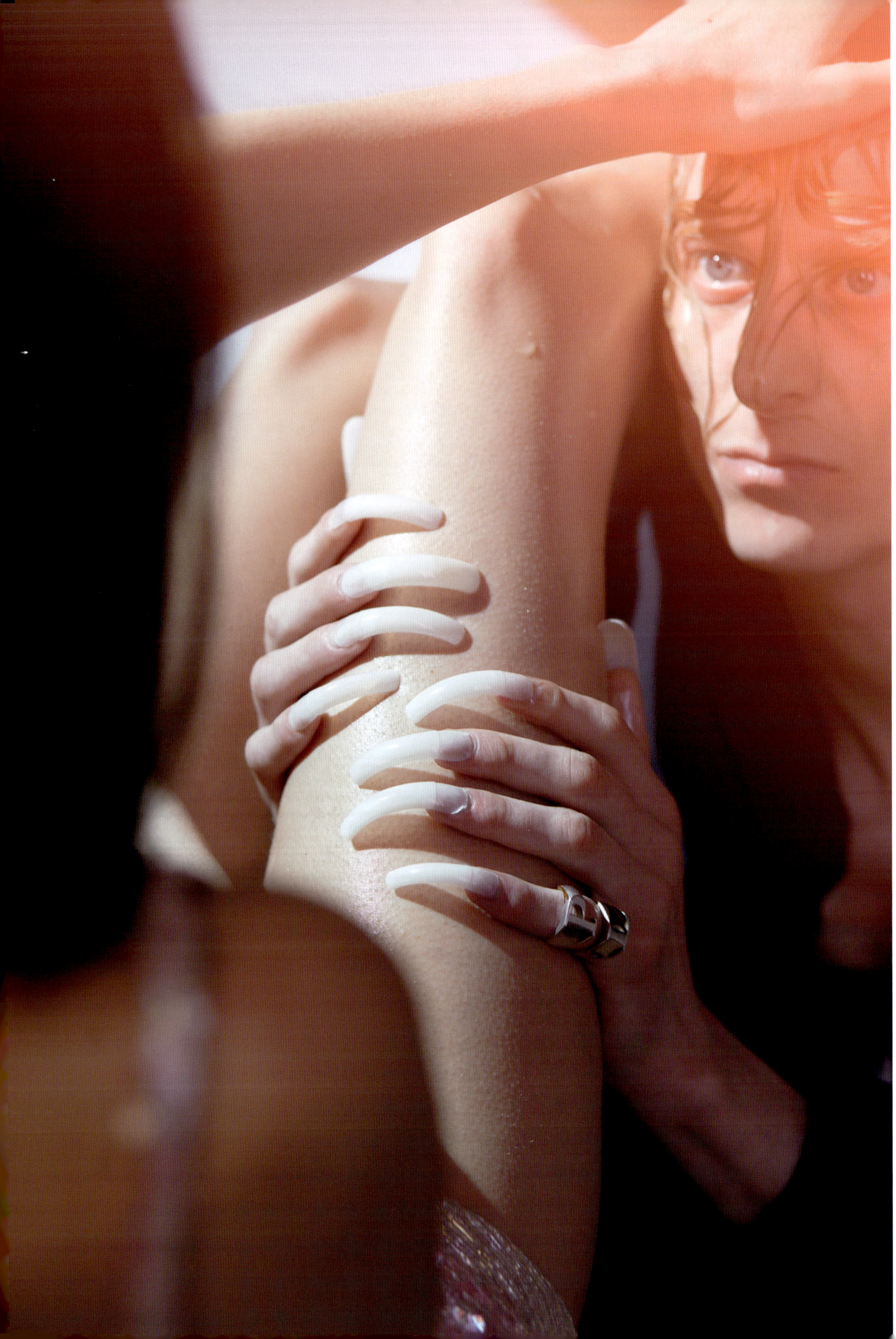

POR
T
FOL
IO

HANNAH VILLIGER'S POLAROID PORTFOLIO

Photography Hannah Villiger
Text Bice Curiger

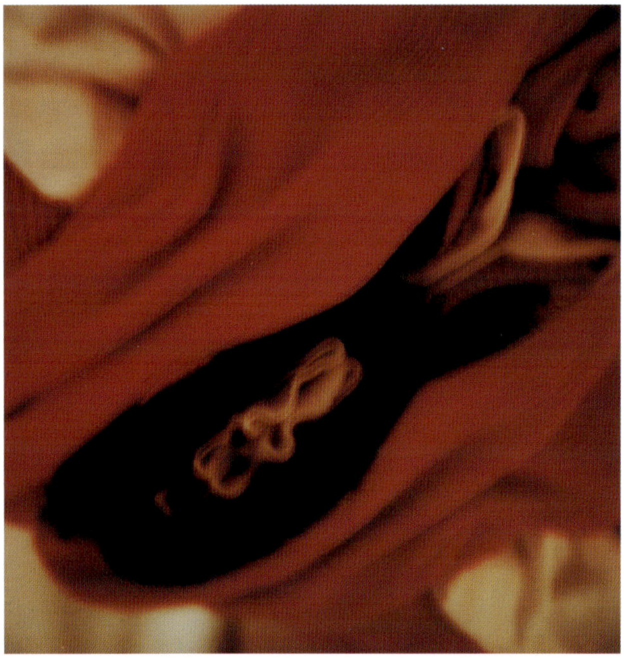

The following pages showcases a selection of the Hannah Villiger's more unknown Polaroids. Villiger, who died in 1997 at the untimely age of forty-six, left behind a wildly underrated body of work.

Hannah Villiger graduated from Luzern's art school in 1974, before spending the 1980s in Paris. She participated in the São Paulo Biennale in 1994, and for the duration of her career was known predominantly as a photographer, though she personally considered herself a sculptor—and rightly so. She famously experimented with using her own body as the subject of her images, often rendering herself fragmented, distorted, twisted and beyond recognition.

She exhibited her Polaroids as enlarged photographs in dynamic ensembles. The Polaroid Portfolio is accompanied by Bice Curiger's 1981 text "Hannah and the Horizon", affording us a poetic insight into the realm of Villiger and Curiger's work during this period.

Bice Curiger co-founded the magazine *Parkett* (1984–2017), was the curator of the Venice Biennale in 2011, and is currently the Artistic Director of the Fondation Vincent van Gogh in Arles, France.

HANNAH AND THE HORIZON*

When trying to describe physical feelings of any kind, we find ourselves shortchanged by language. I arrived at this conclusion after several, always hopelessly crude attempts to describe fundamental moments in Hannah Villiger's oeuvre. The public-at-large is quite capable of registering feelings of repulsion or extreme empathy when blood flows in the movies, when someone is cut, or surgery is performed, or when faced with eroticism, vertigo on a lookout tower or sports—all points on a scale that are clearly designated and defined. But in between lie immense micro-regions, dead lands, where words fail. This is the territory that Hannah Villiger explores. With a well-honed consciousness she masterfully negotiates the overall system of obstruction (of hindrance and enfeeblement). When communication is constantly kept in check, metaphor comes to the rescue. Perhaps this is why Hannah Villiger's work seems so womanly and so strong.

It is conceivable that the vertigo caused by verticals (at the edge of the abyss) has a gentle partner in horizontals (a kind of "window" feeling). When it is very intense, you feel it in your nostrils, your ears, your chest or—in connection with speed—your bottom. The fixed point is not the abyss, but the horizon. When I was a child and we went for a drive on Sundays, I would sit in the backseat and imagine—especially in fast curves—that I was riding a bicycle because I was never given one. Hannah Villiger can do it without a bicycle. That's what I have to think of when I see her photographs of gushing water, swift birds or colliding bocce balls. There is also the mute, squat airship, suspended in the sky, or the burning palm leaf thrown into the air. Here, pleasurable and extremely subtle use is made of the potential of empathy, which in turn makes us aware of our own potential and position as parts of a greater whole.

Hannah Villiger's much enlarged color Polaroids no longer record the vehemence of directly transmitted physical sensations; they have quieted down. "He had teeth like luxury hotels on the beach in Florida and when he closed his mouth, there was a big scar." (Laurie Anderson) These color photographs, usually one meter square, gradually turn into boxes the longer you look at them. Boxes into which you poke your head very, very slowly without noticing, because the pull is so gentle. And damp fog, pointed palm leaves, skin or gazes brush against us, passing by. But there are also pictures, the energy of which is directed outwards, pictures that radiate, so that we already notice from afar that we are being kept at bay. These are the cold pictures, like the eye with a razor-sharp gaze. Once you have stood in front of them, you know that the format of these photographs is incontestable.

Sometimes the subject matter of a picture ignites feelings; other times it is a vessel or catchment for them. In memory, such distinctions are often utterly irrelevant. For this reason, Hannah Villiger's wooden or plexiglas objects crop up again in her photo works. Is Hannah Villiger the fog creeping around the mountain, or is the fog enveloping her? Movement back and forth, sudden clashes and leaps, simultaneous flowing and flying flit through Hannah Villiger's work until a compact whole emerges—like her name, HANNAH...

Translation: Catherine Schelbert

* This article was first published in *Künstler aus Basel*, exh. cat., Kunsthalle Basel (Basel: 1981), n.p.

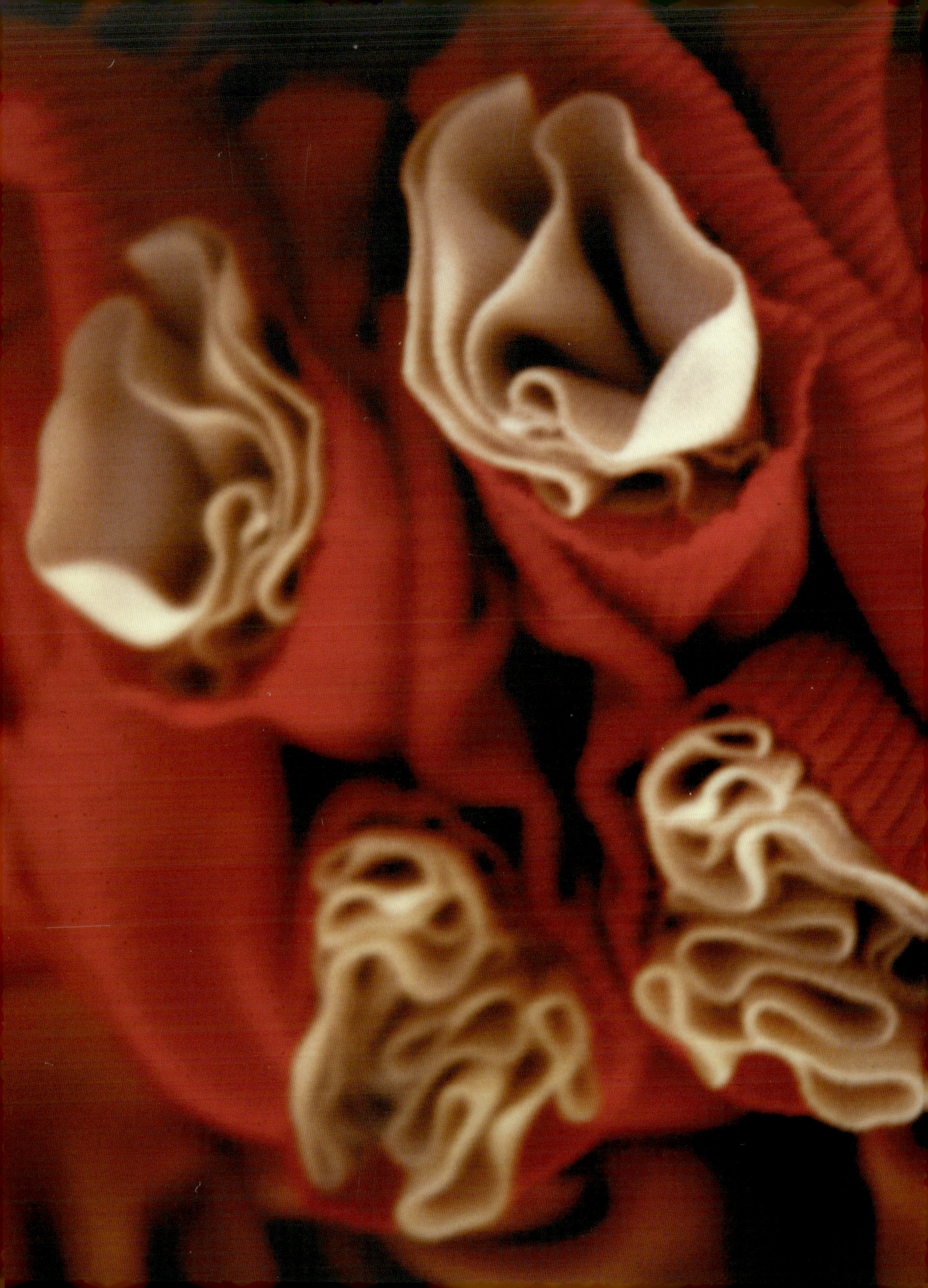

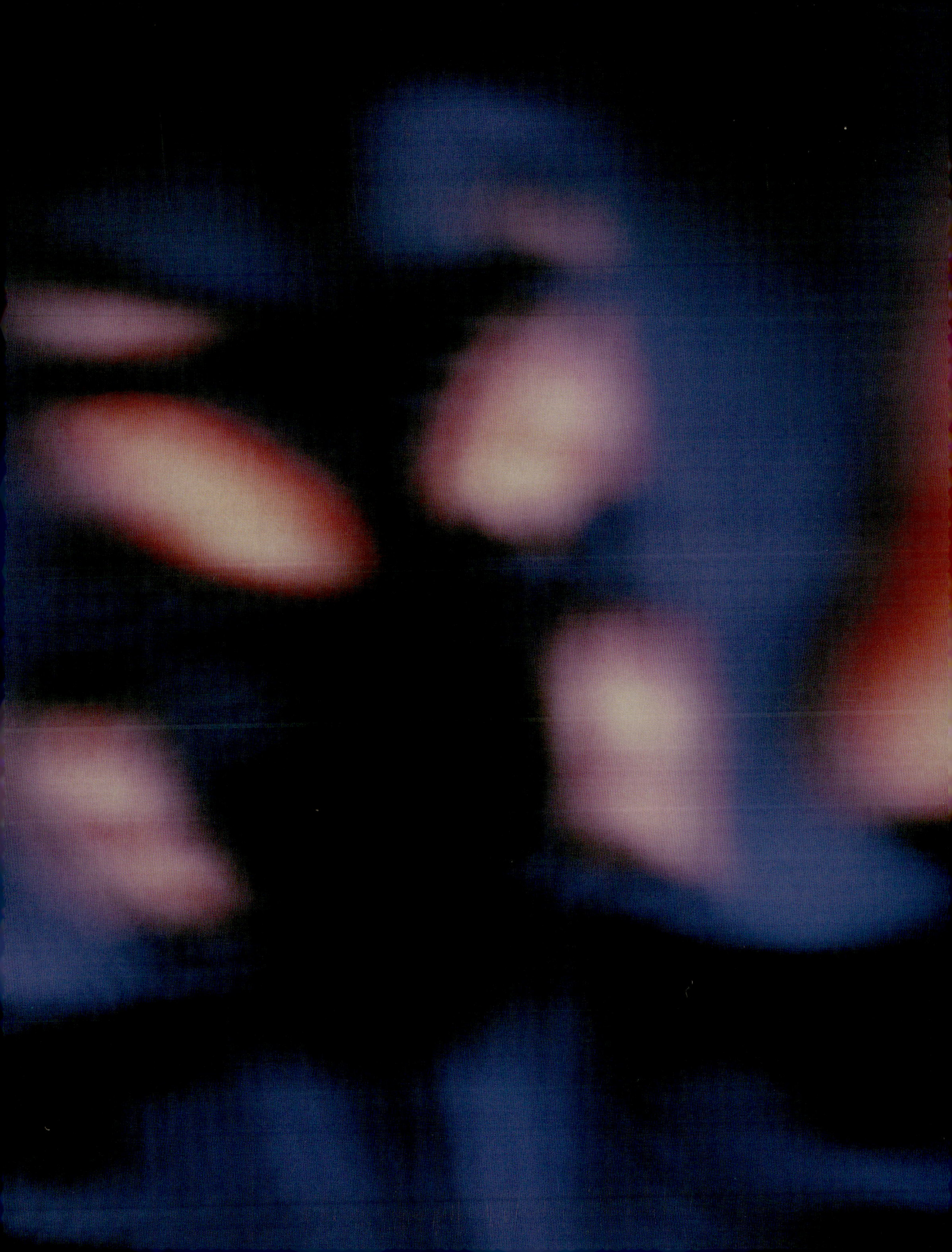

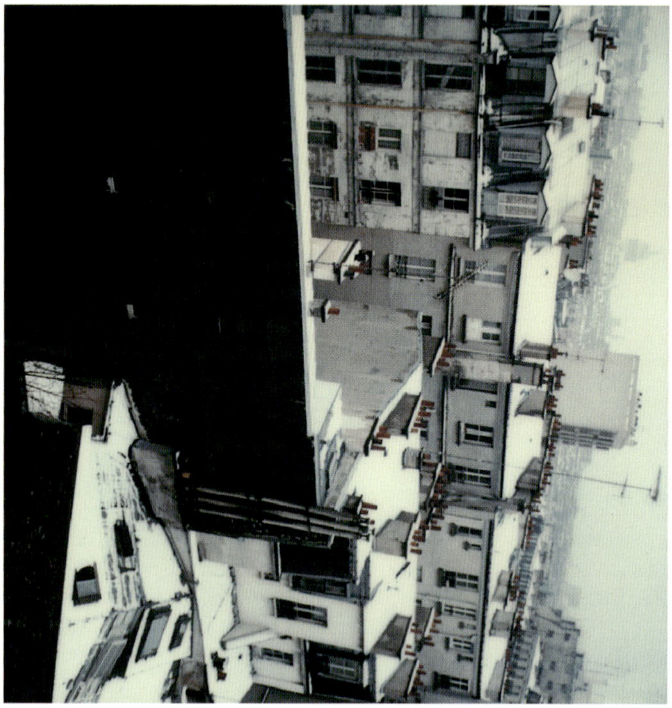

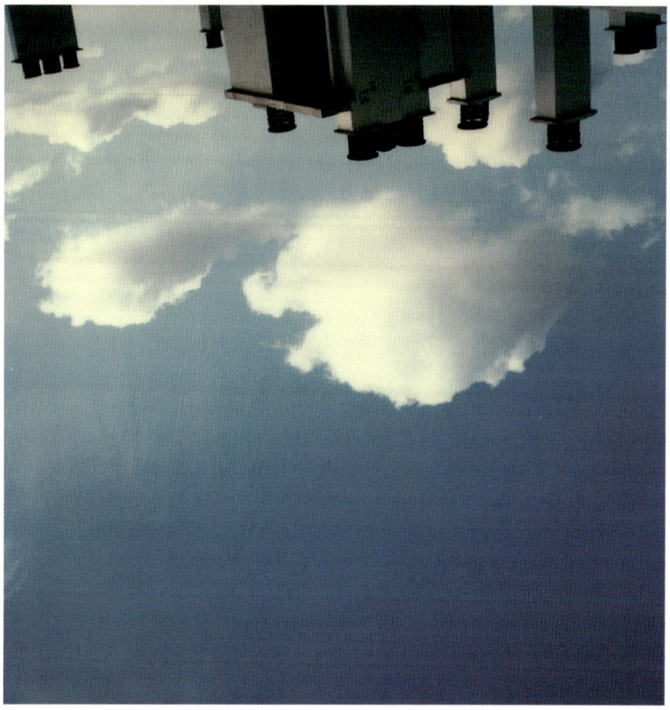

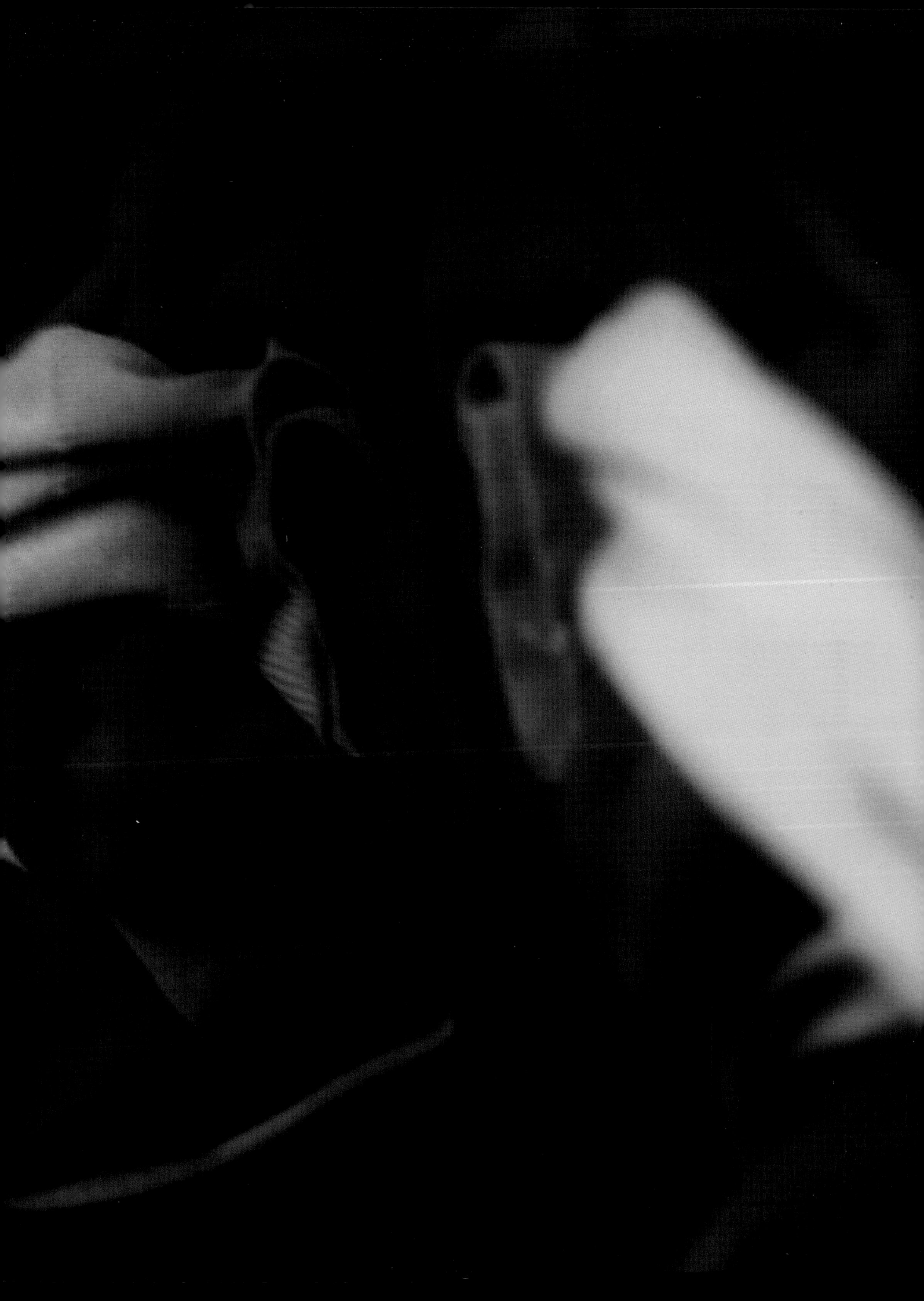

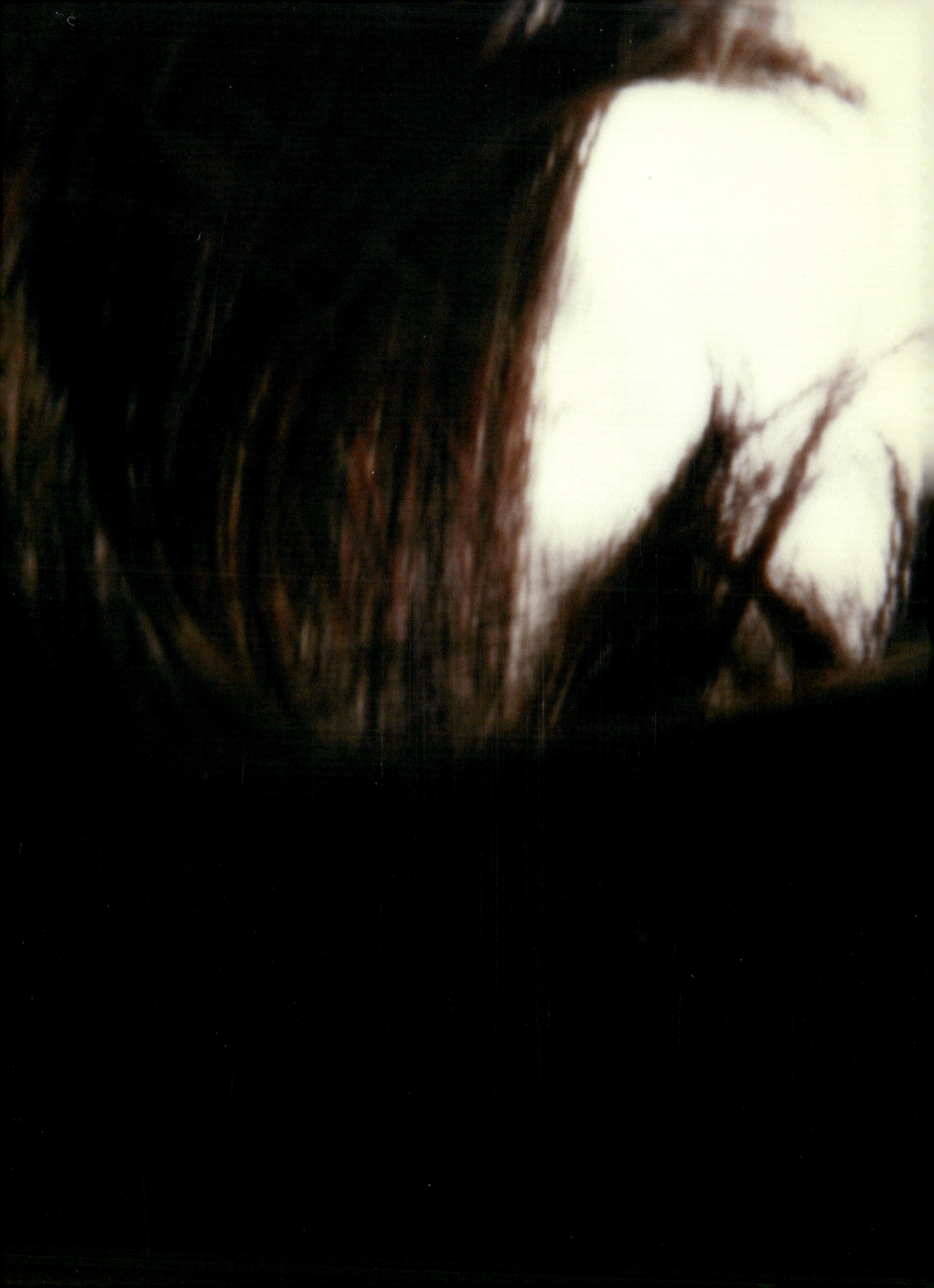

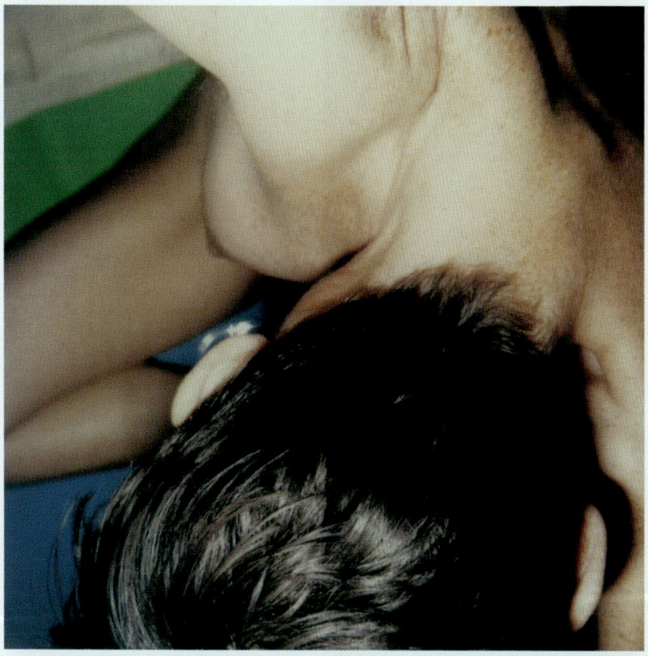
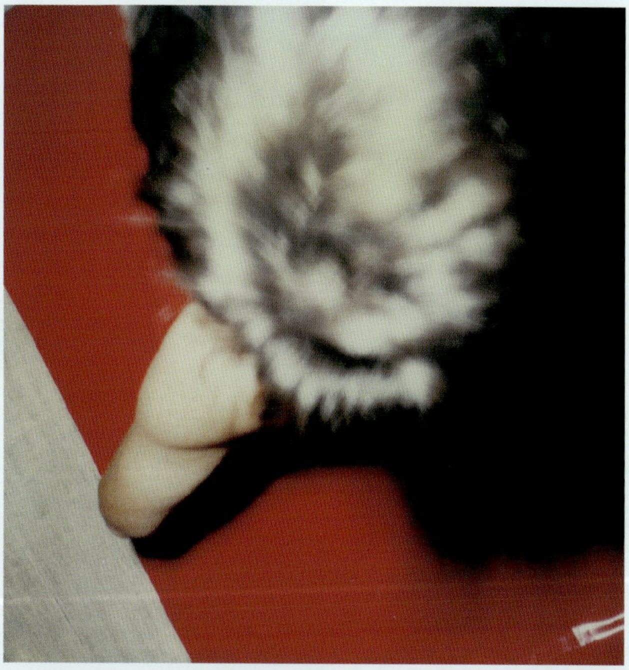
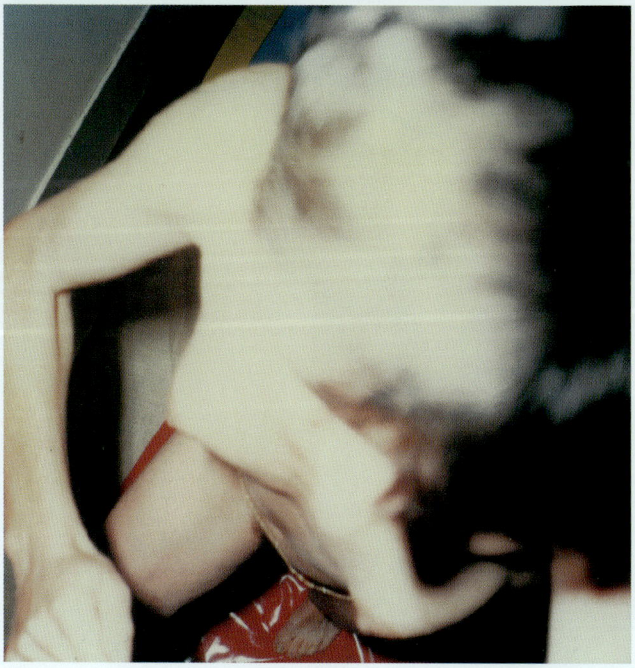
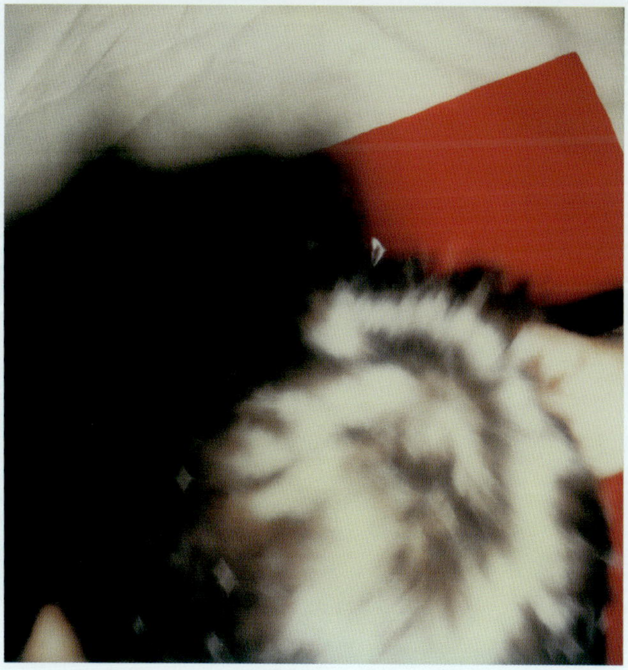

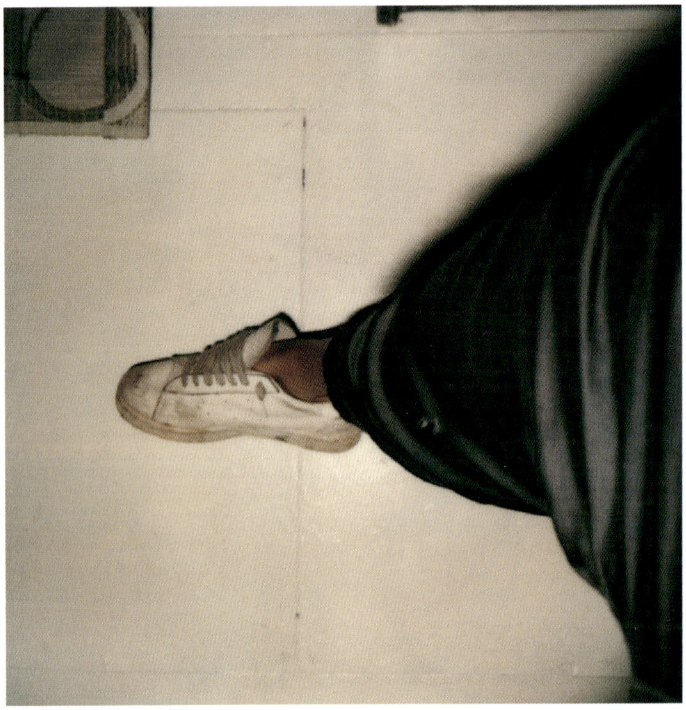

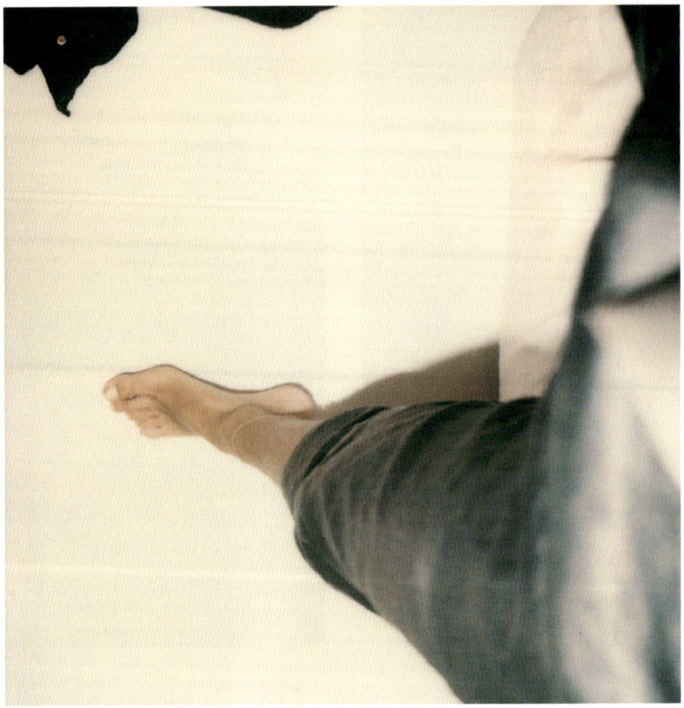

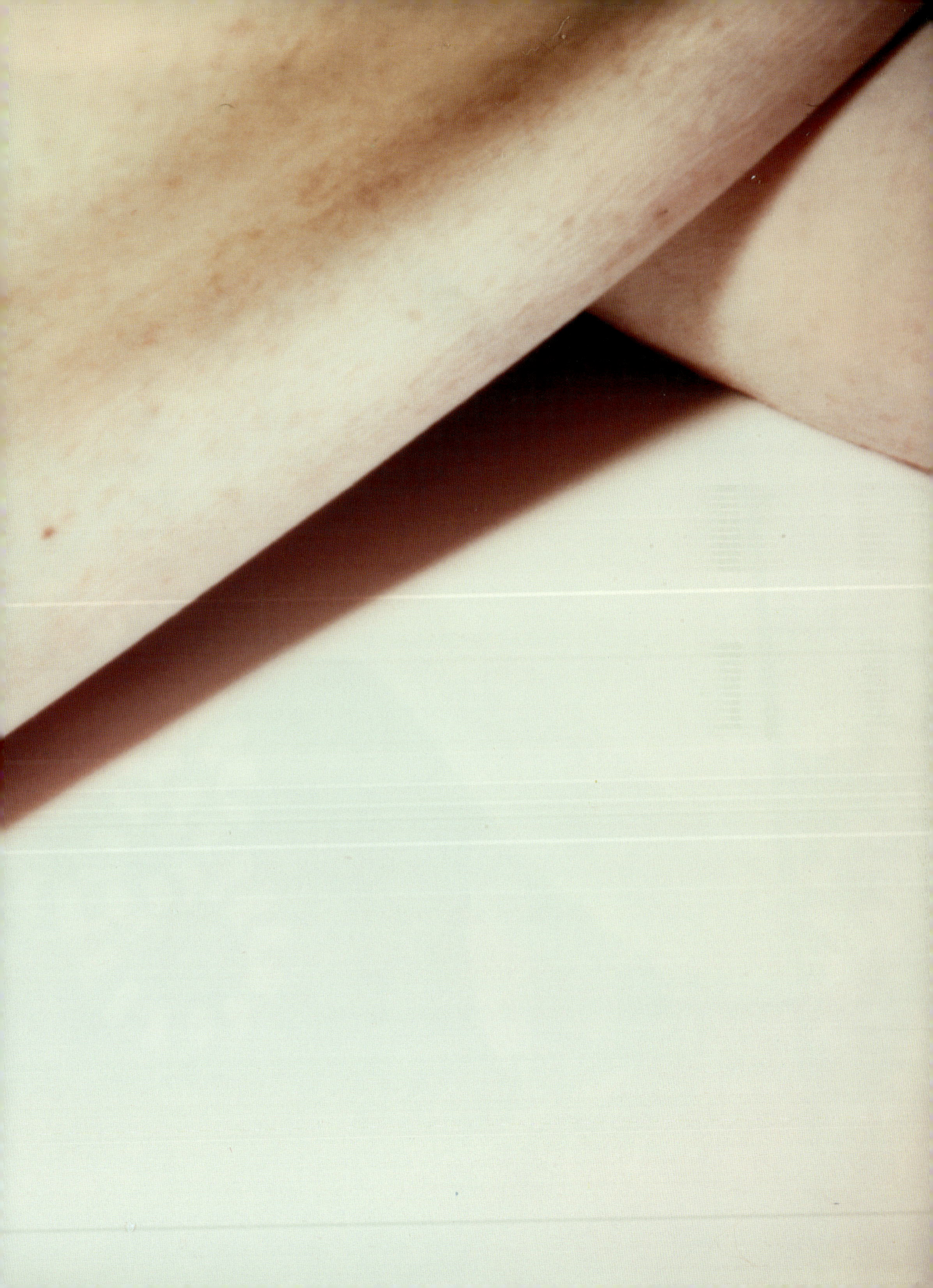

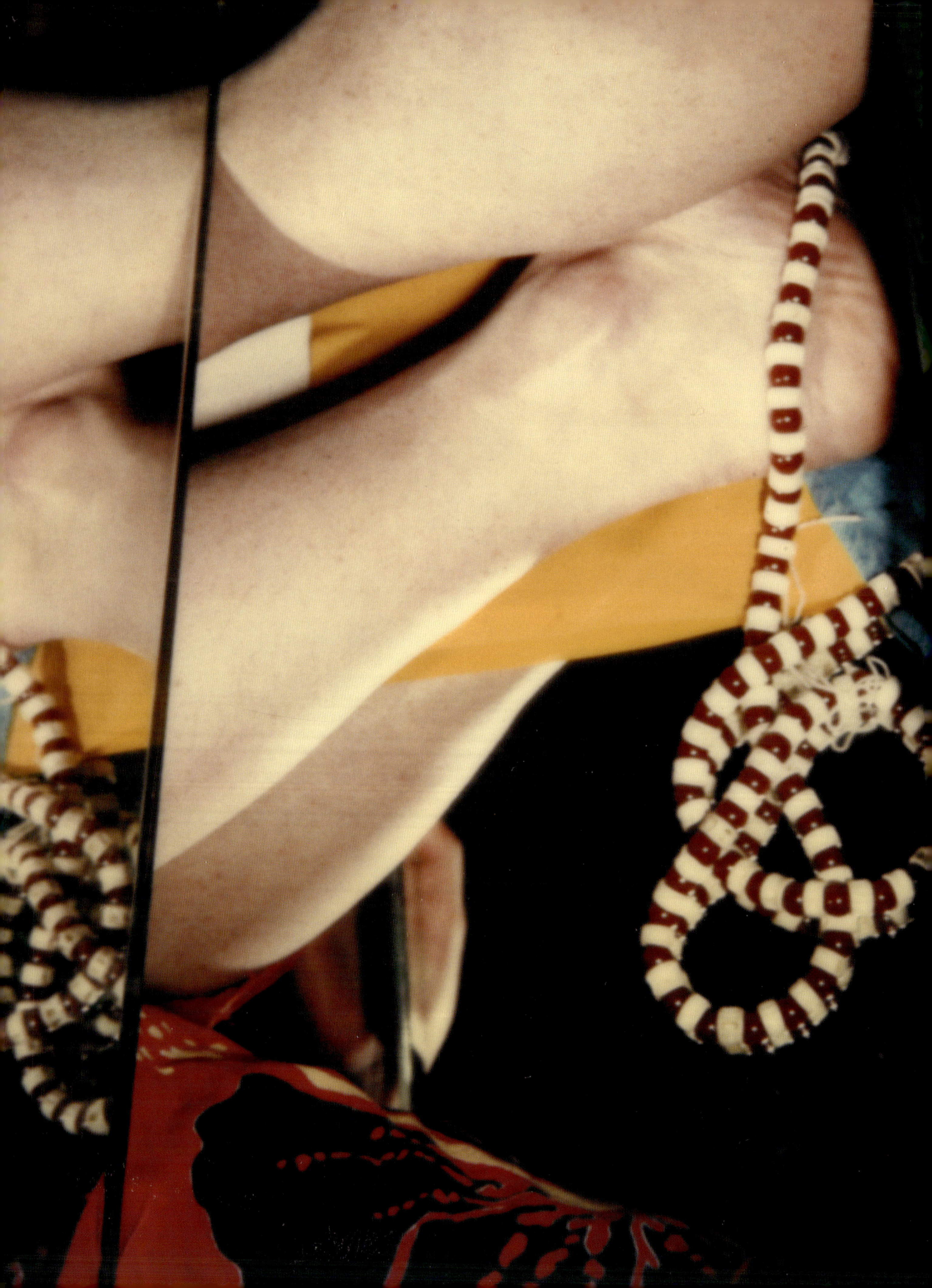

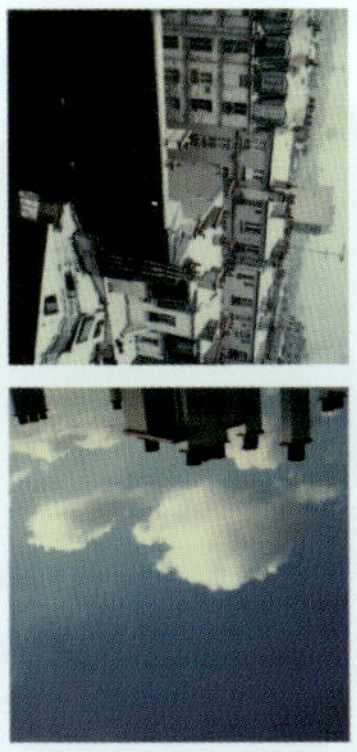

City, 1994/95, two polaroids, mounted on cardboard, 19.5×8.8cm, No. 445, copyright The Estate of Hannah Villiger

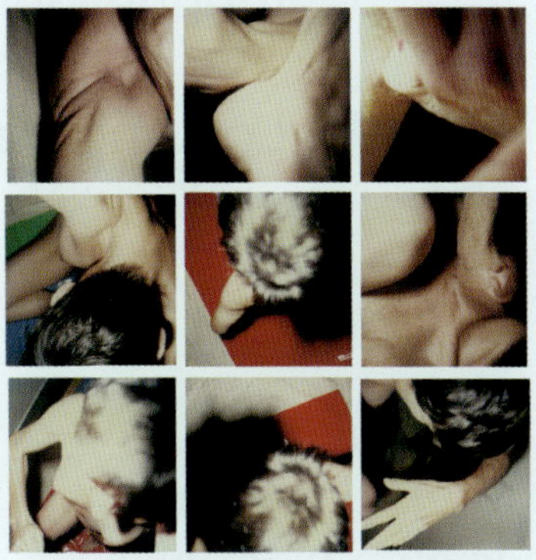

Block XXVI, 1990/92, nine C-prints of polaroids, mounted on aluminum, 385×379cm, No. 395, copyright The Estate of Hannah Villiger

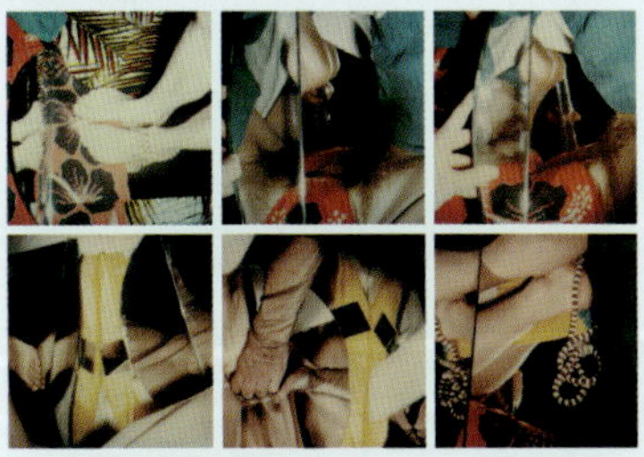

Block XVII, 1989, polaroids, mounted on cardboard, 21×25.5cm, No. 305, copyright The Estate of Hannah Villiger

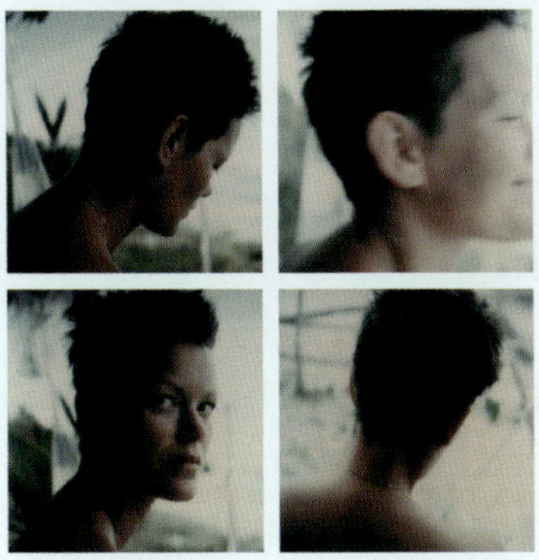

Work, 1980/81, four C-prints of polaroids, each 38×38cm, No. 107, copyright The Estate of Hannah Villiger

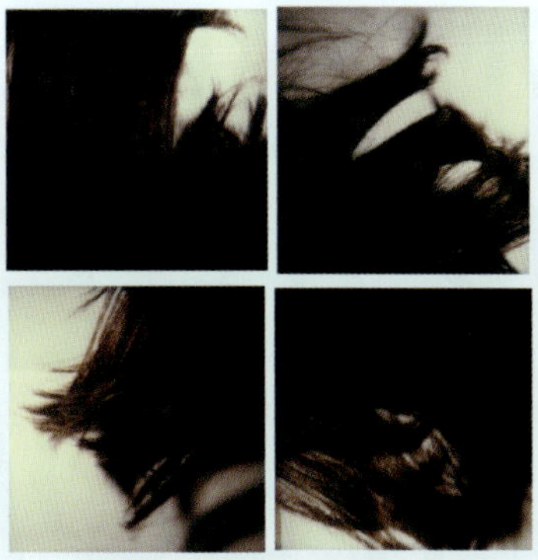

Sculptural, 1996, four polaroids, mounted on aluminum, 21×21cm, No. 466, copyright The Estate of Hannah Villiger

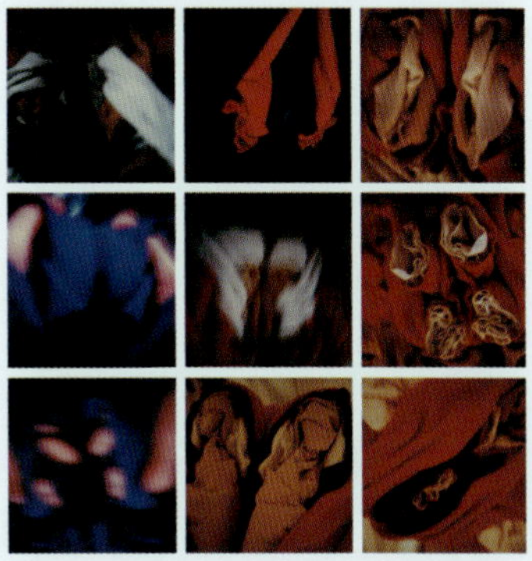

Block, 1996, nine C-prints of polaroids, mounted on aluminum, 385×379cm, No. 476, copyright The Estate of Hannah Villiger

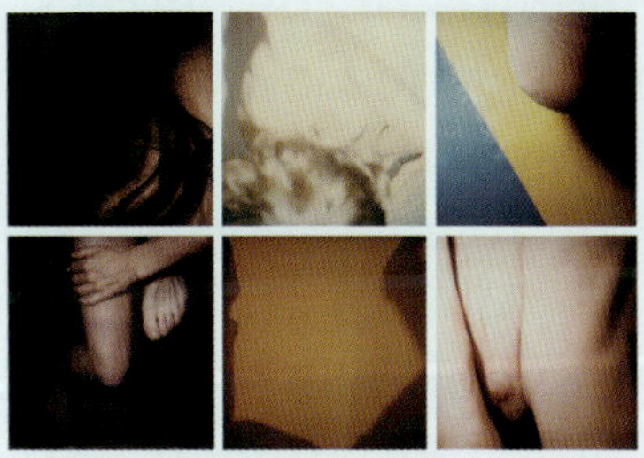

Block, 1997, six C-prints of polaroids, mounted on aluminum, 254×377cm, No. 476, copyright The Estate of Hannah Villiger

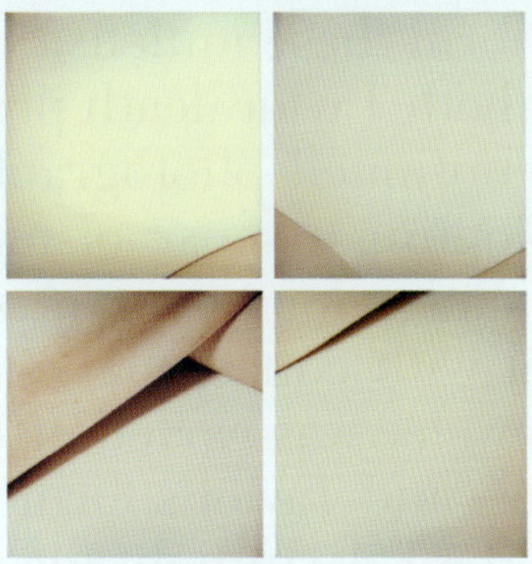

Block XXXV, 1994, four C-prints of polaroids, mounted on aluminum, 258×254cm, No. 394, copyright Cabinet des estampes du Musée d'art et d'histoire, Geneva; The Estate of Hannah Villiger

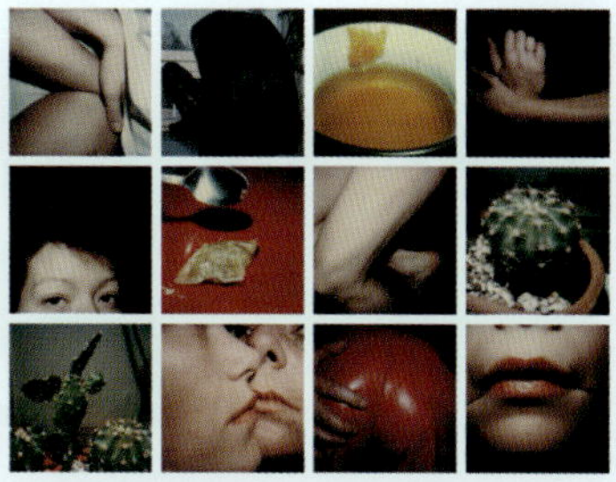

Work, 1980/81, twelve C-prints of polaroids, mounted on aluminum, 355×475cm, No. 90, copyright Aargauer Kunsthaus and The Estate of Hannah Villiger

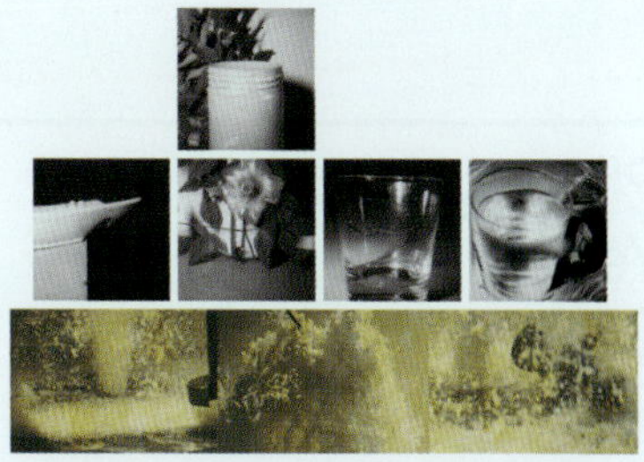

Needy/Sculpting, 1982/83, three coloured black/white photographs and five black/white prints of polaroids, mounted on aluminum, 286×411cm, No. 140, copyright The Estate of Hannah Villiger

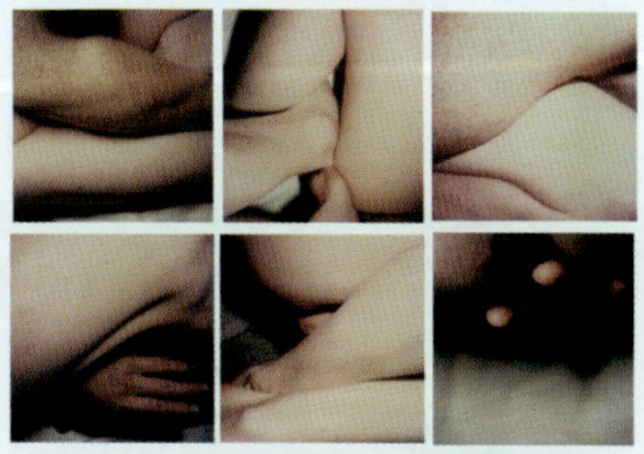

Block XX, 1990, six C-prints of polaroids, mounted on aluminum, 255×379cm, No. 308, copyright The Estate of Hannah Villiger

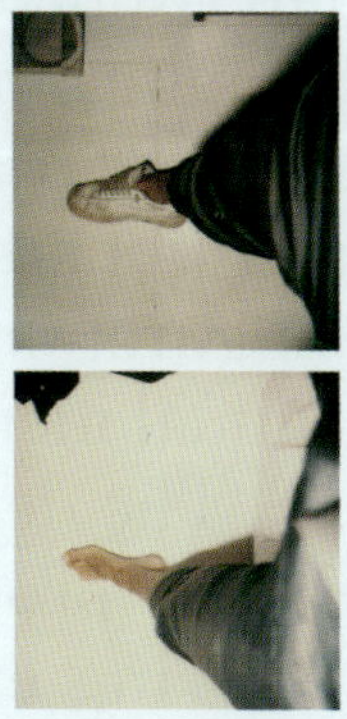

Work, 1981, 2 C-prints of polaroids, each 38×38cm, No. 106, copyright The Estate of Hannah Villiger

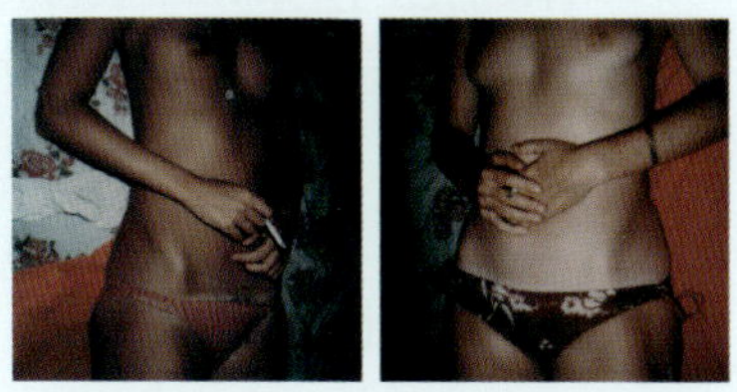

Work, 1981, 2 C-prints of polaroids, each 38×38cm, No. 105, copyright The Estate of Hannah Villiger

CATHERINE OPIE'S *ELIZABETH TAYLOR*

Photography	Catherine Opie
Year	2010–11
Courtesy	Regen Projects, Los Angeles

Catherine Opie and Elizabeth Taylor shared an accountant. One day, the accountant offered to introduce Opie—a long-time admirer of Taylor's AIDS advocacy as it was reflective of her own work as a supporter of organizations such as Act Up and Queer Nation—to the Hollywood legend. And so in 2011, she began shooting at Taylor's home during the final months of the actress' life.

It would be fair to describe Catherine Opie as a documenter of American landscapes, irrespective of whether they are physical, political or ideological. Having toggled between portrait, landscape and studio photography in conceptual and documentary styles for more than twenty-five years, Opie's work is often as much about the photographical medium as it is her subjects. She chronicles communities like an anthropologist—high school football players, bondage practitioners, Malibu surfers, the crowd at President Obama's first inauguration, lesbian couples across the U.S.—and explores the individual identities that form these milieus.

The death of Elizabeth Taylor death profoundly altered Opie's creative process. She continued photographing as Taylor's estate was being executed, adopting a sense of movement. Having until that point shot mostly static, documentary-style images, Opie was now able to experiment with conceptual, staged work. In the moments before Taylor's jewelry was carted off to Christie's to be auctioned, for example, Opie and Taylor's former assistant laid out the jewels on the couch in the LA-sunlight for a series of abstract pictures. "It was a moment of homage," Opie says. "We would never have [done that] if she'd been alive."

On the last page of this portfolio is a suite of photographs provided by the auction house in charge of selling Taylor's belongings.

Elisabeth and Richard

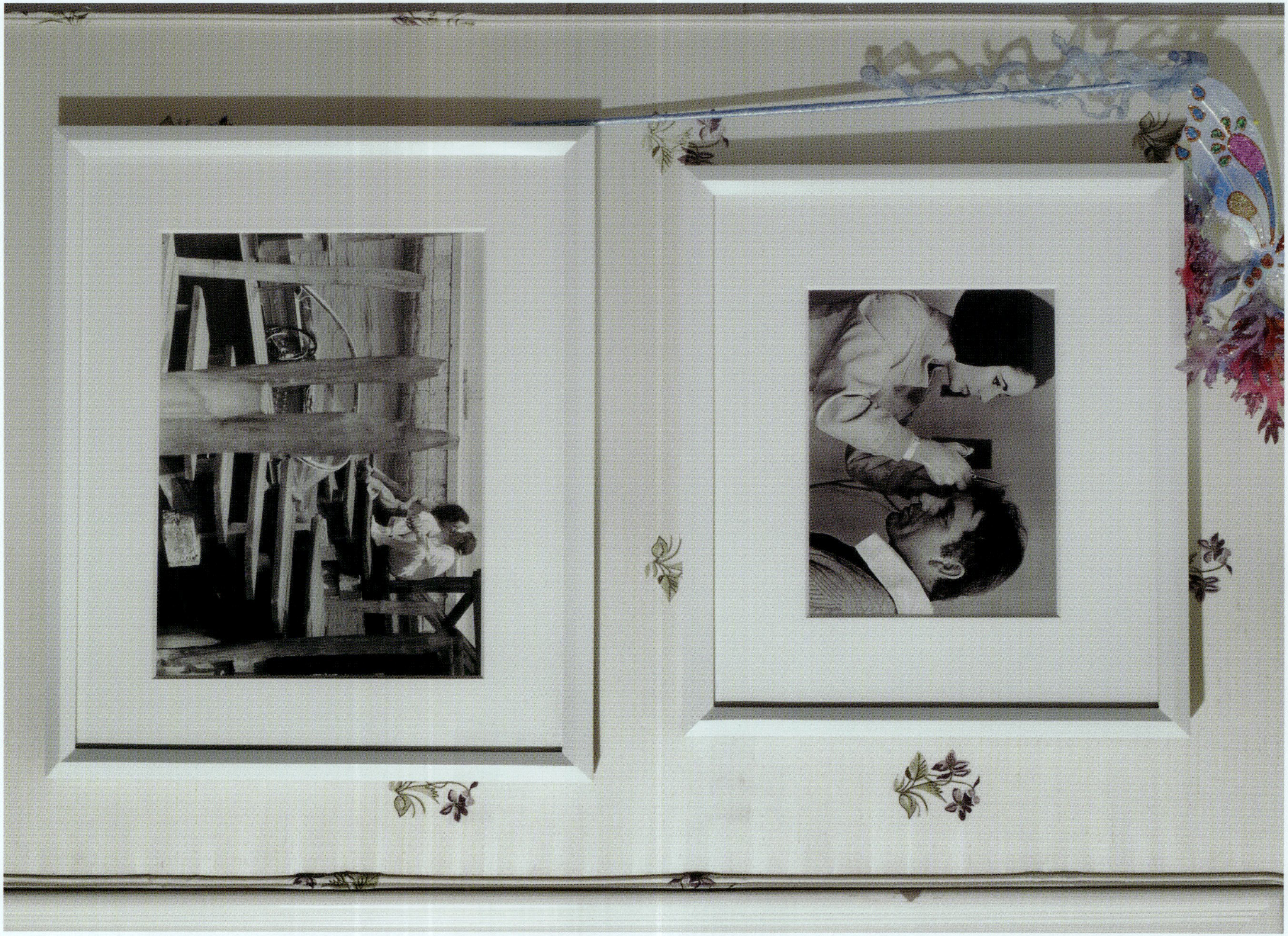

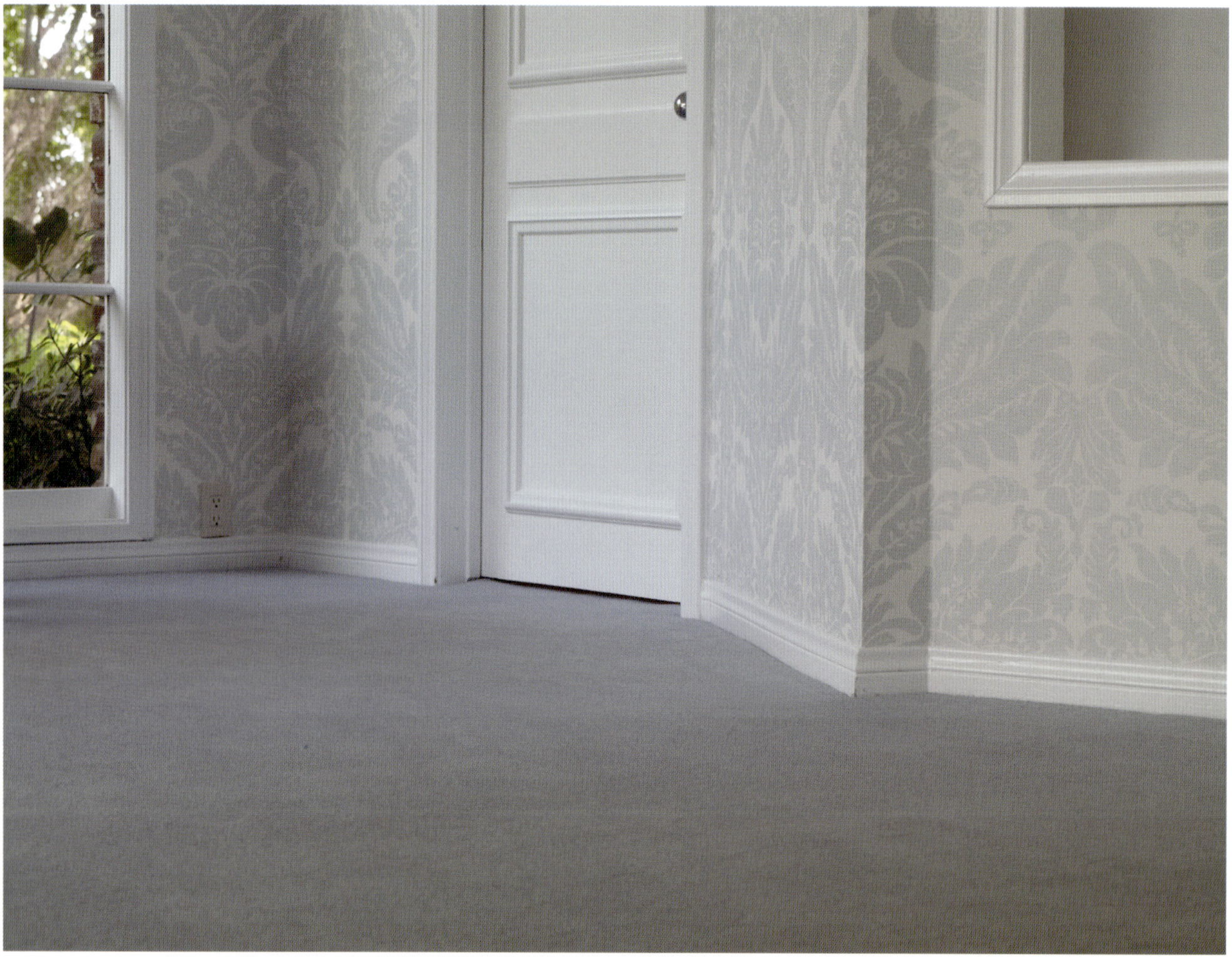

Blue Room Corner

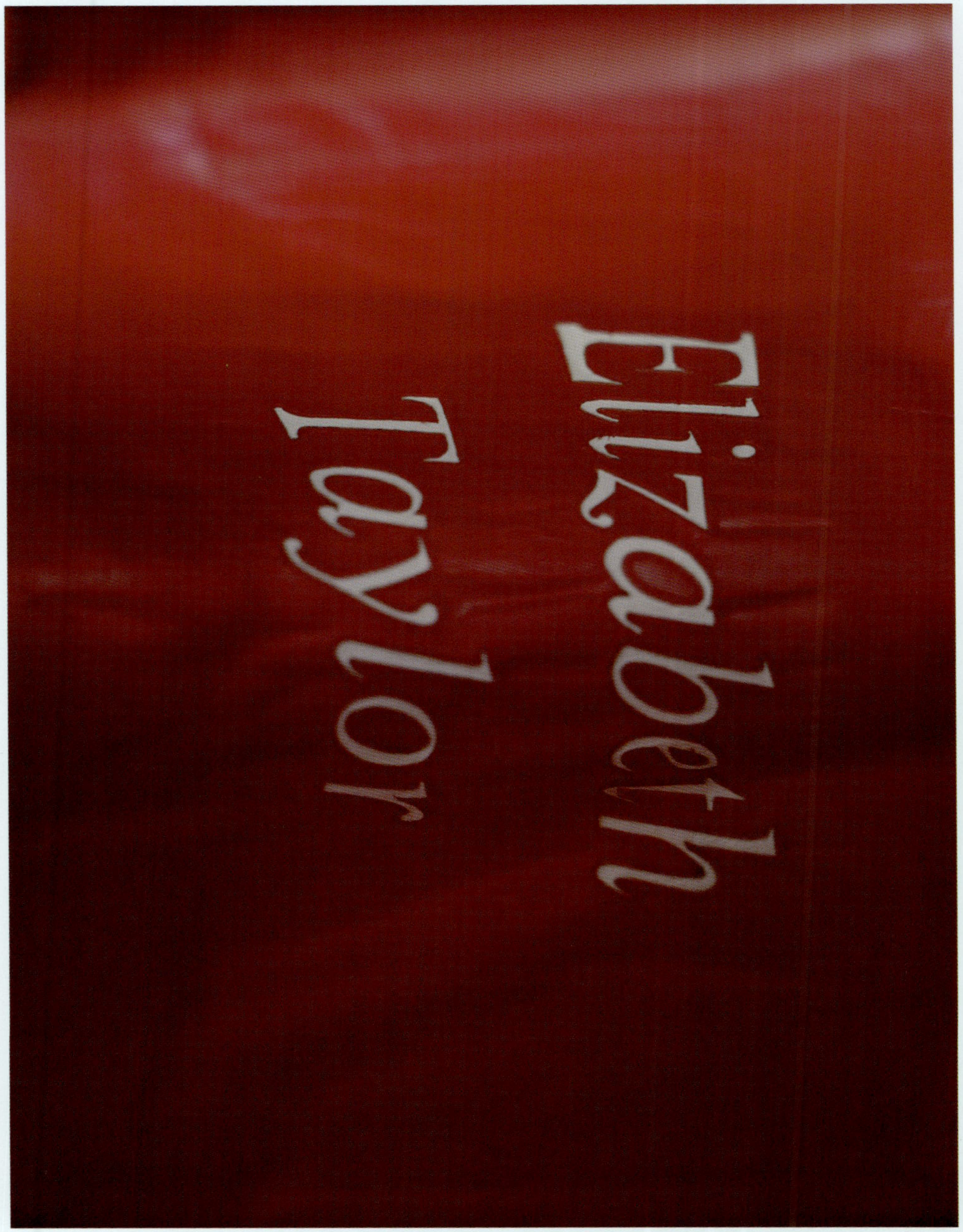

Red Directors Chair

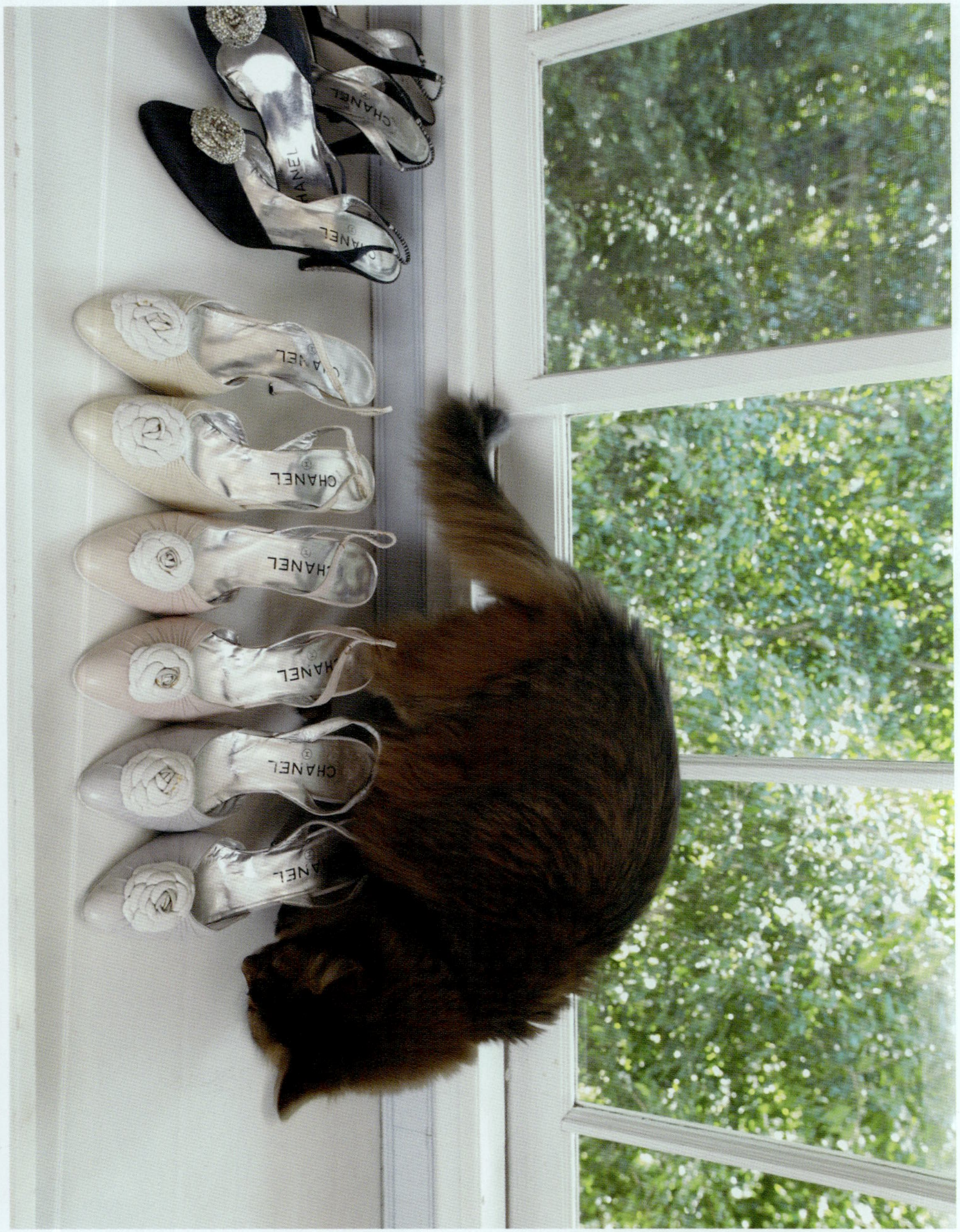

Fang and Chanel

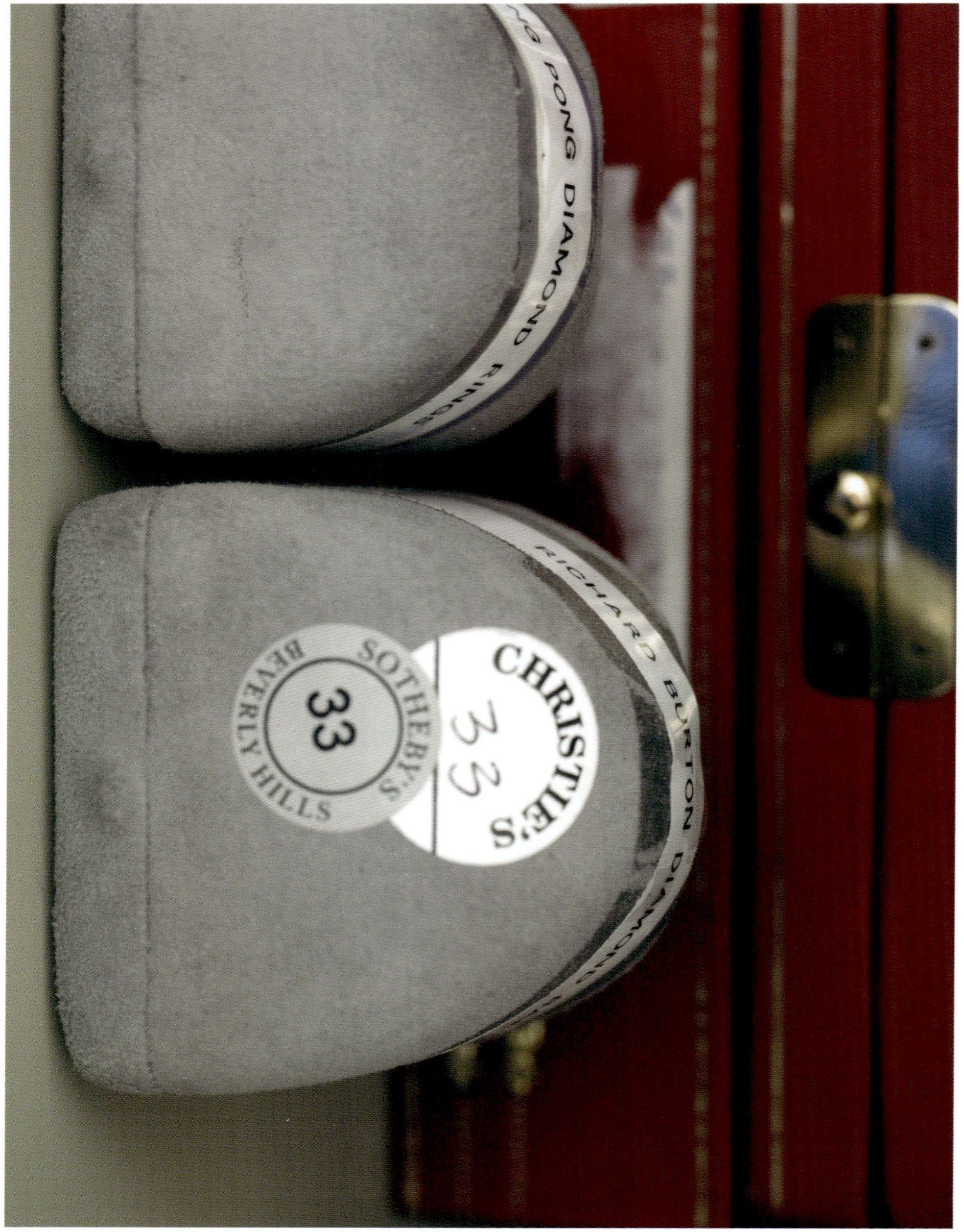

Jewelry boxes

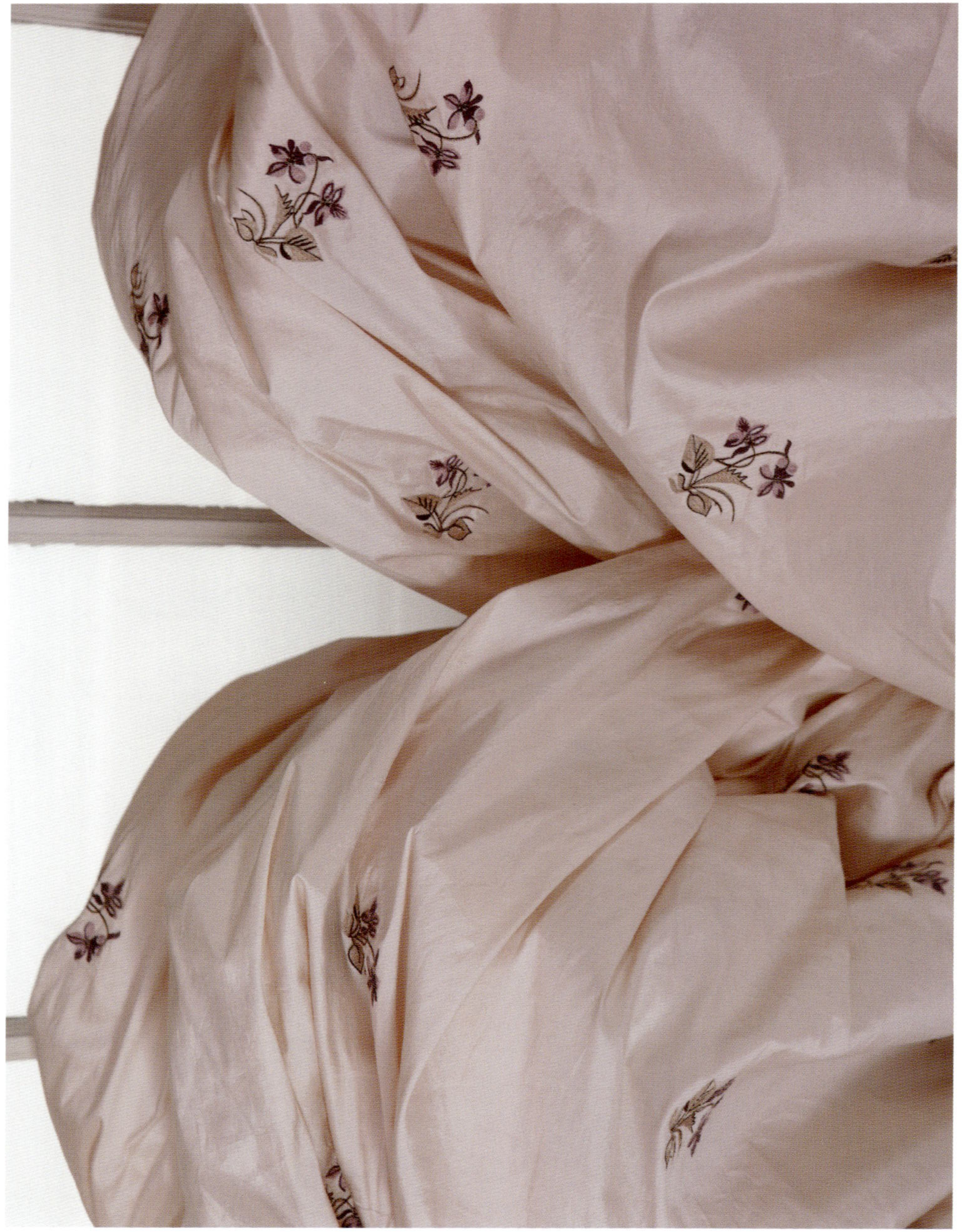

Balloon shades

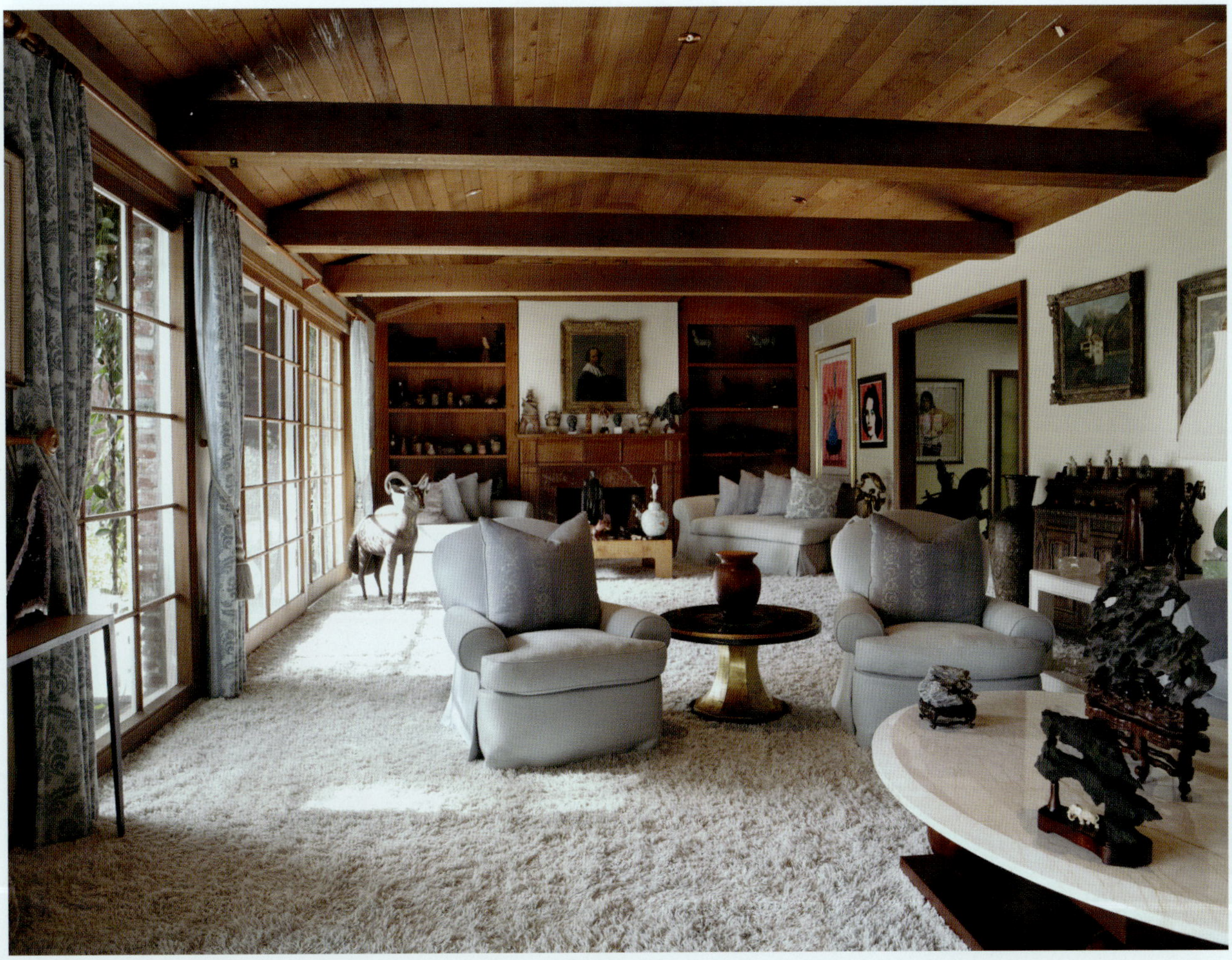

Livingroom West view

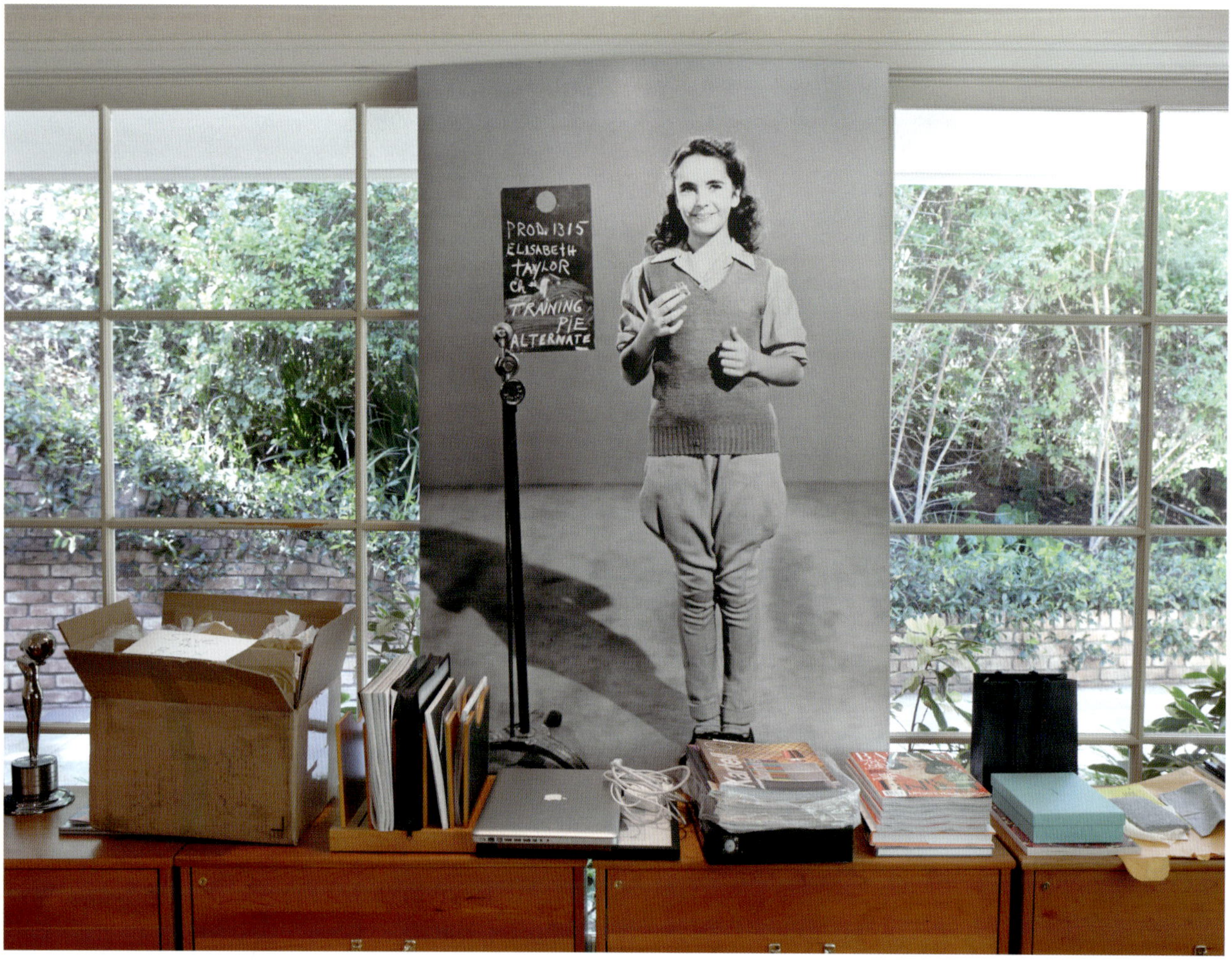

National Velvet costume

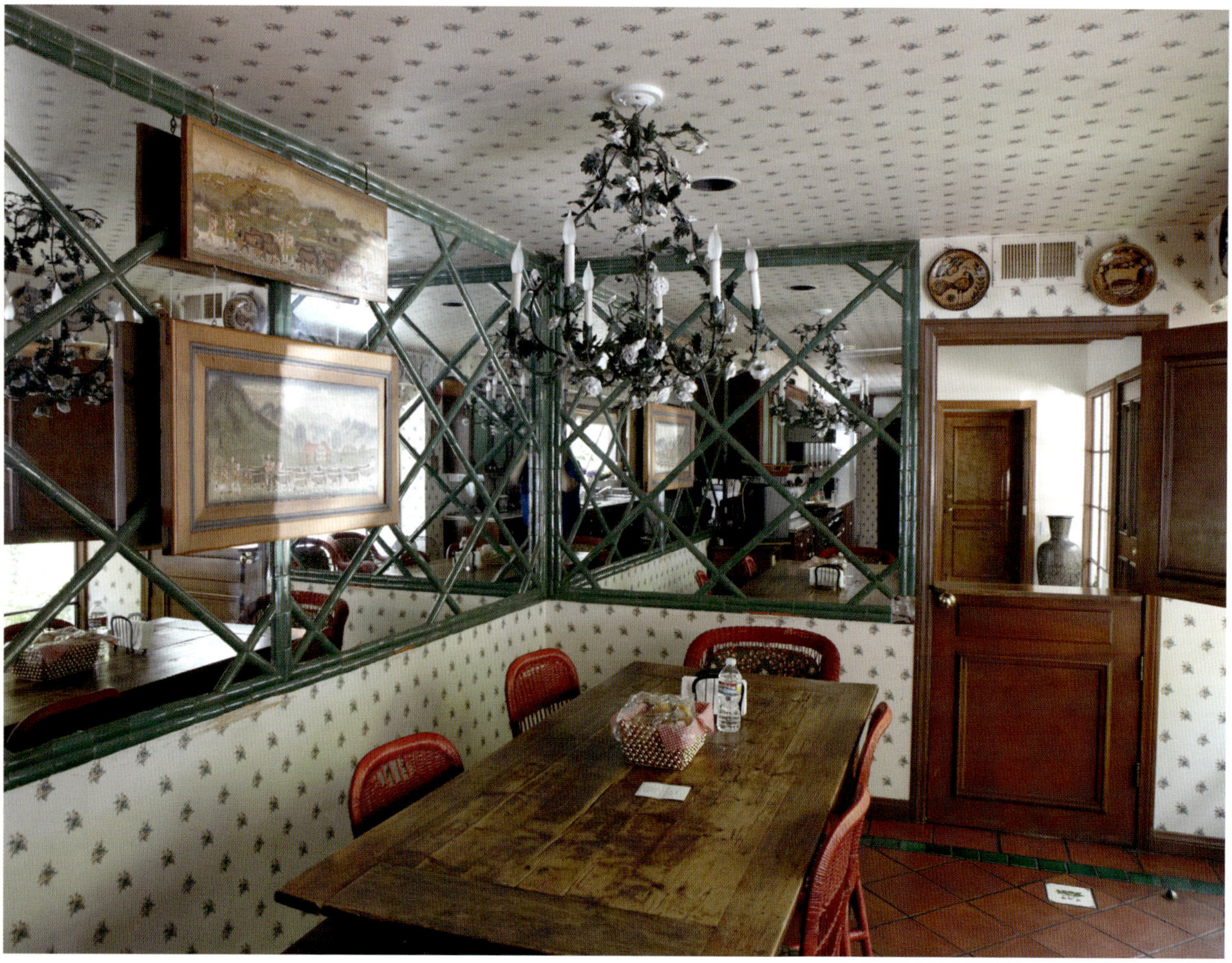

Kitchen table

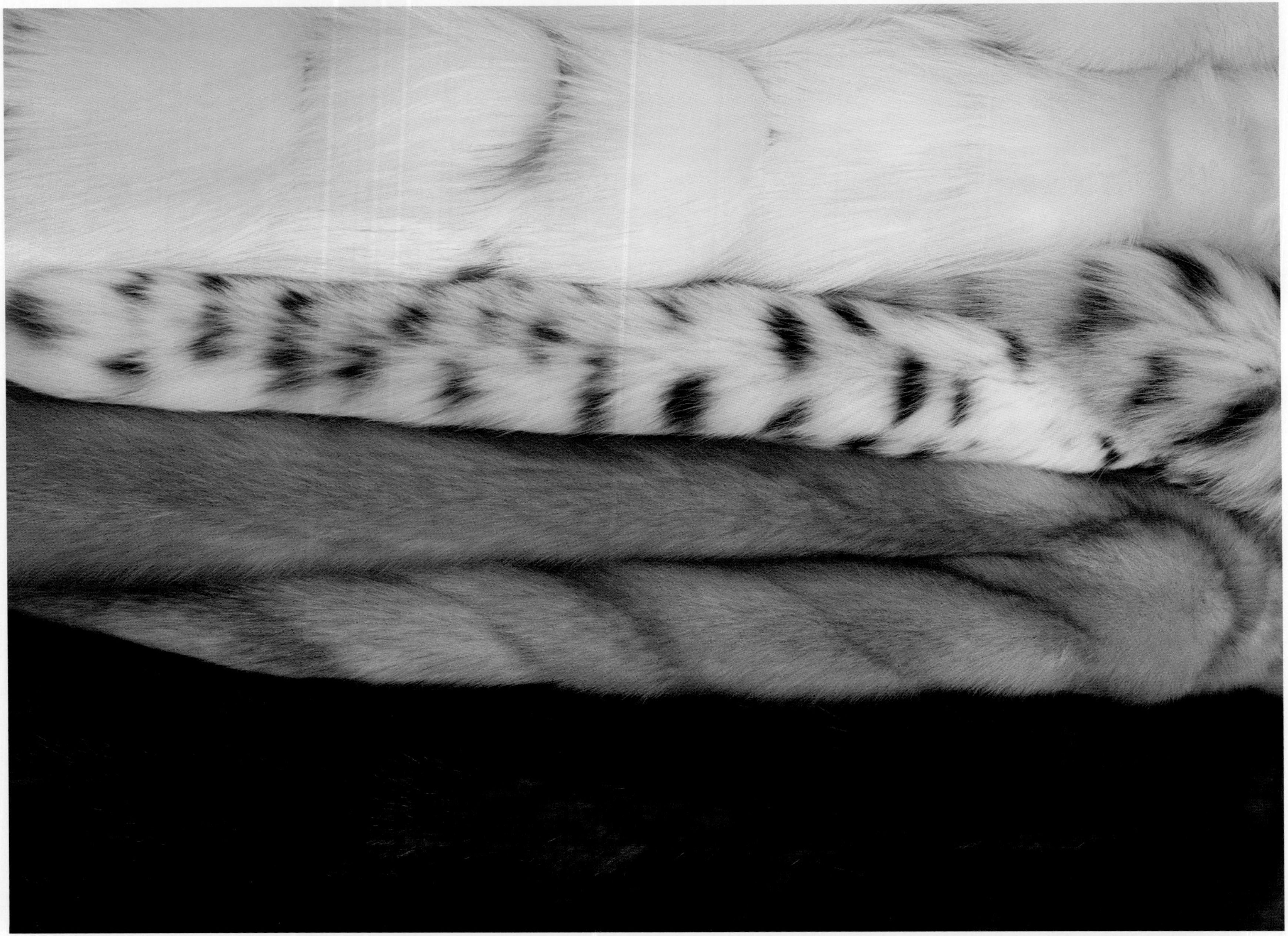

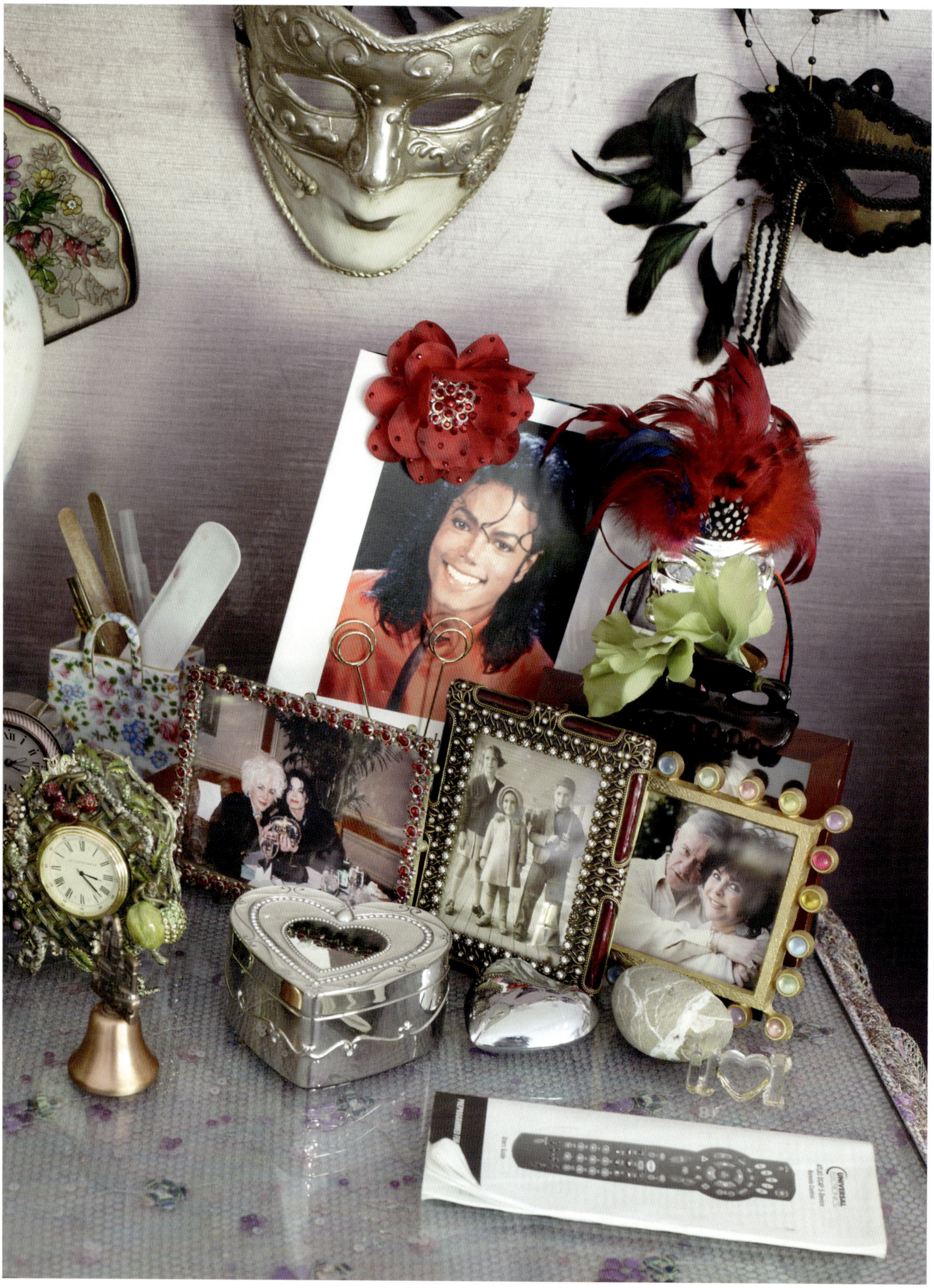

Bedside table

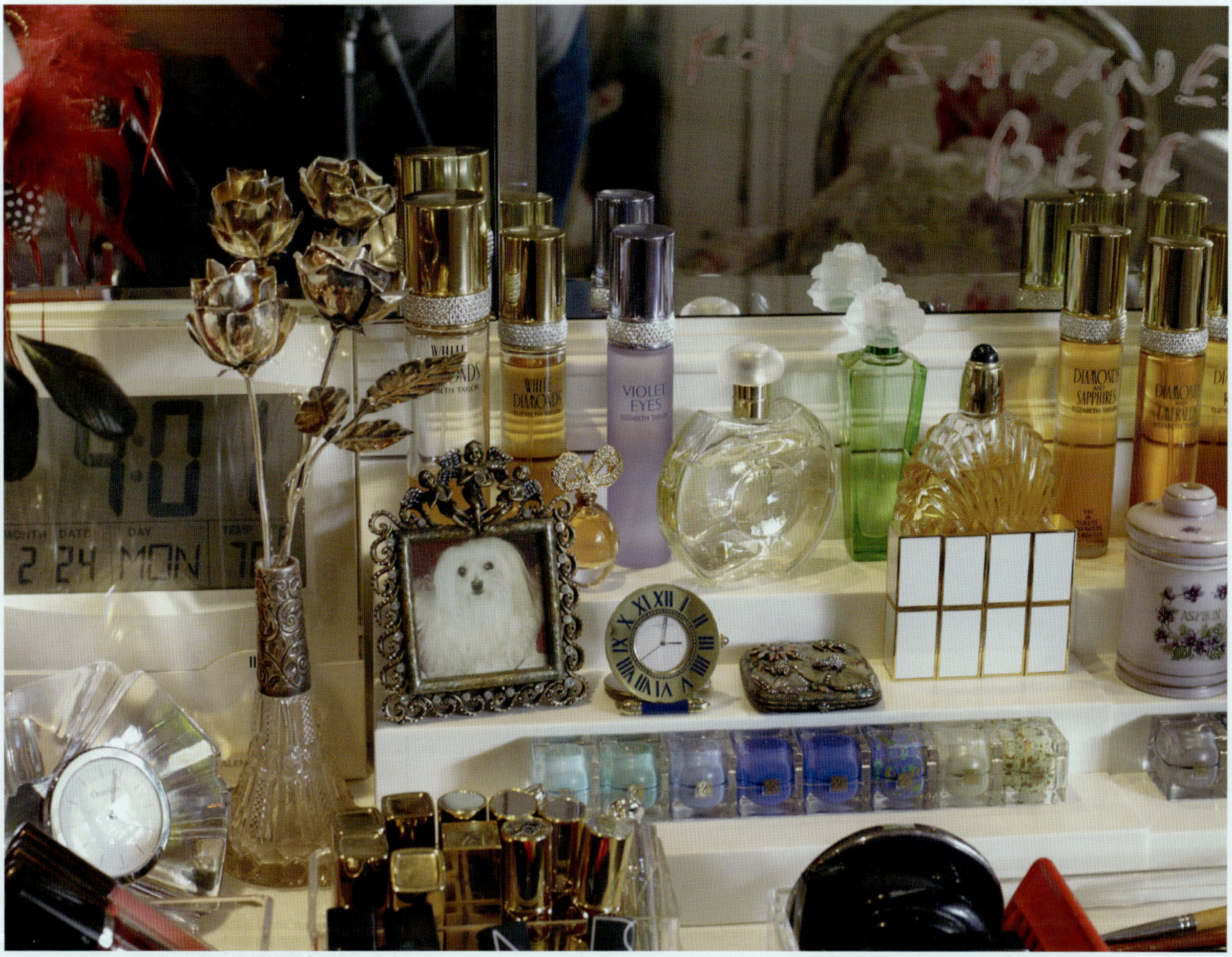

Makeup table

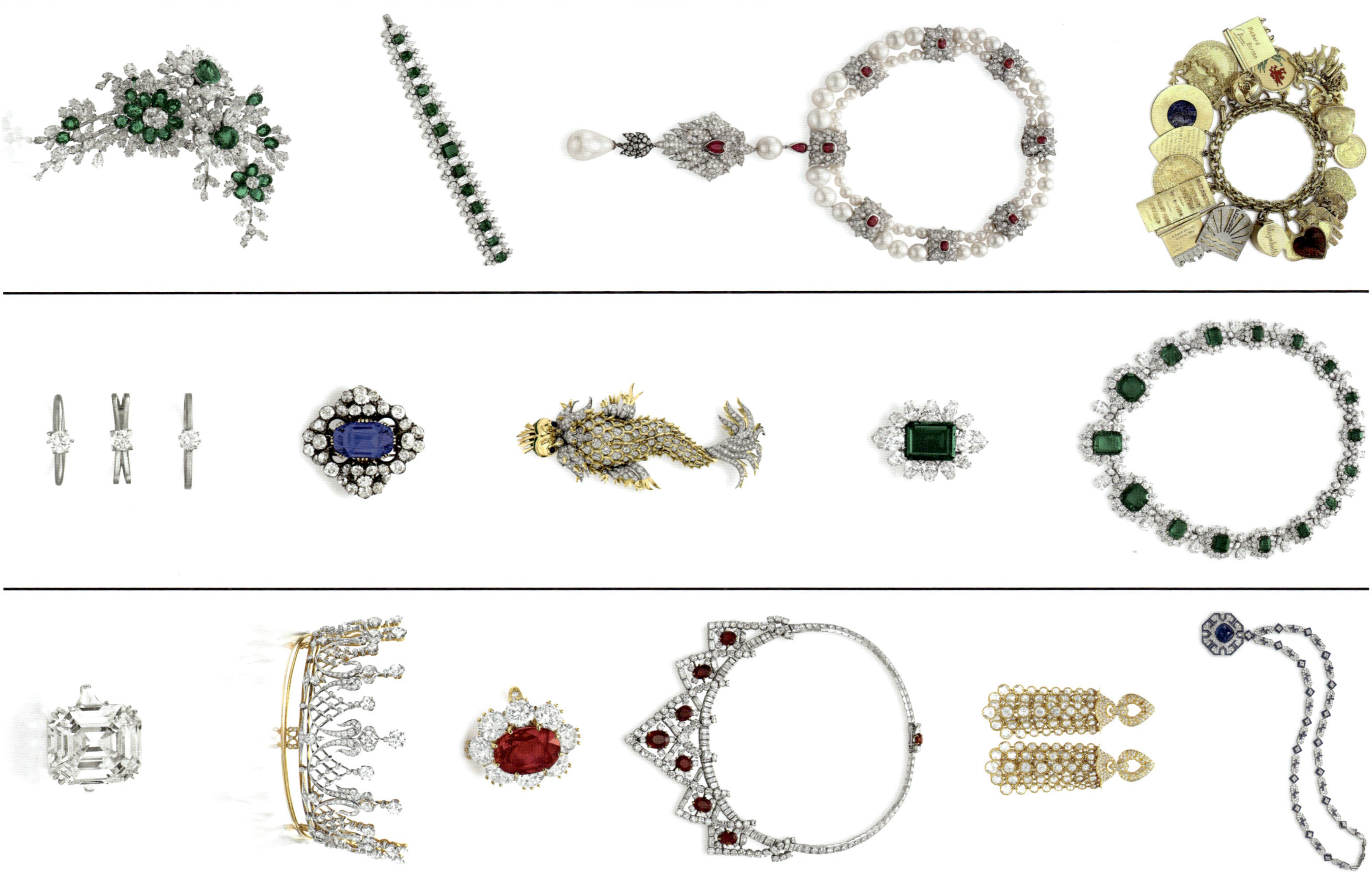

Jewels from the Estate of Elizabeth Taylor. Auctioned by Christie's December 2011, New York. © Christie's Images

GALLERY

TAKEOVERS, JOINT VENTURES, AND CONTIN-UATIONS—THREE GALLERISTS IN CONVERSATION

PROVENCE AW 18/19, included a survey of gallery closing letters. A selection of emails, notes, and press statements that detailed the various reasons as to why a gallery chose to wind down business, and how they communicated this to the outside world.

With *Takeovers, Joint Ventures, and Continuations—Three Gallerists in Conversation*, we continue investigating the format of the contemporary gallery, seeking to uncover the motivations and consequences of these intriguing business tactics.

In recent years, the so-called "program gallery" has been under pressure. Perhaps it always was, but the gallery market has been fluctuating as of late. What alternatives exist for a gallery to survive today, besides sustained growth and becoming a global chain?

In early February, we met with Esther Schipper, proprietor of the eponymous Berlin gallery. In 2015, Esther Schipper GmbH acquired Johnen Galerie—also in the German capital. We wanted to find out a bit more about how she felt about this takeover, four years on.

Following the sudden passing of Berlin gallerist Barbara Weiss on New Year's Eve in 2016, the directors of her eponymous gallery, Daniel Herleth and Bärbel Trautwein, made the decision to continue her work. PROVENCE met with the pair earlier this year to speak about this continuation, and the challenges associated with inheriting a gallery with a history as grand as Weiss'.

PROVENCE had the chance to speak with Gisela Capitain in Cologne and at Art Basel Hong Kong. The conversation touched upon her own gallery ongoings in Cologne, but focused on the joint venture Capitain Petzel—an art gallery founded in 2008 in conjunction with New York gallerist Friedrich Petzel.

GISELA CAPITAIN

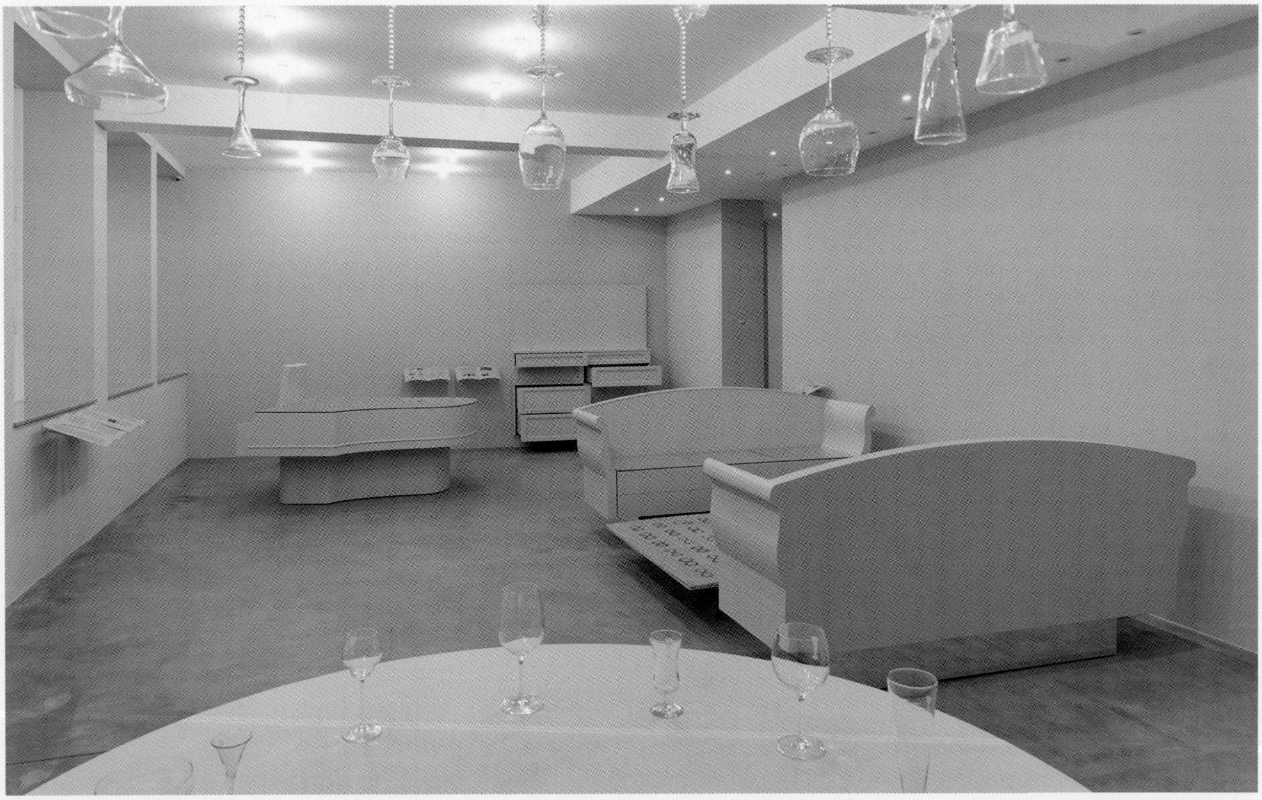

View of Barbara Bloom's 2015 exhibition "RSVP" at Gisela Capitain, Cologne / Courtesy of Barbara Bloom and Gisela Capitain, Cologne

PROVENCE: We were interested in talking with you since you were the driving force behind your Berlin-based joint venture with Friedrich Petzel. We were curious to hear more about how this began?

Gisela: Well, we both had the idea. We kind of came up with the thought in Miami, when Friedrich was still participating. We wanted to have a partnership in Berlin because so many of our artists would like to exhibit there, and we wanted to offer them a platform and opportunity to show with us. It also had to do with the fact that you don't want to lose an artist to other galleries in Berlin, simply because that city is such an important place as far as the contemporary art canon is concerned.

PROVENCE: When I came to your booth at the fair, you were talking with Christian Nagel. It's interesting to think about how you decided to keep your main gallery in Cologne and begin this joint venture, almost like a showroom, in Berlin. Nagel completely left Cologne, but has now returned to reopen his gallery space there. Was it wise to stay?

Gisela: Well, I never wanted to leave Cologne. Germany still has two parts: the West, with its tradition for fine arts and its history, specifically the '80s, and then there's Berlin, which reopened post-reunification with a new spirit and hype.

So, it made a lot of sense to keep the gallery in Cologne. It's in the center of Europe so you feel much more flexible in terms of travel. You can be in Belgium, France, the South or Switzerland in no time. On the other hand, Petzel and I wanted to keep our main spaces, so he's the partner from New York, I'm the partner from Cologne, and we have a shared partnership in Berlin. We wanted to develop a distinct program for Berlin, so it actually isn't only a showroom. We have mutual artists there, for sure, but we also represent artists with whom he's not working in New York, nor I in Cologne. So that's a mix of both programmes, but also something different.

HE'S THE PARTNER FROM NEW YORK, I'M THE PARTNER FROM COLOGNE

PROVENCE: So it's also a company for itself?

Gisela: Yes, this is its own company. This is its own business, its own entity. A very clear joint venture.

PROVENCE: Just now before our interview, you were talking with your gallery colleague about strategies, and of course you exchange information when you travel around to do fairs et cetera. Did you have any previous collaboration with Friedrich Petzel? Did you do fairs together?

Gisela: Well, we've known each other for a very long time. Friedrich was my very first gallery assistant in Cologne when I opened the space in 1986. At the time he was an art history student. He stayed with me for almost two years, I think, before moving to New York. I helped him with his first job in New York at Metro Pictures and after that, he started his own gallery. So this is how we know each other. It formed the very important basis of trust and respect we have towards each other, a crucial factor when doing business in cities other than your own.

> FRIEDRICH WAS MY VERY FIRST GALLERY ASSISTANT IN COLOGNE, WHEN I OPENED THE SPACE IN 1986.

PROVENCE: That's a very beautiful base for a good collaboration.

Gisela: Absolutely.

> "FRANCHISE GALLERIES" [...] FUNCTION LIKE BIG ORGANIZATIONS, LIKE ONE OF THOSE HUGE FASHION BRANDS

PROVENCE: It also explains why, even before the joint venture, you had so many mutually represented artists.

Gisela: Yes, exactly. And I think the advantage of this collaboration is that we have our own businesses, and a mutual partnership that enables different situations and energies. Also, the business models in Germany differ to those in the United States as far as visas, German taxes, German laws regarding artist rights and, for example, money laundering go. There are many different things to pay attention to. Someone from New York would lose their mind and patience over in Germany. So in our case, it made sense to form a partnership, but not merge completely.

PROVENCE: It also makes total sense to me that it has its own structure. This allows it to form its own identity, which that proved difficult for galleries that have outposts in multiple cities.

Gisela: Exactly. But this model is completely different. Anyhow it's incomparable. These "franchise galleries" present whatever they want to show, wherever they want to show it, globally. They function like big organizations, like one of those huge fashion brands, which is perhaps the future of this industry, but not for us.

PROVENCE: So it's a generational model?

Gisela: Yes.

PROVENCE: But on the other hand, you've probably heard of Lars Friedrich? He worked for Christian Nagel for many years, and what he's trying to do with his program in Berlin, follows your type of gallery model. It's not necessarily very successfull in terms of finance, but he's been doing it for a couple of years already.

Gisela: Yes, and he is very courageous. I think he needs not only a good amount of energy but also...

PROVENCE: ...Patience.

Gisela: I think the one advantage we still have is that our joint venture offers not only a distinct program, but also an individualized approach as to how we operate, how we talk to collectors and institutions, and how we build our network. It's not like a brand. We manage to maintain our individuality, character, and a system where we still have to fulfil the artists' expectations and wishes, not only offer them exhibition opportunities in ten different countries at the same time.

PROVENCE: Do you feel that the gallery is under pressure?

Gisela: We always feel under pressure. No matter when or where. Here, at an art fair, this pressure is more visible. It's less stressful at my gallery in Cologne because its definitely more provincial.

PROVENCE: Yes, but it's also your home environment.

Gisela: Yes, there I can maintain some distance to the world's mad happenings. I can define what I want, where I want to go, and how I would like to do things. So I couldn't have a second gallery in New York—that would definitely drive me crazy.

PROVENCE: So, no joint venture in Shanghai?

Gisela: No.

PROVENCE: It's not necessary?

Gisela: I think it's more interesting to start cooperating with galleries who have their main branches here in China, in one of these "booming" cities. I think it's much more rewarding to develop common interests with them. If you have similar ideas regarding good art, how you like to work with an artist and ethics, cooperation can be very interesting. It offers you more possibilities because here, they have their own networks here having been working here for so many years. It makes much more sense to make them your allies, not your competitors.

> IT MAKES MUCH MORE SENSE TO MAKE THEM YOUR ALLIES, NOT YOUR COMPETITORS.

PROVENCE: Are there galleries that you look up to here?

Gisela: Yes. The longer you're here and the better you get to know them, the easier it becomes to recognise the potential for a future collaboration.

PROVENCE: But it's not that you have started to represent Chinese artists in your program?

Gisela: Well, we were lucky enough to find the Hong Kong artist, Samson Young, during our very first Art Basel Hong Kong. It was the best possible moment for us and we are still extremely happy and grateful that we met him because he's had such an amazing career since—he's already internationally renowned.

PROVENCE: And the piece that he produced with the Cologne Symphony Orchestra, that was probably arranged through you, with an exhibition that you held at the same time?

Gisela: Actually, it had to do with a project which we helped organize at the Venice Bienniale. The conductor who worked on the symphony with him saw his work at the Biennale and contacted us, and so we helped with putting them in touch and a little bit financially, so that the collaboration could happen in Cologne with this wonderful, private orchestra.

PROVENCE: Great!

Gisela: And it was a really good experience, I have to say. We were there for the recording. It was amazing!

MAKING IN-HOUSE MAGAZINES ALSO HAS A LOT TO DO WITH CONTROLLING AN ARTIST'S WORK. IT MEANS THAT YOU HAVE ALL PARTS OF AN ARTISTS PRODUCTION AND PRESENCE COMPLETELY UNDER CONTROL.

PROVENCE: I have an interest in magazines, and earlier, when you compared the gallery industry to the fashion industry, it made me think of several galleries that are now publishing their own in-house magazines. Is this another sign that some galleries are starting to run like small fashion houses? Do you think the fashion world is becoming a blueprint for the direction the art world is heading, and how art brands are being built?

Gisela: It looks like it. This is their interest. But making in-house magazines also has a lot to do with controlling an artist's work. It means that you have all parts of an artists production and presence completely under control.

You pay the art critic, you do the research yourself, and you help the institutions that need funding for exhibitions since public budgets have been cut. Many aspects of this former art world are more or less gone.

PROVENCE: It really is crucial to develop these alternative models of gallery collaborations where you remain equal parties, instead of crushing all other galleries, or simply getting squashed yourself.

Gisela: Yes, it is a tough moment for that. It's win or lose, as you say. So I hope these collaborative models will be in for the long run.

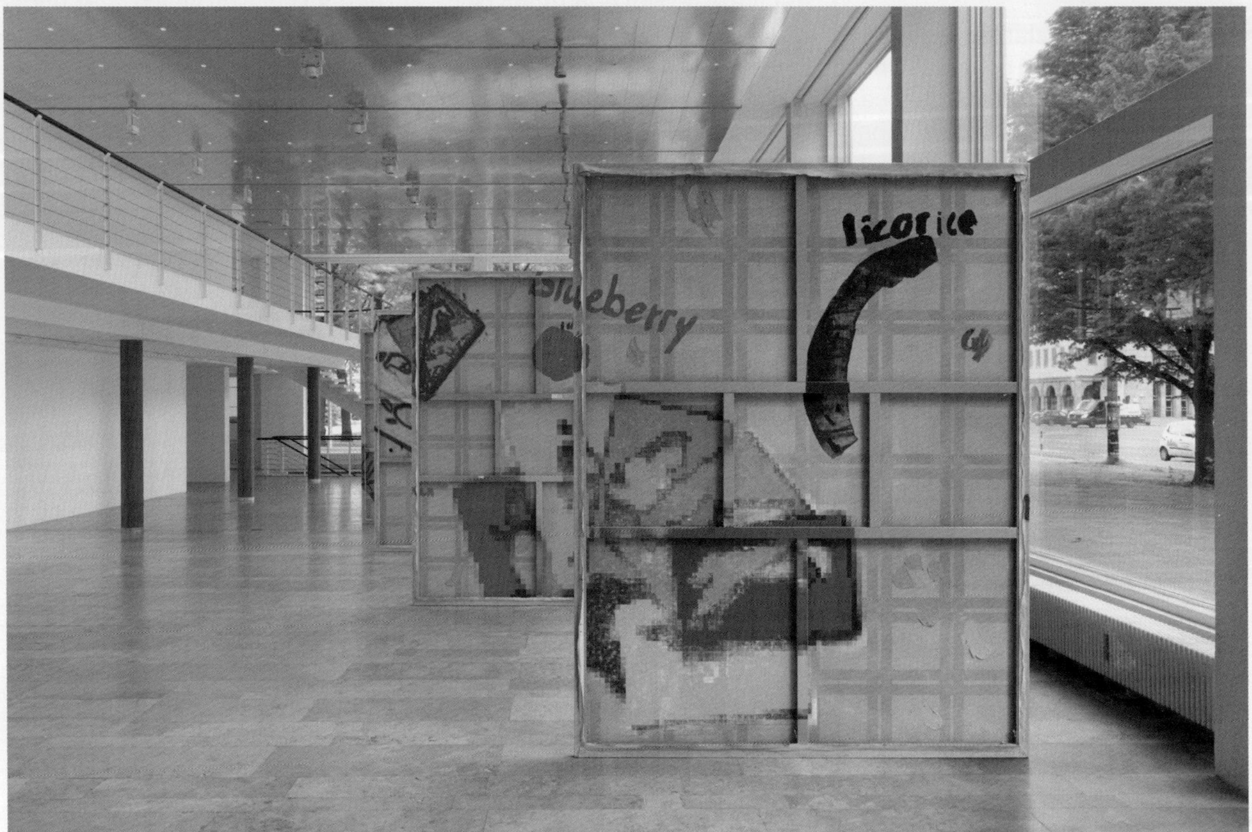

View of Laura Owens' 2015 exhibition at Capitain Petzel, Berlin / Photo by Jens Ziehe / Courtesy of Laura Owens and Capitain Petzel, Berlin

ESTHER SCHIPPER

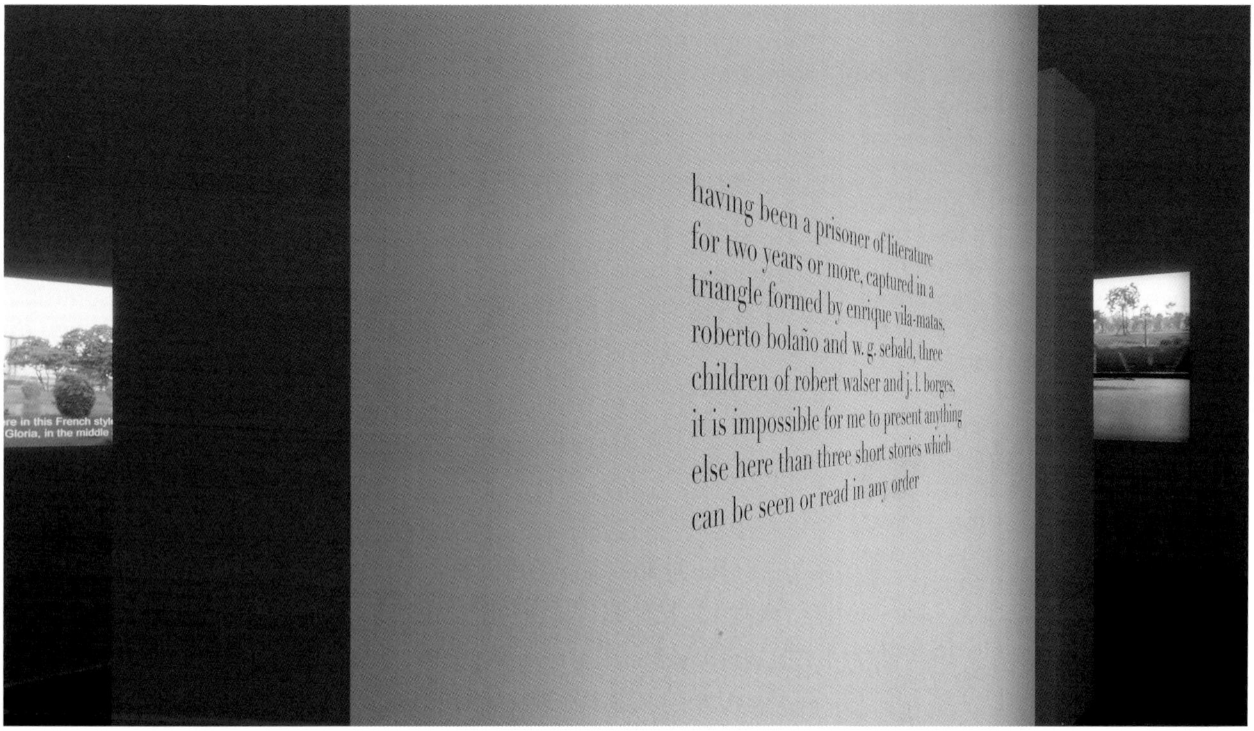

View of Dominique Gonzalez-Foerster's 2008 exhibition at Esther Schipper's previous location in Berlin / Photo Carsten Eisfeld / Courtesy of Dominique Gonzalez-Foerster and Esther Schipper, Berlin

PROVENCE: In 2015, it was announced that you had begun a partnership with Jörg Johnen. Was it like a merger? Or what would you call it?

Esther: It was a classic takeover. In 2013, a friend and collector who had spent most of his active career in mergers and acquisitions approached me. He told me that Jörg was considering his options regarding stepping down. The globalization of the art market, the challenges that come with it and the increasing pace were not things Jörg wanted to pursue in the future. He worked with many artists I was friends with, or were very close to artists that I represent, so I was very intrigued by this proposition. It took a year and a half of numerous discussions with lawyers and accountants and various specialists until we decided that this was the best way to go. It's very difficult to put a figure on businesses like ours, ones that are so deeply personal, which is why we decided to announce our plan to the art world using a rather precise press campaign, instead of discussing it in advance. We were very much aware that it was a rather unconventional model.

PROVENCE: Not common at all.

Esther: I've been thinking a lot about how our businesses are so dependent on our personas, which can become challenging since you cannot run and grow a business all by yourself. Growing a business cannot be done by one person alone; it has to be done by a team, or many teams. Advising and selling art is often based on an especially mature and trusting relationship. Therefore, building a high-performing yet personal business is the biggest challenge for a gallerist, I would say. You see quite a lot of colleagues from the previous generation that keep working until an advanced age, and this makes you consider how it can be possible to step down. So, for me it was interesting to think about how to integrate and take over what has been a gallery; the memory, the archives, the history of sold works, all these things that are a big part of our work. I am convinced that one of the biggest assets of the gallery is a well-maintained archive. I am able to tell you who bought what, at which time, under which conditions—even after thirty years. This continuity is just as important for the artist as it is for a client. And Johnen Galerie put in lot of work to have this continuity.

GROWING A BUSINESS CANNOT BE DONE BY ONE PERSON ALONE; IT HAS TO BE DONE BY A TEAM, OR MANY TEAMS.

PROVENCE: Bärbel and Daniel from Galerie Barbara Weiss also said that they feel comfortable continuing Galerie Barbara Weiss because the gallery left such a well-kept archive. There are collectors coming to them saying, "With Barbara, we used to get a

20% discount," and then they can check the old invoices and see that they were never 20% discounts, it was always 10%.

Esther: I think the key reason as to why Jörg wanted to step down were the changes and adjustments required in order to be visible in the global art market. The drastic changes after 2008 redefined the business. It is slowly reshaping itself, but it is very different from what it used to be. Before 2008, a good program and a good eye were enough. If you showed the right artists at the right times, sales were almost guaranteed. This is how Jörg and all of us did our jobs back then. Times have changed. Today you can have incredible exhibitions by great artists, but they will not be seen, unless you take part in all the major art fairs, run an active social media campaign and are somehow present in different places at the same time.

PROVENCE: But you don't want to become a global chain either, right? You're comfortable with this size. But can a gallery of this size survive?

Esther: That's a good question. We're already represented in different places, but not with an exhibition space.

PROVENCE: But with representatives in Asia and China?

Esther: Yes, also in Spain and France. But there's no physical space yet, though I'm actually working on having smaller office spaces in a couple of places.

PROVENCE: How about China? Ten years ago it was still all about New York, but now, the younger artists we're meeting here in Hong Kong are all aiming at Shanghai. It seems that a complete shift of focus towards China is happening right now. So I guess you also have people here and begin working with artists here?

Esther: Yes and no. There's a part of my biography that is linked to this part of the world.

PROVENCE: You were born in Taiwan?

Esther: Yes! A big challenge for businesses operating in Asia is actually the cultural difference. Luckily, I never experienced those differences so strongly. I was even completely fluent in Mandarin as a child. I can safely say that Beijing feels more like home to me than Moscow. About ten years ago, we began to notice that more and more Asian clients reached out to us, people who were interested in starting a conversation about purchasing works but also about exhibitions and collaborations. I quickly became extremely interested in exploring all these new possibilities. It's not an easy path for a lot of reasons. The market is very different from what we are used to. For instance, in China, there is no history of commercial art galleries the way we know it, though there's a longstanding tradition of collecting art.

PROVENCE: All of these galleries are like twenty years old, maximum.

Esther: It depends on what country we are talking about. In Mainland China it is rather recent, but the situation is different in Japan, Taiwan, or Korea. Generally speaking, the market in Asia is growing and changing very quickly, and it is very clear that this will continue. It's certain that the people of China will be so much more present, and it's something we need to understand and accept. It's a challenge, but challenges are good.

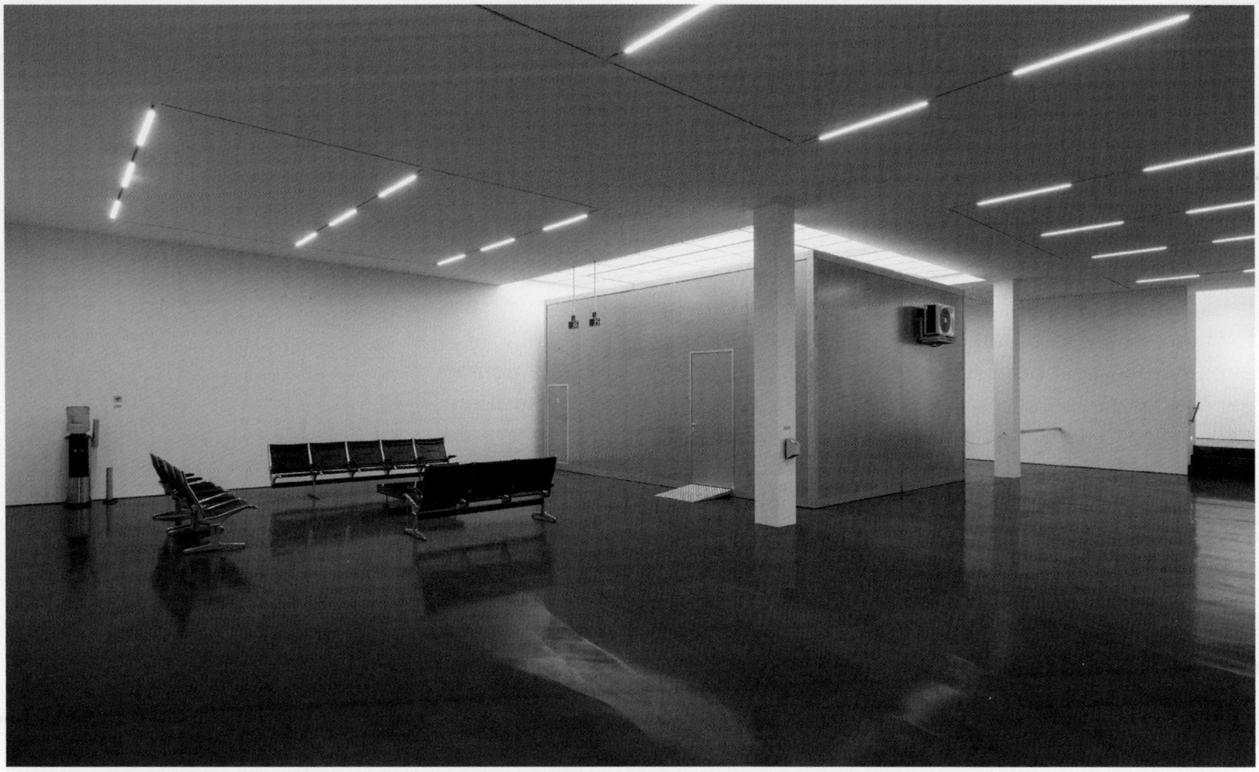

View of Simon Fujiwara's exhibition "Empathy I" in 2018 at Esther Schipper's current location in Berlin / Photo Andrea Rossetti / Courtesy of Simon Fujiwara and Esther Schipper, Berlin

DANIEL HERLETH AND BÄRBEL TRAUTWEIN OF GALERIE BARBARA WEISS

PROVENCE: Daniel, when did you start working for Barbara Weiss? You joined the gallery first, right?

Daniel: Yes, I started working for Barbara in 2013.

Bärbel: I was still working for another gallery at that time. In 2014 we began Oracle, our project space in Berlin. Barbara would come by from time to time to see our exhibitions. One day she invited us to do an exhibition in her gallery. That's how our collaboration with her began.

Daniel: While we were working on that exhibition—it was an exhibition with Peter Fend—she asked if we would be interested in working closely together with her, and if Bärbel could imagine working for her gallery too. Barbara had already learned about her medical condition, and she wanted to make sure that the gallery could continue to function as she focused on her recovery. It was a very difficult situation from the beginning. As Barbara was working mostly from home, we visited her constantly and spoke on the phone several times each day. She was also present at special occasions at the gallery, such as openings, for example.

PROVENCE: You mentioned earlier that Barbara herself was optimistic until the end, and believed that she would recover.

Daniel: Yes, for a very long time we didn't talk much about her illness. She wanted the gallery to keep working. That was the reason she had asked us to work with her, and this was the constellation we were working in and focusing on. It was only relatively late, when her condition aggravated, that we began talking about the possibility of a continuation.

Bärbel: For Barbara, it then became very important to know that the gallery would continue.

Daniel: The idea was, and still is, that we continue to work with her program and in her spirit. Yet it was also clear from the beginning of our collaboration that there would be changes. Barbara maintained very close relationships to the artists she worked with, and she made sure as much of this was passed on to us as possible.

After Barbara passed away, many questions remained unresolved. While it was clear that the gallery should continue, the question was how to do so on a practical level. So, in the following weeks, everyone involved including the artists, her husband Kasper König, her parents, some lawyers, and the two of us discussed the process and agreed to do it the way we have.

BARBARA HAD ALREADY LEARNED ABOUT HER MEDICAL CONDITION, AND SHE WANTED TO MAKE SURE THAT THE GALLERY COULD CONTINUE TO FUNCTION AS SHE FOCUSED ON HER RECOVERY. IT WAS A VERY DIFFICULT SITUATION FROM THE BEGINNING.

PROVENCE: This certainly doesn't sound easy. A gallery is usually not just a business, but also a very personal structure, with many things standing and falling with the gallerist.

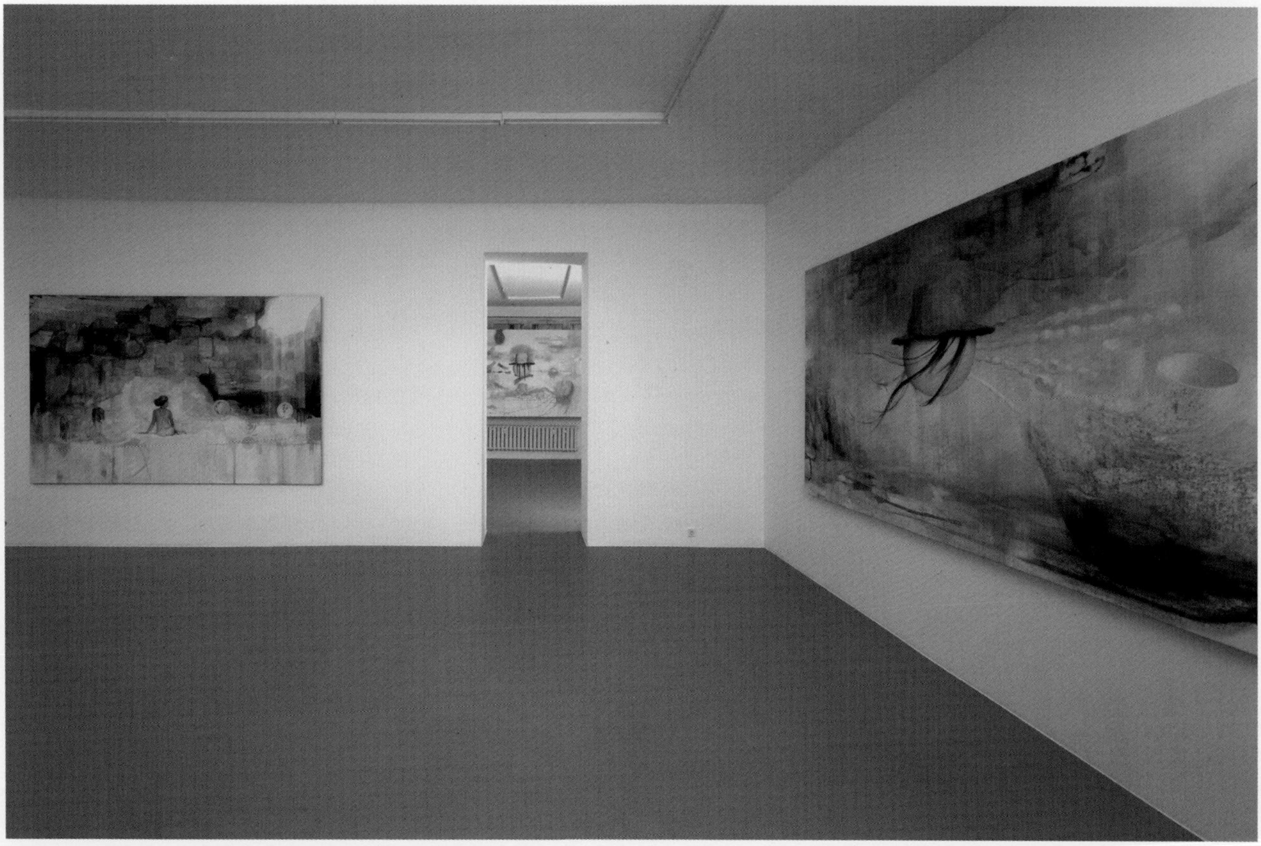

View of Monika Baer's 2003 exhibition "Jäger" (2003) at Galerie Barbara Weiss' former location, Zimmerstraße 88, Berlin

Bärbel: Sure, we had to keep up the business and deal with these problems at the same time. And the gap Barbara left was very large. We didn't have time to develop a plan for the future right away. That only came afterwards. We had to figure out how everything worked and how we wanted to react to this and that. So it has been more of a process. Additionally, we also feel that the art market is changing at the moment, and it affects us too. But it's not necessarily negative; it's a change.

Daniel: Personally, I think that art and dealing with art is something that young people will always look for and engage with, but it's clear that today, even young art is quite expensive, meaning there is a certain threshold to overcome in order to become a collector.

PROVENCE: Did you ever consider changing the name of the gallery after you took it over? In recent times, when the great Fashion houses themselves have been taken over following the death or departure of their founders, whoever took over the brand eliminated the former head's first name, as seen in the cases of Maison Margiela, Dior and Saint Laurent.

Daniel: And the same holds true for galleries. I think that the first name is usually "deleted" when the gallery reaches a certain size or starts to have partners. Barbara herself was not very much concerned with the gallery's name when we discussed the future, in the sense that the name could be changed as long as the work of the gallery would continue.

Bärbel: Maybe at some point the name will change, if we feel that this is the right thing to do. You have to build your own story, and it's of course important for us to create our own identity, through the work we are doing. We never wanted to simply administer the inheritance of Barbara Weiss, and she didn't want that we do so either.

PROVENCE: Another question is the incredible capital that the gallery brings; the artists you work with. You mentioned Oracle before, which represents a younger generation. Are you also getting young collectors?

Bärbel: Yes, definitely. I mean that's important for every gallery. I'd say, that with younger artists come younger collectors. Thankfully, a new generation has arrived. But, of course, it's also crucial that the old collectors remain, those who have accompanied the artists and the gallery for a long time, and still continue to do so. This commitment is very special.

Daniel: It's interesting because when we look in the files, we can see that the situation was rarely static. Barbara's gallery emerged from her association with Michael Wewerka. They had already worked for one year as Galerie Wewerka & Weiss. When she opened her own gallery, she took on not only artists with whom she had already worked with, but of course also new ones. Since then, the program has continually evolved. Actually, only Maria Eichhorn and Raoul De Keyser have been there from the very beginning. Also, if you consider how the prices for contemporary art have developed over the last twenty years, and all the other changes that came along with this; international art fairs, art as investment, et cetera, you'll see that Barbara's

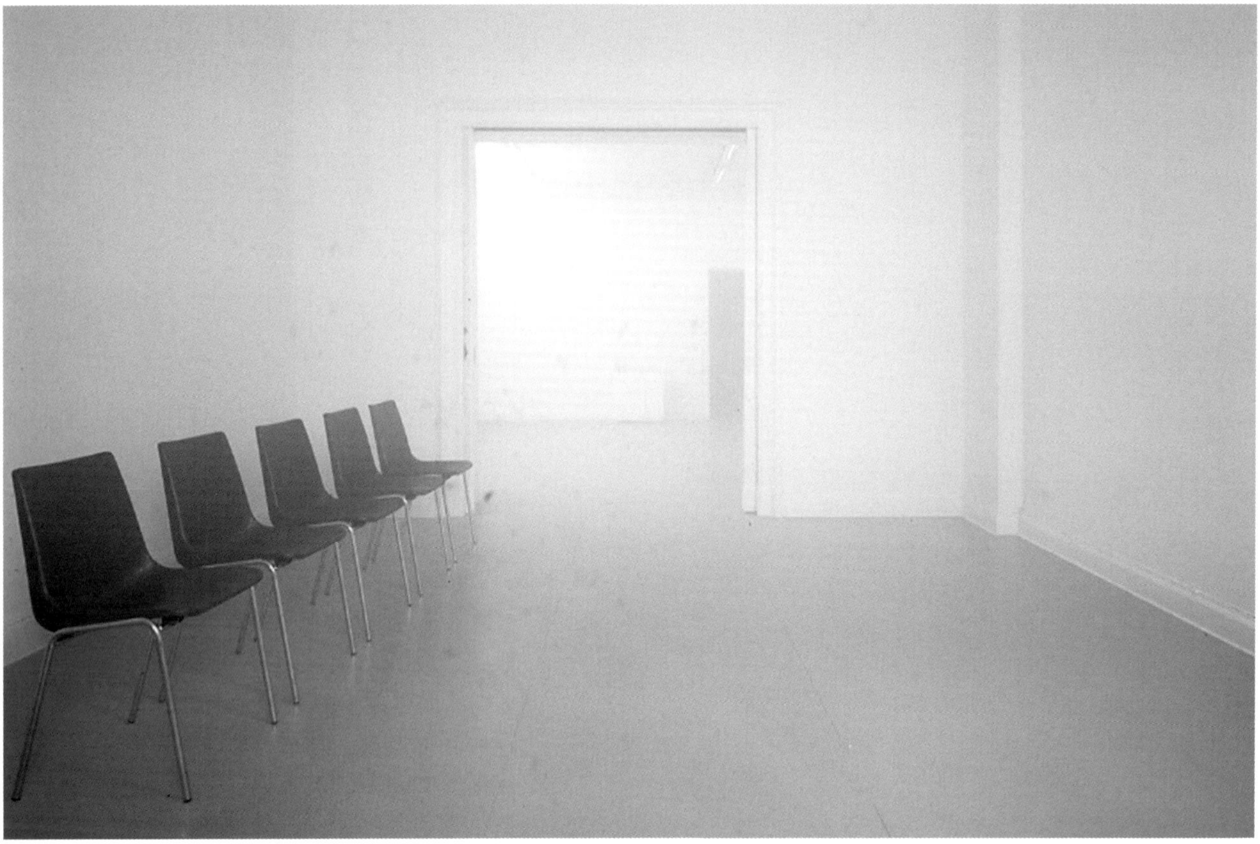

View of Maria Eichhorn's 1991 exhibition "Meer. Salz. Wasser. Klima. Kammer. Nebel. Wolken. Luft. Staub. Atem. Küste. Brandung. Rauch" at Galerie Wewerka & Weiss, Pariser Str. 92, Berlin

situation wasn't one of relative stability. There were always dynamic changes.

PROVENCE: There's really a structural change occurring at the moment, as far as the art market is concerned. And I don't think that anyone really knows where it's going.

Bärbel: No, totally. Of course, we talk a lot and sometimes we think, "What kind of development is this?!" But, on the other hand, it is much more international today and, like in most fields, also in the art world things gravitate towards larger structures.

PROVENCE: These big gallery chains didn't exist before. They work more like large corporations.

Bärbel: Exactly, but it's also related to what we spoke about before regarding fashion houses. Because when the houses continue, some of the traditions, though preserved, will be reinterpreted. I recently saw a documentary on Alexander McQueen and in one scene, where he becomes the head designer at Givenchy, the house employees look at each other and ask, "How can we do this now?" And in the end they all become closer in some way. So, I think that those moments can be productive, even though it might not always seem that things will work out.

Daniel: The majority of the founders of these large galleries are still very present, but this will inevitably change in the next few years, so it will be exciting to see how this will unfold. In our situation with Barbara it was different, given that she wasn't forced to end her tenure due to her age. When you are confronted with that issue in your seventies or eighties, it might be easier to say, "OK. I did it, and now it's over." But I think Barbara always saw her gallery as a joint endeavor with her artists, and she felt a great responsibility towards them. This project has not come to an end. I think this is why she felt the gallery should continue; and this is what we are doing.

PROVENCE: I can imagine that the Galerie Barbara Weiss files are an incredibly archive to study. Have you considered making parts of this public, perhaps curating an exhibition about Barbara's role as gallery director?

BARBARA ALWAYS SAW HER GALLERY AS A JOINT ENDEAVOR WITH HER ARTISTS, AND SHE FELT A GREAT RESPONSIBILITY TOWARDS THEM.

Daniel: Yes indeed. It is fascinating to see what it meant to run a gallery in Berlin in the '90s. Of course, it was also international, but it was also very personal, and there was not a lot of money around. Everything was either handwritten or sent by fax! We actually talked to Kasper about the possibility of making an exhibition around Barbara's work as a gallerist. There is already a bit of distance to the '90s Berlin scene, and it would be quite interesting to explore all of this, especially since the archive is so vast. It would be exciting. Hopefully we can realize this in the future.

REPORT

FEMME FATALE

Conversation with Cao Yu

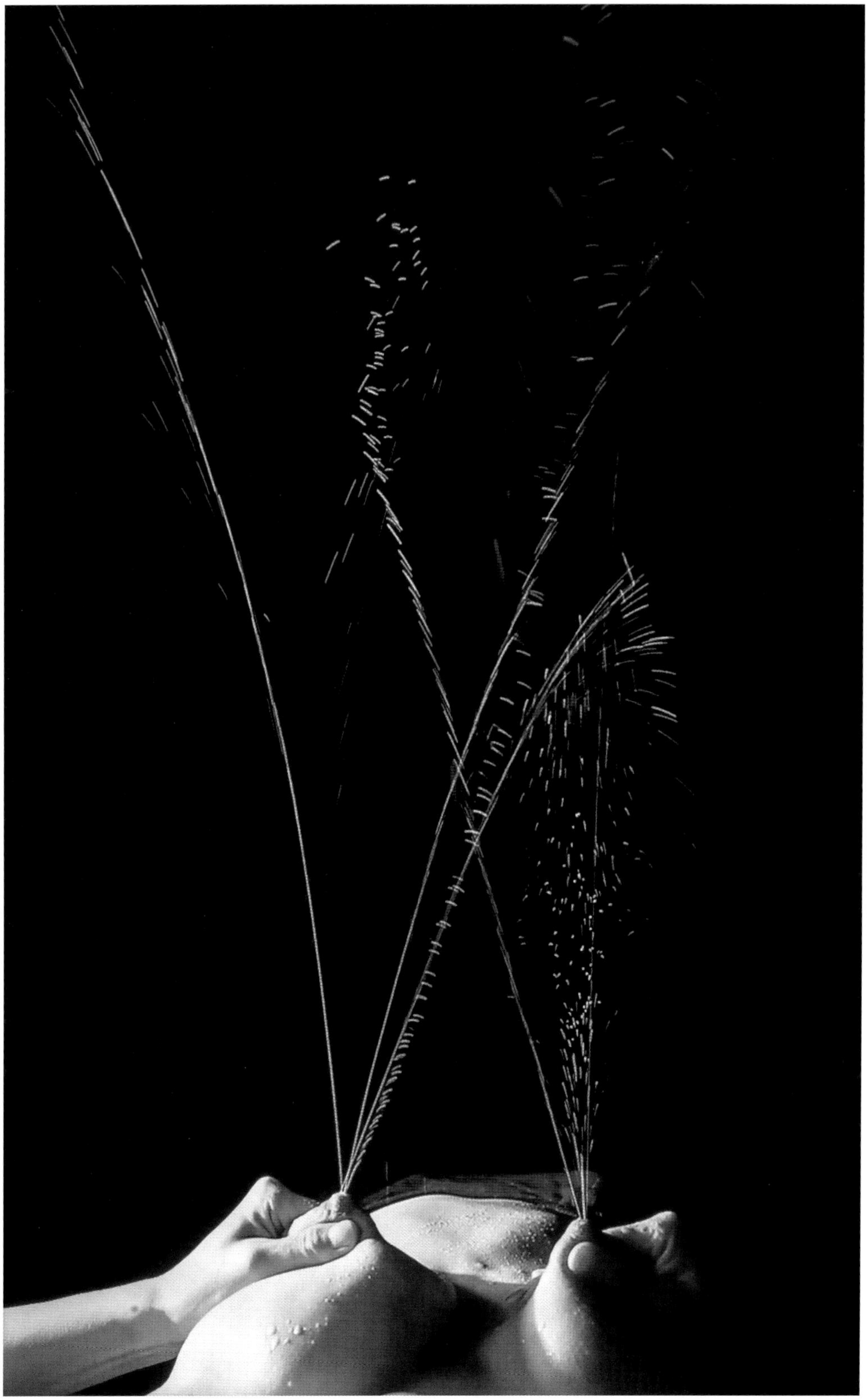

Cao Yu, *Fountain*, 2015 / Single channel HD video (colour, silent) / Courtesy of the artist and Galerie Urs Meile, Beijing-Lucerne

The following conversation between artist Cao Yu and PROVENCE was conducted in Beijing shortly before Yu left for her first solo show at Galerie Urs Meile in Luzern.

Cao Yu was born in 1988 in Liaoning Province, China. She lives and works in Beijing and is most well known for *Fountain* (2015); a silent video loop in which the artist repeatedly expresses milk from her breasts. In the video, we see the artist laying on her back—an unusual position for breastfeeding—and, as the title suggests, squeezing her breasts until milk spurts upwards, as water would from a fountain. During our talk, Yu explained how she took titular inspiration from Marcel Duchamp's *Fountain* (1917), and paid homage to Bruce Nauman's *Self-Portrait as a Fountain* (1966/67).

PROVENCE: What is your background in? What did you study, and where?

Cao Yu: I graduated from the Central Academy of Fine Arts in Beijing where I studied sculpture. There were many things I learned during this period that honestly, I could have done without. Curriculum aside, I was truly interested in the so-called "misuse" of materials, machines and tools; the concept of how one's body can be deformed. Getting "hurt" in the process of art production. For example, cutting oneself with a chainsaw whilst woodworking, or hitting one's hand with a stone carving hammer.

PROVENCE: Does art pay your rent?

CY: After graduating from art school I began working a "regular" job but ended up quitting, as I felt that I had become too distracted from my artistic practice. Plus, I have two children and a husband, who also happens to be an artist. I have a lot going on and having a day-job on top of things was just too much. I want to remain independent, despite the financial risk. I prefer to live a life of crises and conflicts, not one of false peace.

PROVENCE: Do you remember your first encounter with art?

CY: When I was ten years old, I remember my teacher asking us to sketch a jar and apple. Every time I finished a sketch, I began to question whether that image was all I wanted, whether it was the way we must take to art, whether I had to spend my whole life on a piece of paper.

PROVENCE: Your upcoming show at Urs Meile Luzern is titled "Femme Fatale", why did you choose this title? How do you feel about categorization in general? How do you feel about the polarization of women and men? Are you interested in overlaps, or questioning the boundaries of gender?

CY: The title of this solo exhibition comes from a yet-to-be exhibited work, which incidentally continues a theme I initially explored in my first solo show. The work *Fountain* is a dialogue and extension of a series of classical works that relate to the concept of fountains throughout art history.

"Male" and "female" are extremes of the gender binary. Though I am a female, I never draw lines between the genders. I'm often moved before great artworks, pieces of literature and films before I even find out the artist's name or gender.

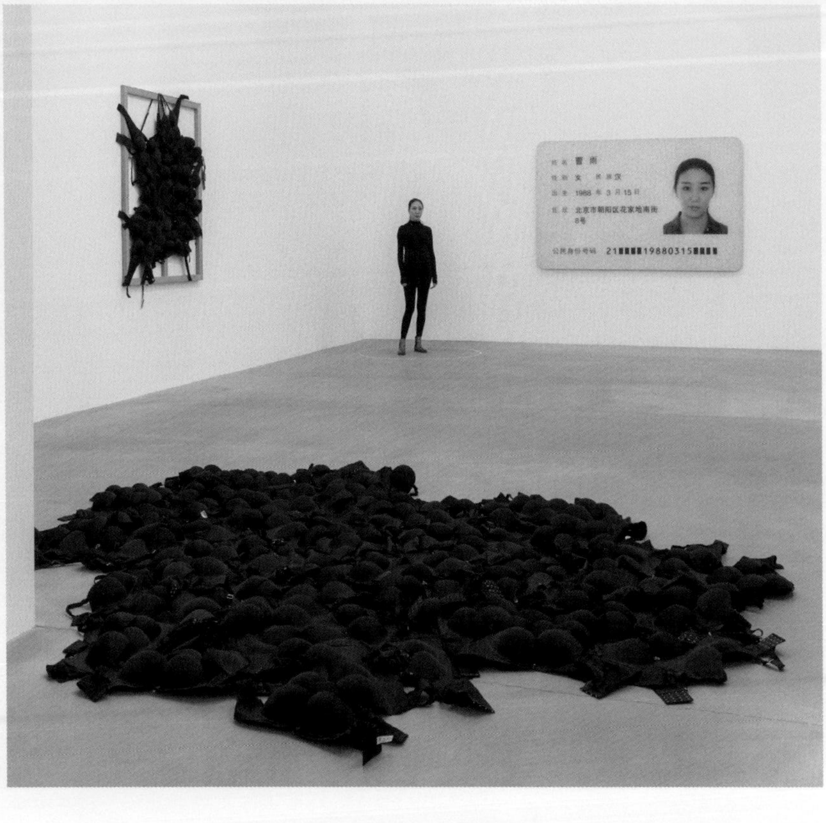

Cao Yu, *The Colorful Clouds*, 2017 / Black bras, 10 × 300 × 345 cm / Courtesy of the artist and Galerie Urs Meile, Beijing-Lucerne

DON WE NOW OUR GAY APPAREL —A DAY AS AN EXTRA ON THE SET OF *THE NEW POPE*

Text and photography Edgars Gluhovs

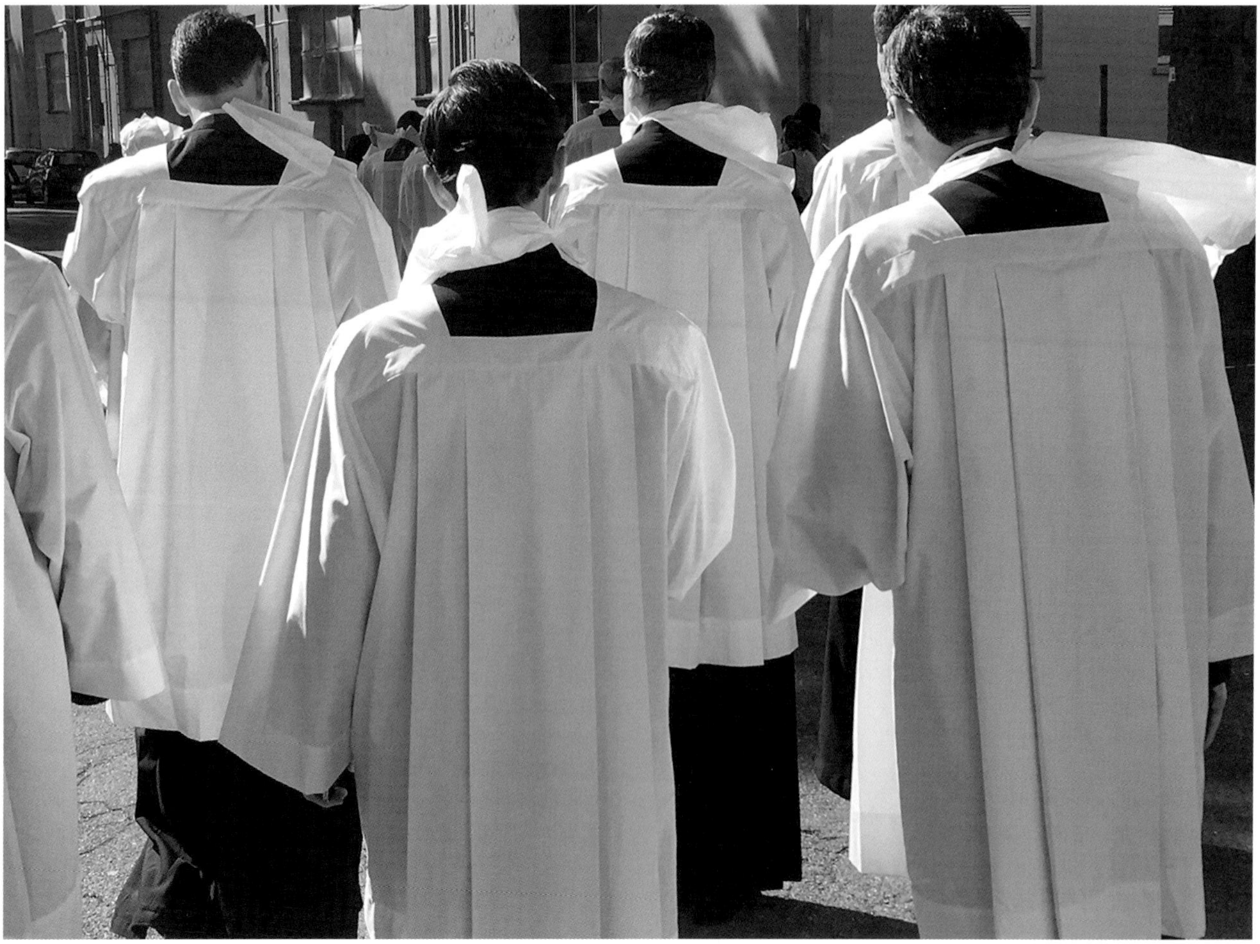

In 2015, artist Edgars Gluhovs made his Italian artistic debut at the Latvian Institute Rome. The exhibition marked the artist's resignation from private banking and his total dedication to an artistic practice, as well as his unforeseen entry into the world of Roman cinema. Gluhovs had a cameo as a barkeeper in the twenty-four hour blockbuster exhibition "The Street" at Cinecittà Studios in 2016, and earlier this year, he returned to the eternal city's film studio to shoot Paolo Sorrentino's *The New Pope*. Herewith, Gluhovs shares his experiences from the set.

Paolo Sorrentino's television series *The Young Pope* premiered on HBO in the autumn of 2016. Starring Jude Law as the fictional Pope Pius XIII, it was a spectacle of Vatican intrigue, lush scenography, and exquisite costumes.

I was living in Rome at the time and some of the scenes had been filmed in the house that was my temporary residence. The view from the window of the Papal apartments in the first episode was the same as that from my own bedroom, and the night-time confession scenes were filmed on the terrace where we enjoyed afternoon drinks. Quickly, we became fans of the show and later that year I organized a group exhibition titled "Young Popes" in the tower of that same building—in order to fill the void as we awaited the second season, as the press-text stated.

I JOIN THE SMALL CONGREGATION, INHALE AN ESPRESSO AND PROCEED THROUGH THE STUDIO GATE.

Two years later and in Berlin, my phone rings on a December afternoon, an Italian number: "Edgars Gluhovs? This is the casting agency working for Paolo Sorrentino. We have your details on file. Would you like to be a priest in the upcoming series *The New Pope*?" It takes me a few moments before I remember that, indeed, someone introduced themselves to me as working for Sorrentino's casting agency at a party in Rome once, took my picture, and wrote down my details "for future reference." The role in question is only that of a background actor (or "background artist" as Ricky Gervais' character refers to himself on *Extras*), but acknowledging the serendipity and looking for an excuse to escape the Berlin winter for a few days, I do not hesitate: "Yes, with pleasure." I agree to participate in one day of filming. That's all I want.

A few days later, the shooting date for the scene is confirmed. I arrive in Rome the evening before the shoot and go to bed early in order to be on set by 7 a.m.

The filming is to take place on a soundstage in the Cinecittà film studios. During the early morning metro ride, an elderly man sitting opposite to me reads a newspaper while wearing a non-descript winter jacket, black trousers, black shoes, and bright red socks. I am willing to bet my lunch that he will step out at the Cinecittà stop, walk through the studio gates, into a dressing room, and emerge in the full regalia of a Cardinal of the Holy Roman Church.

There is a small kiosk on wheels by the metro stop where the Cineccità proletariat have their morning coffee before putting in a good day's work. Wanting to fully be part of it all for that one day, I join the small congregation, inhale an espresso and proceed through the studio gate.

Even though I am early, the hallway in the wardrobe department is already full of people. There are men of all ages, a few women, most of them still in their street clothes while a priest and a Papal Swiss Guard, fumbling with his helmet, mingle amongst them.

Presently, an assistant invites me to follow him through a door and I find myself in the hair and make-up department where I am directed to take a seat. To my distress, a hairdresser is already approaching, scissors and clippers in each hand. While I realize that his intention probably isn't to give me a monk's ring-hairdo, I quickly decide that any kind of physical intervention is above my pay-grade. Anyways, who knows what kind of damage the man has in mind. I protest in a most polite but resolute manner. Somewhat surprised that I am declining what he considers to be an offer of a free hair-cut, the hairdresser contents himself with a few touches here and there, fumigates me with a generous amount of hair spray, and sends me off.

There is a queue leading to the dressing room from which, one by one, cardinals and bishops emerge to cheers of approval from fellow extras waiting their turn. Seeing me leafing through a book that I brought along, a middle-aged priest-in-waiting turns to me and attempts to make small talk. "Are you studying to be a cardinal?" he asks in Italian. I am never particularly talkative at such an early hour and besides, there is the serious business of finally putting on my priest costume that I am keen to get on with. "Hmmm," I reply. "Did you understand what I said?" he persists, eager for a sign of appreciation for his little joke. "More or less," I answer. He turns away, visibly disappointed.

The dressing room is abuzz with activity. Assistants are rushing around, there are extras in various stages of *déshabillement*; rows of garments hang on the rails in the strict order of the ecclesiastic hierarchy. I swiftly undress and put on the clothes pre-selected according to my size and tagged with my name. Black trousers, a pair of black oxfords, white shirt, black cassock, collar, surplice. There are thirty-three buttons to close on the cassock—a task that I, aided by a wardrobe assistant, perform with great efficiency.

The black socks are my own, naturally from Gammarelli—the official tailor to the Pope and the purveyor of socks intended for clergy. Sometime in the previous year I had put together a small show dedicated to this brand. The socks were available for purchase during the show and decorated the room in colorful arrangements of silk, wool, and cotton. I want to inject a bit of the real deal into the day's proceedings, even though my effort will likely go unappreciated.

Dressed as simple priest, I am slightly envious of the cardinals and bishops in their deep reds and rich purples. Were I a real priest, perhaps I'd really study on so I could advance in rank, so as to be able to wear those clothes.

DRESSED AS SIMPLE PRIEST, I AM SLIGHTLY ENVIOUS OF THE CARDINALS AND BISHOPS IN THEIR DEEP REDS AND RICH PURPLES. WERE I A REAL PRIEST, PERHAPS I'D REALLY STUDY ON SO THAT I COULD ADVANCE IN RANK, SO AS TO BE ABLE TO WEAR THOSE CLOTHES.

But, the cassock sits well, and I can pay full attention to what is going on around me. We are now in a large hangar serving as a waiting point—a limbo of sorts. Finally I can see all of the costumes at once. There must be a few hundred extras. They are sitting on rows of white plastic chairs, alone and in groups, chatting, looking at their phones and drinking coffee.

If one puts their mind to it, almost any man you pass on the street looks like a potential priest. Just imagine him in clerical attire. Casting a group of priests really can't be that difficult. Nevertheless, some physiognomies were clearly chosen to catch the eye: a small, almost dwarf-sized young priest with bulging eyes, an imposing bishop with a great white beard, a number of elegant, patrician looking ambassadors with perfect hairstyles.

I pass by two cardinals taking pictures of each other "Would you take a photo of us together?", one of them stops me. "By all means," I take his phone and do my best. "Bravo. And now one with you?", he says. "Oh, ok"—I first pose with one cardinal, a small man with a sugary smile, then with the second, a sterner one wearing spectacles. I too try to look stern. I have decided that today, I will be a very serious looking priest.

I AM SURPRISED TO SEE [THE DIRECTOR] CHEWING ON A CIGAR, WHICH STRIKES ME AS A BIT OF A CLICHÉ.

Little by little, production assistants group everyone by clerical hierarchy: priests are placed with priests, bishops with bishops and so forth. When dealing with such a large group of people, it quickly becomes apparent that a strict hand is necessary, lest some cardinals begin bumping into one another, or a lone bishop wanders off the set. One by one, the groups are escorted and led across the Cinecittà grounds to the set. It looks like an informal procession. The sun is already up and the bright robes flutter in the light breeze.

The scene being shot is a funeral mass celebrated at St. Peter's Basilica. For this purpose, the soundstage has been semi-converted to look the part. The marble floor ornament is recreated in linoleum, there are rows of pews, the Bernini Baldachin columns and the Pope's throne. A white coffin is placed at the center. The background will be added digitally via bluescreen.

I am seated on a pew, towards the back, flanked by a priest on each side. This turns out to be a bit of a peanut gallery, as the bishops and the cardinals are closer to the altar and the main action. Swiss Guards line the aisle. An ancient little lady in a nun's habit, all bent, shriveled, and seemingly half asleep, is sitting on the pew behind me. She is called Marcellina and is the focus of continuous caring attention from her fellow extras as well as the crew and director.

Ramon Garcia, playing the plump Cardinal Aguirre, rolls onto the set and gives everyone an enthusiastic "buongiorno." Other actors quietly take their place. The cameras are positioned, and there is a call for silence as the director's assistant explains what is being required of the day's "background artists."

Several sequences are to be shot. There is the entrance of Silvio Orlando in his role as the endearingly scheming Cardinal Voiello, the speech he will give, the entrance of the new Pope (played by John Malkovich), and the Pope's brief address to the congregation. All that is required of the extras is to sit, stand, turn our heads following the cardinal and the pope with our gaze, make signs of the cross, say one or two phrases in ceremonial Latin and look solemn throughout the proceedings.

Paolo Sorrentino seems relaxed but looks scruffy, like many directors tend to look, for some reason. I am surprised to see him chewing on a cigar, which strikes me as a bit of a cliché.

Then, the clapperboard goes clap, and it's action. I follow the instructions, which really isn't much as far as acting goes. I behave more or less as I would in a real mass: observe the surroundings, the congregation, and try to keep up with this ritual, which is a bit exotic to me.

Each sequence requires shots from several angles and, invariably, several takes. An actor is out of step, somebody looks into a camera or—to general consternation—a phone rings, which happens repeatedly despite the desperate admonishments from the director's assistand.

Costume and make up assistants dart about the pews in between takes—brushing hair, adjusting a sleeve or a collar, powdering a bald head and adding an artificial tear here and there. There are bits of gossip exchanged among the extras: "What scene is coming up," "What is this and that actor's name," and "What has happened to Jude Law's Pope Pius XIII at the end of the first season?"

At lunch, everyone is handed large sheets of thin white plastic, to be tied as a bib around the neck lest the pristine costumes—heaven forbid—get maculated by some sauce. Back in the large waiting hangar, the faux Vatican elite are served meals in cardboard boxes that look like oversized in-flight meals. Bishops, nuns and cardinals, balancing on flimsy plastic chairs, dig into cold roast beef, potatoes, and oranges. There is a queue of people in red, black and purple, attempting one by one to squeeze into a small bathroom-stall. Splendid as the costumes may be, they present quite a challenge in that particular regard.

After a spell in the sunshine where more photos are taken, cigarettes are smoked and gossip is exchanged, we are back on set. The morning's palpable sense of curiosity and amusement has, by this time, given way to a somewhat more get-on-with-it feeling of professionalized routine.

The pace picks up. The scenes are being shot and reshot. Turning to look around, standing up, following the Pope with our eyes, answering his Latin blessing, not looking into the camera, again and again.

Papa Malkovich exudes calm and authority, sliding serenely up and down the aisle during his sequence, performing the sacramental rituals at the altar and blessing the congregation. In between takes he disappears from view or waits languidly on his throne.

My mind wanders a little. I think about the fact that there hasn't been a bearded Pope for a few centuries, I mentally transpose that famous scene from *Being John Malkovich* onto this set, and I remember Peter Sellers in *The Party*, unwittingly sabotaging an entire shoot. I wonder what it would take for me to get kicked off the set. A few ideas spring to mind.

As the afternoon progresses, there are audible sighs and mutterings going through the rows of my fellow clergy who are starting to get tired. At last, Silvio Orlando nails his lines, no ringing phones interrupt the scene, and the "background artists" look just right. It's a wrap and there is some general, albeit tired, rejoicing and applause. As before, everyone is lead to the wardrobe by rank. Our priest group exits last. In the pocket of my cassock is a souvenir I take along with me: an authentic-looking booklet with the mass' program, handed out to everyone to hold and leaf through during the shoot. It is designed and printed specially for this scene and is emblazoned with the new Pope's insignia.

Notwithstanding the lavatory experience, I find that I have already gotten quite used to the costume over the course of the day. Defrocked and changed back into my regular clothes, suddenly, for a brief moment, I feel a little strange.

DEFROCKED AND CHANGED BACK INTO MY REGULAR CLOTHES, SUDDENLY, FOR A BRIEF MOMENT, I FEEL A LITTLE STRANGE.

It is already dark when I step outside. The cardinals, bishops and nuns—once again indistinguishable from an average Roman—are slowly trickling out of the studio. I walk towards the metro to head back into the city. Here and there, I see the occasional red sock flashing in the dark of the evening.

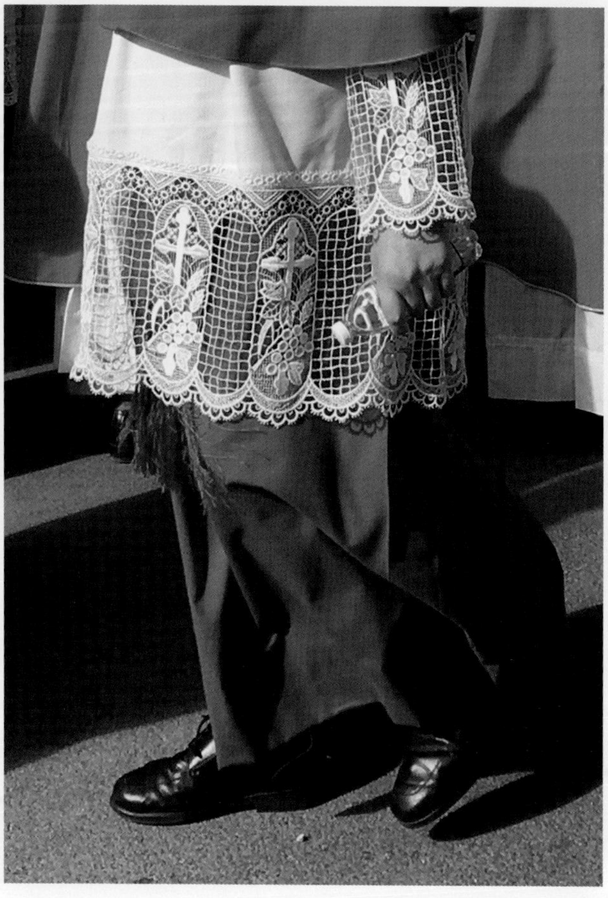

UNTITLED BUILDING— ON CADY NOLAND

Text — Inka Meißner
Photography — Stefanie Pretnar

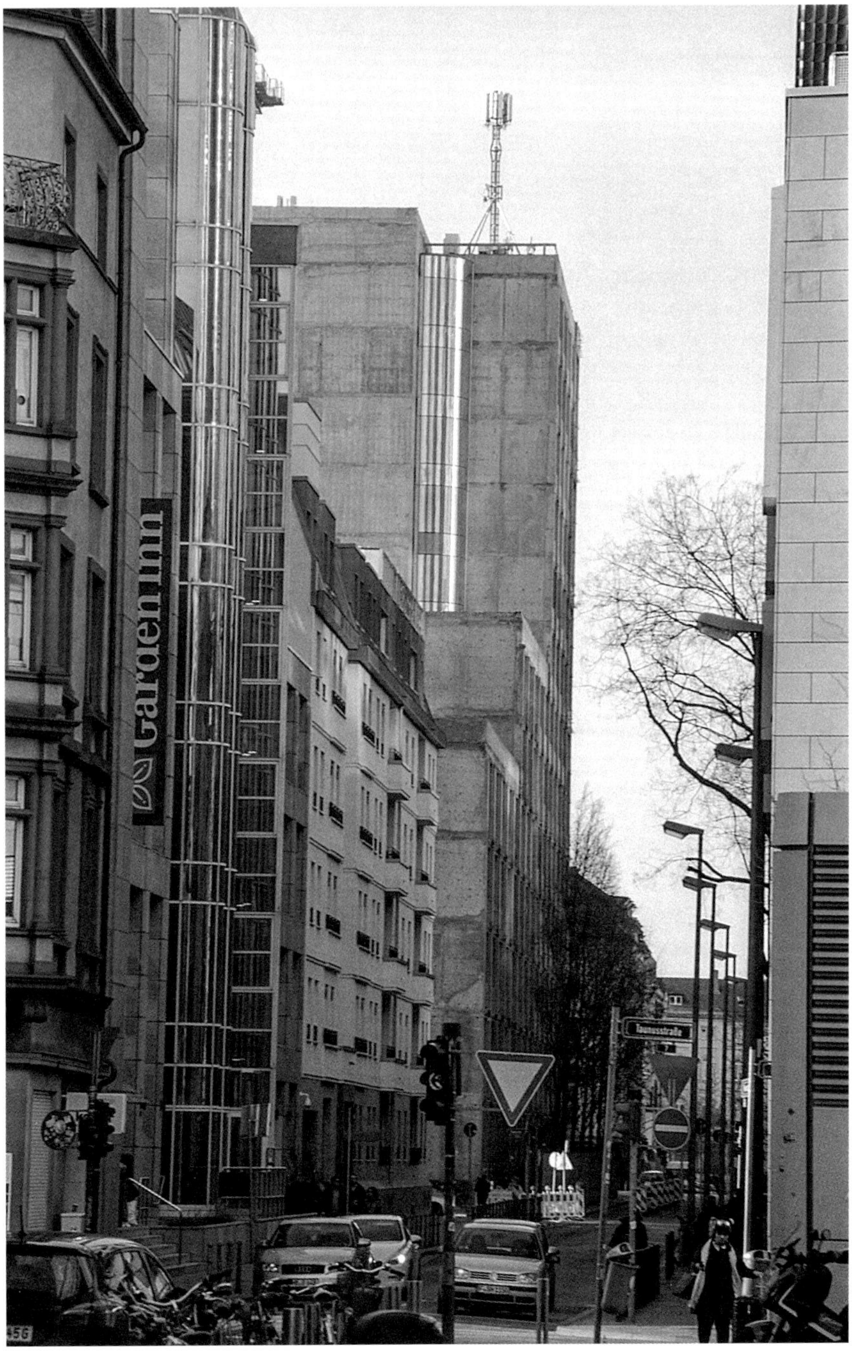

In *Untitled Building—On Cady Noland*, Inka Meißner and Stefanie Pretnar offer their personal perspectives on the work of artist Cady Noland, and her recent exhibition at the Museum für Moderne Kunst (MMK) in Frankfurt.

Cady Noland was born in 1956 in Washington, D.C., the daughter of color field painting pioneer Kenneth Noland. She rose to fame in the late 1980s before abruptly ending her artistic practice by the end of the 1990s.

Today, in Trump's America, Noland's work is more alive and relevant than ever, as social circumstance becomes increasingly reflective of the Reagan Era.

Inka Meißner is an artist based in Berlin. She recently contributed to the Cady Noland Symposium at MMK.

Stefanie Pretnar is an artist and photographer living in Frankfurt. For this contribution, she didn't photograph Noland's exhibition, but instead rendered the atmosphere of the show into a suite of architectural photographs.

Experiencing the month of April alongside the works of Cady Noland has been a wild ride.

When I first saw the exhibition at the Museum für Moderne Kunst in Frankfurt, I felt as if the artist was looking back at me while I looked at her works—and she didn't like it. Her imaginary eyes were resting on the back of my head, like a laserpointer, so I went for a spin, going through the exhibition at a quicker than normal pace. Marked by bouts of guilt and streaks of good old reason. But at some point, an interesting event took place—my own paranoia departed, and I found myself finally able to see the paranoia of the world, as it is contained in Noland's artworks.

A friend of mine who grew up in Frankfurt told me how for her, the MMK always turned into a haunted house when she passed through it and contemplated the art; I understood her comment as a compliment. The architecture allows the artworks to develop their very own sense of self-conciousness since the spacial situations do not repeat themselves—there aren't two rooms in this building one would enter in a similar way.

Watching while being looked at; staring at the holes, and the holes stare back—just as the dark joke won't leave the scene. Through the holes in Noland's work, one can see the museum itself. And there are plenty of holes; holes perforate the famous upright cut-out of Lee Harvey Oswald, *Oozewald* (1989), suspected murderer of John F. Kennedy, the holes for the head, wrists and ankles, guillotine-style, in her numerous guillotine-sculptures[1]. They expose the white walls of the museum as well as the spaces between those walls—staircases, niches and breakthroughs. A remarkable moment unfolds on the first or second floor when a corral gate adorned with a horse's headgear leads into a comparably petite gallery, in which you will find a smaller work of Noland's, *Percussion and Cartridge Revolvers* (1984). It consists of a manual for firearms mounted on a wooden plate, a wooden stick, several snap hooks, handcuffs, a whistle, leather buckles, a cord and various metal rings. It shares the space with Bill Bollinger's 1968 artwork *Pipe*, comprised of two aluminium tubes attached to each other with a plasitic hose.

Connecting the dots with a decided projecting brushstroke, the paranoia reaches beyond this physical realm and into the wider context of art and its historization. On the ground floor hangs a painting by Kenneth Noland (strangely enough, the colors match those used in a permanent wall painting by Günther Förg in the stairwell). When one is looking from what must be the north side of the building, the piece *Dead Space* (1989) shifts into the viewer's gaze, overlaying the work with a number of metal pipes, arranged in a prison bar-like construction that reaches almost all the way from the ceiling to the floor. Whatever came ahead of Noland's blank envisioning seems strangely naïve, as if the shapes and materials were still hanging around at the play yard, ready to be arranged along modernity's formal tropes, not yet seeing the pattern.

The museum was planned, designed and build during the same period of time Noland spent constructing her distinct, artistic intuition on the other side of the Atlantic. MMK as we know it today opened to the public a year before Noland's participation in documenta IX in 1991. On the MMK's Wikipedia page[2], one finds a quote by its architect, Hans Hollein. Said quote goes more or less as follows: "There cannot be a neutral room in the museum, but only distinctive rooms in different sizes and grades of circulation with which the artworks can enter a dialectical relationship of reciprocal exponentiation."

This loss of an outside, the disappearance of an objective or timeless place that had only ever been imagined—be it for the part of the observer, spectator, recipient or the artwork itself—is obviously a postmodern condition. But when the actual reality of this is revealed in a physical experience, an encounter with the tangible protagonists of this scaled down, cybernetic system (that the field of art outlines as well) doesn't feel as comfortably established as the long-serving term "postmodernity" might suggest.

In their lectures at the symposium on Cady Noland two days before the writing of this text, both Larne Abse Gogarty and Peter Osborne addressed the fact that at the very core of bourgeois identity-formation, specifically of that that informs the inherently capitalist US-American social fabric, lies the neccessity to own property. (I don't have the space to reliably reconstruct their arguments, I simply wanted to recap one moment that stood out to me as being crucial.) When private property lies at the core of self-affirmation; other people are dangerous and objects exist only to be owned or desired. Within the tools responsible for securing and defending oneself and one's property then lies the essence of bourgeois sculpture.

Exhibited in the context of a fine art institution, these tools seem to touch upon the categories that the art world created for them, such as the "readymade". But what happens is that the pieces Noland had chosen for her artistic endeavour enter the picture from a structurally different angle. In unmasking the sculptural genre as the disguised symbol for an ideology of self-made ownership, the objects exhibited become either the weapons they intended to be, or items of sociological interest. The extent to which this is a fundametally different genre is yet to be proven, however it does expose the uncanny self-similar relationship between things as being tools of harm or objects of art.

From here on, the different pieces and their choice of matter dig into several areas of the capitalist's bourgeois psychoscape, both grand and petite. A central breeding ground is located in the basement workshop, as Diedrich Diedrichsen laid bare in his lecture, tracing back the materials to where they are charged up with their fatal ideological (mis)understandings at this historical moment. Another is the obvious shape of the fence and various models of a town square's facilities, fitted for torture and killing. It extends to its visual and medialized counterparts in the form of images in which the violence of the object relations is encoded in increasingly abstract ways.

In an exhibition of that size, the limited range of materials and motives in Noland's ouevre becomes obvious. The constant repetition doesn't only expand on the decreasing complexity of image-content, form and surface that the progession of capitalism is confronting us with; it also narrows down the obsessive need for protection and destruction to its basic signifiers, revealing the banality of some of today's operative mechanisms, which are otherwise rather difficult to decipher.

Finding a note to end on is not easy. April too is ending and, in a last bout of paranoia, I asked myself if there was a way of possibly releasing the aggression inscribed in the way Noland relentlessly addressed the atrocities of the meta-game[3]. From the postmodern cultural feedback loop, into wherever the artist might have wanted it to come to a rest.

But that's when the dark joke resurfaces, or maybe I just realize that there are quite a few jokes that I just don't get. If Noland's work wouldn't point out the systemic roots of what plays out as a political aesthetic these days, as dangerous and brutal as it is perceived in such a seductive way, the potential humor inscribed in some of the pieces would come much closer to the fore. Her well-informed, bold way of assembling materials tells of an utter disinterest in institutionlized ideas of sculpture, that is in a way reminiscent of artistic practices such as that of Isa Genzken. The shopping carts and baskets—*Full of Action*[4]—carry home whatever you or your car needs to keep running... I'll leave it at that for now.

1 Like f.e. *Tower of Terror*, 1993, *Gibbet*, 1993/1994 and *Beltway Terror*, 1993/1994
2 https://de.wikipedia.org/wiki/Museum_f%C3%BCr_Moderne_Kunst
3 This is how Noland frames the social aesthetics of US-American society back then in *Towards a Metalanguage of Evil* (Stuttgart/Kassel: Edition Cantz/Documenta, 1992), 5: "The game is a synthesis of tactics, played out in the social arena, in which advantage can be gained in an oblique way."
4 One work, a shopping cart filled with rims is titled: *Cart Full of Action*, 1986, and a metal basket carrying sturdy metal chains and a jumper cable is titled: *Basket of Action*, 1988

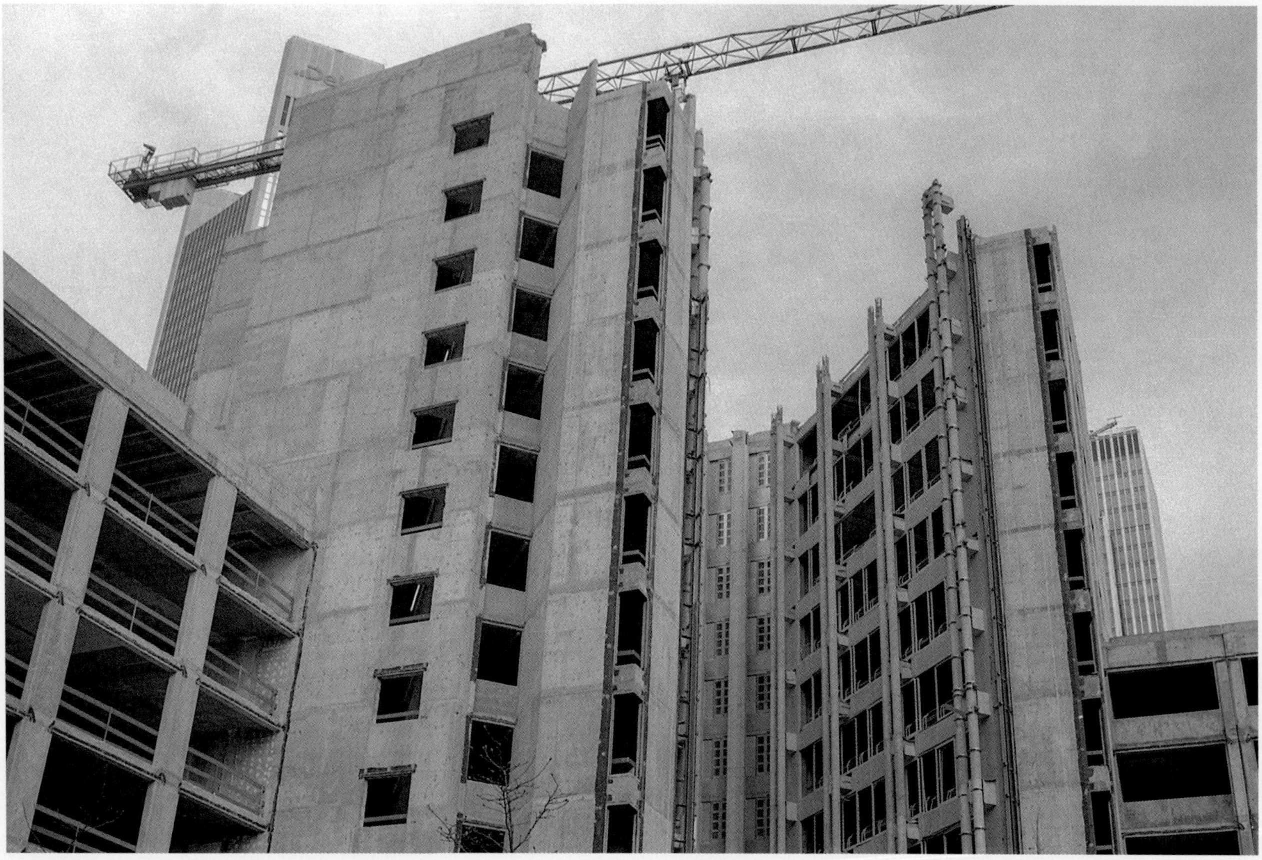

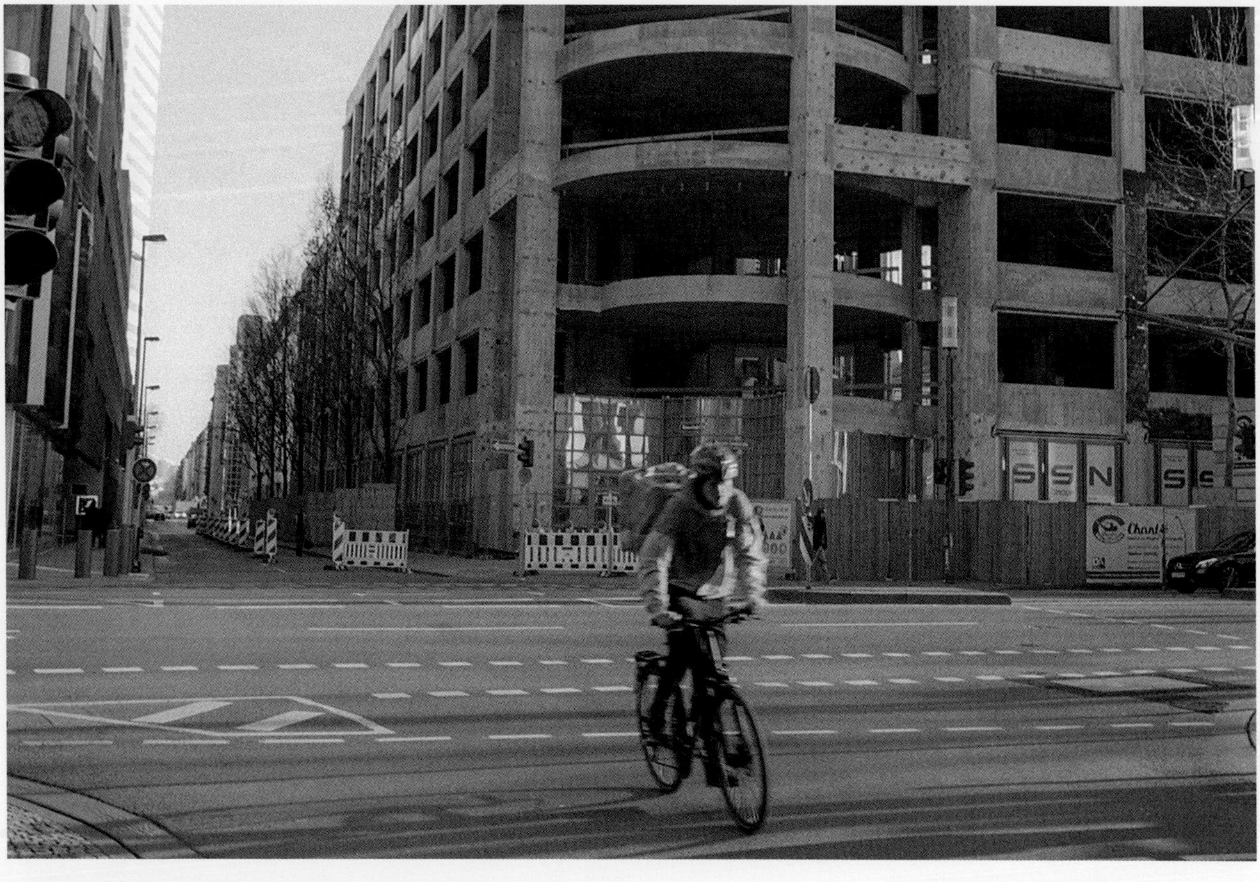

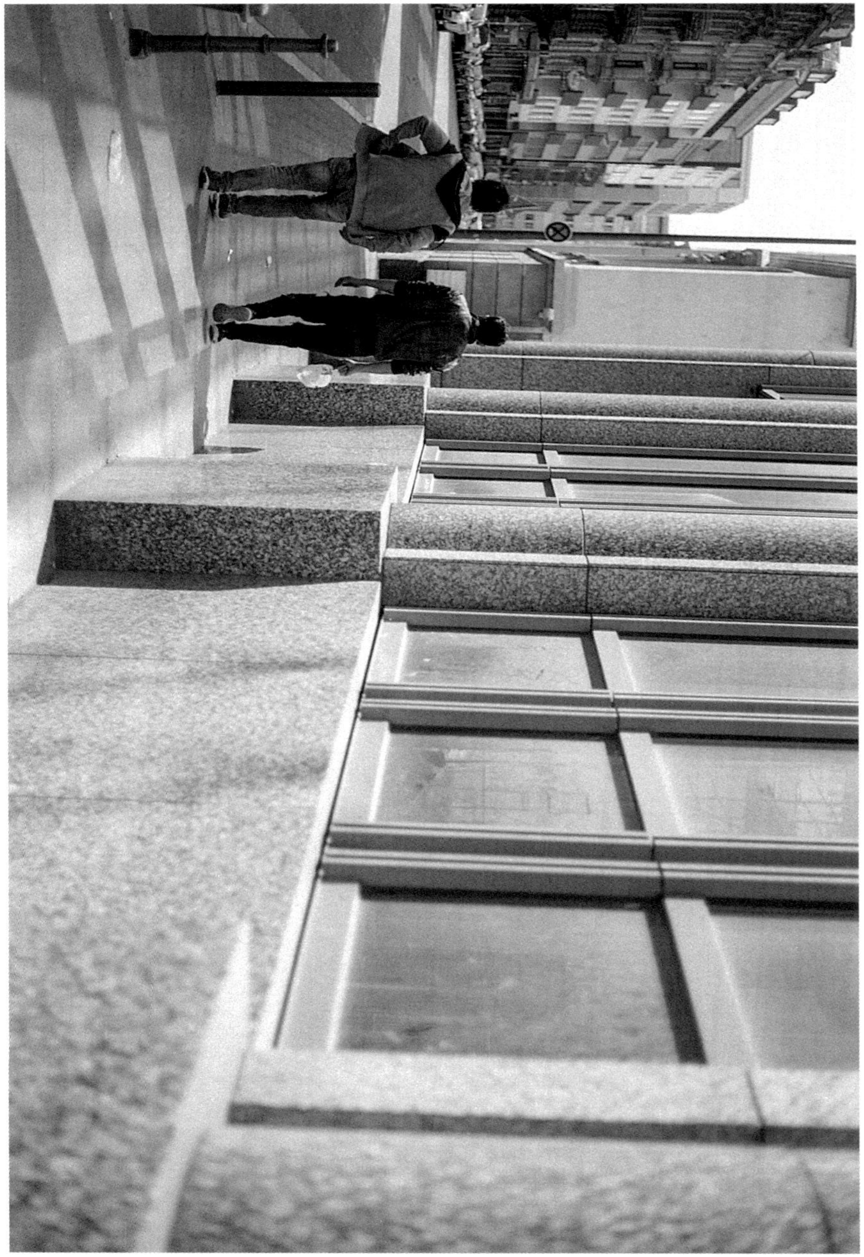

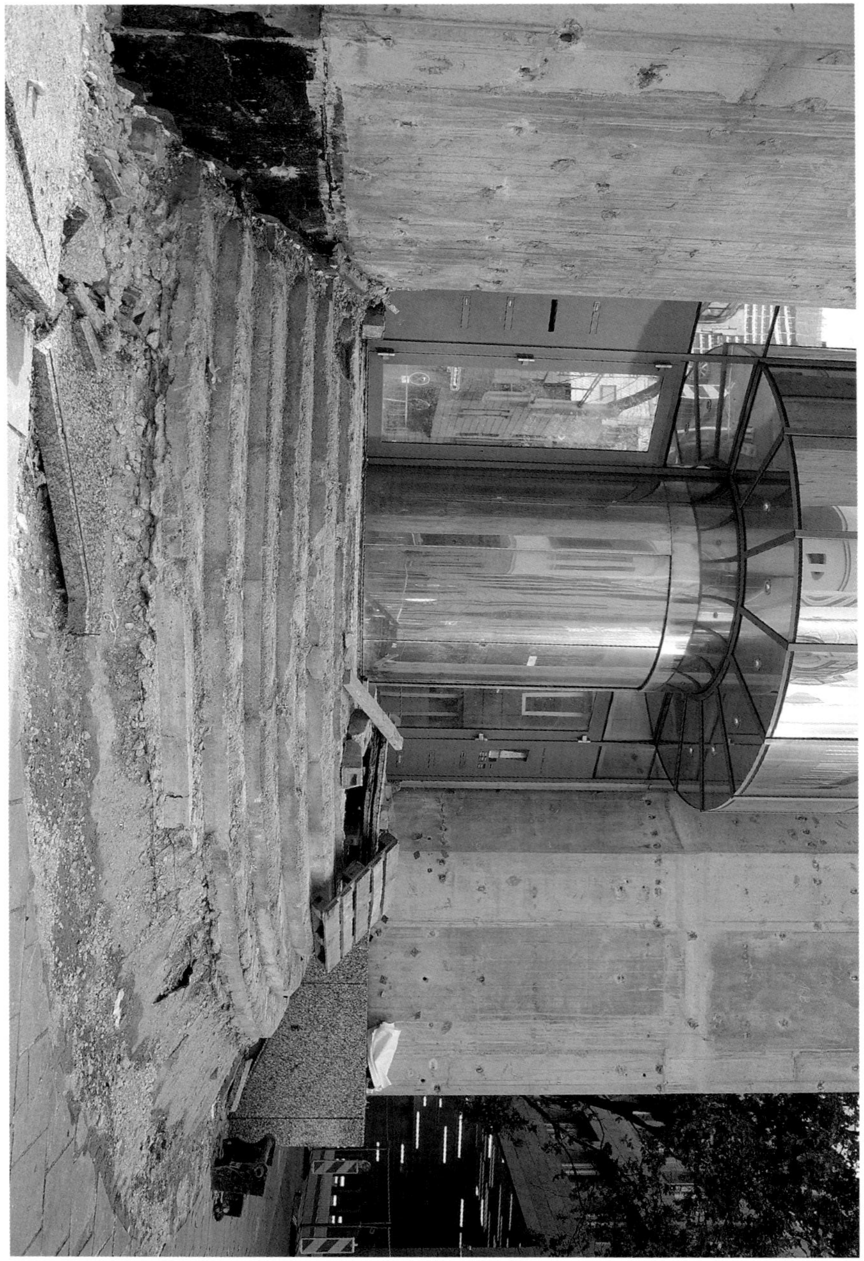

LIT ER ATU RE

RELEVANT READINGS

Violence of a structural nature is no less brutal than its physical counterpart. The everyday presence of structural violence causes a mute paralysis. The definitions of gender based on symbolic, cultural, and physical boundaries are as hard and clear as they are painful to experience. Upbringing, cultural attribution, existing power structures, social codes, religious traditions, and biological manifestations unite to form a violent normative framework that governs body, sexuality, identity, and behavior.

The following selection of books accompanied "Performing Society: The Violence of Gender", an exhibition curated in 2019 by MMK Frankfurt director Susanne Pfeffer at Hong Kong's Tai Kwun Center for Heritage and Art.

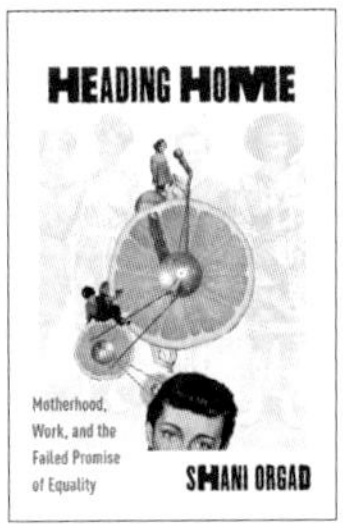

Shani Orgad: *Heading Home. Motherhood, Work, and the Failed Promise of Equality*
Columbia University Press, 2019

In today's advanced capitalist societies, women are encouraged to "lean in." The media and government champion women's empowerment. In a cultural climate where women can have it all (seemingly), why do some working professional women—lawyers, financial managers, teachers, engineers et cetera—give up their careers after having children to become stay-at-home mothers? How do they feel about their decision, and what do their stories tell us about contemporary society?

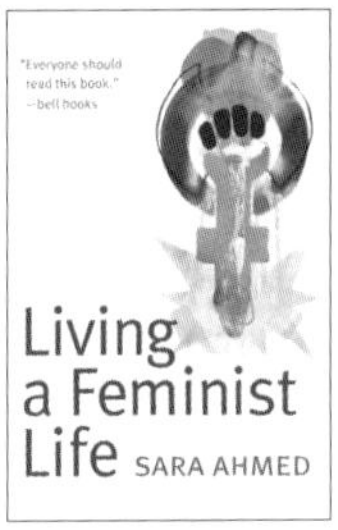

Sara Ahmed:
Living a Feminist Life
Duke University Press, 2017

In *Living a Feminist Life*, Sara Ahmed demonstrates how feminist theory was generated from everyday situations, and the ordinary experiences of being a feminist in the home and work environments. Building on the legacies of feminists of color in particular, Ahmed offers a poetic and personal meditation on how feminists become estranged from the worlds they critique—often by naming and calling attention to problems—and how feminists learn about worlds from their efforts to transform them.

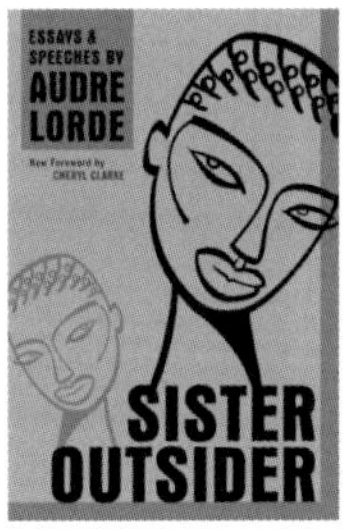

Audre Lorde:
Sister Outsider
Ten Speed Press, 1984

With *Sister Outsider*—an essential anthology—Lorde explores the conditions of marginalization and American white patriarchy from her unique position as a poet, activist, mother, feminist and black lesbian. The book catalogues a series of Lorde's essays and speeches, all ruminating the theme of her identity. *Sister Outsider* is often lauded as being a direct precursor to contemporary feminist theory, as it considers the complexities of intersectional identity in a candid voice.

Jack Halberstam:
Trans.*
A Quick and Quirky Account of Gender Variability
University Press of California, 2017

The last decade has seen an exponential increase in the public discourse surrounding issues facing the transgender community. Though increased visibility invites power, it has also incurred regulation, both in favor of and against trans-identifying people. What was once regarded as a disorder has become an accepted articulation of gendered embodiment, as well as a new site for political activism and political recognition. What happened in the last few decades to prompt such an extensive rethinking of our understanding of gendered embodiment?

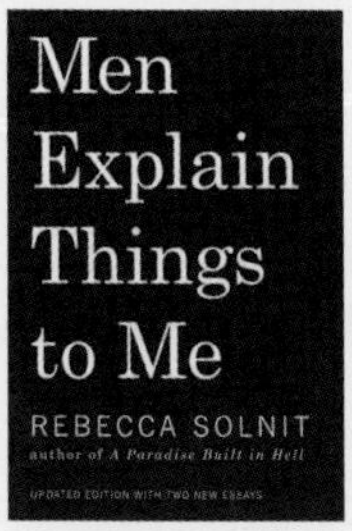

Rebecca Solnit:
Men Explain Things to Me
Haymarket Books, 2014

In her comic, scathing essay, *Men Explain Things to Me*, Rebecca Solnit considers what tends to go wrong in conversations between men and women. She writes about "mansplaining", the phenomenon in which overconfident men explain things to women inaccurately, operating on the assumption that the woman they are talking too knows little to no detail about the topic at hand, when in fact the female explainee knows more than the male explainer. Solnit asks why this arises, and how this aspect of gender-based conflict functions, using personal and hilarious anecdotes to support her argument.

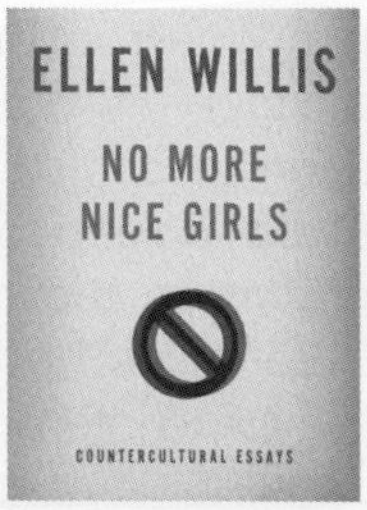

Ellen Willis:
No More Nice Girls.
Countercultural Essays
Wesleyan University Press, 1992

With characteristic intelligence, wit, and feminist insight, Ellen Willis addresses democracy as she sees it: "a commitment to individual freedom and egalitarian self-government in every area of social, economic, and cultural life." In *No More Nice Girls*, Willis confronts the conservative backlash that slowly eroded the democratic ideals and advances of the 1960s, as well as the internal debates that have frequently splintered the left.

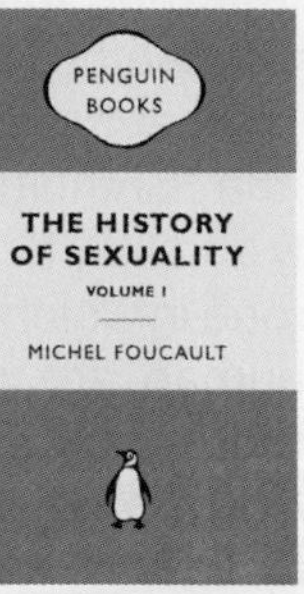

Michel Foucault:
The Will to Knowledge.
The History of Sexuality, Vol 1
Éditions Gallimard, 1976
(French edition)

Here, Michel Foucault offers an iconoclastic exploration as to why we feel compelled to continually analyze and discuss sex, and an investigation into the social and mental mechanisms of power that cause us to direct the questions of what we are to what our sexuality is.

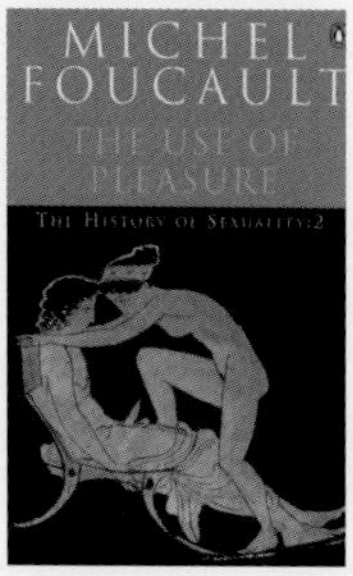

Michel Foucault:
The Use of Pleasure.
The History of Sexuality, Vol 2
Éditions Gallimard, 1984
(French edition)

In the sequel to *The History of Sexuality*, Foucault, the brilliantly original French thinker analyses how the ancient Greeks perceived sexuality. Throughout *The Uses of Pleasure*, Foucault analyzes an irresistible array of ancient Greek texts on eroticism as he attempts to answer the following two questions: How did sexual experience become a moral issue in the West? Why were other appetites of the body, for example hunger, and collective concerns, such as civic duty, not subjected to the numberless rules and regulations and judgments that have defined, if not confined, sexual behavior?

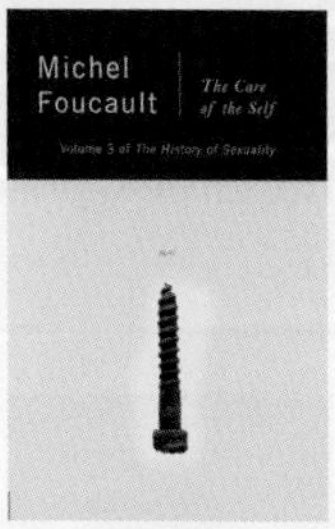

Michel Foucault:
The Care of the Self.
The History of Sexuality, Vol 3
Éditions Gallimard, 1984
(French edition)

In this, the fourth volume of the seminal *The History of Sexuality* series, Michel Foucault takes us to the Golden Age of Rome, revealing a subtle yet definitive break from the classical Grecian vision of sexual pleasure. He skillfully explores the whole corpus of moral reflection with close reference to philosophers Plutarch,

Epictetus, Marcus Aurelius and Seneca, as well as the leading physicians of the era. Through the course of the volume, Foucault uncovers an increasing mistrust of pleasure and a growing anxiety regarding sexual activity and its consequences.

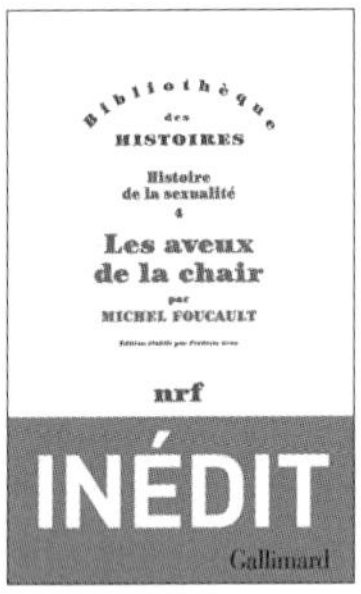

Michel Foucault:
Confessions of the Flesh.
The History of Sexuality, Vol 4
Éditions Gallimard, 2018
(French editions)

The fourth volume of *The History of Sexuality* was incomplete at the time of Foucault's death in 1984. Éditions Gallimard published *Confessions of the Flesh* in French with the title *Les aveux de la chair*. The volume tackled Christian doctrine from between the eleventh and fourteenth centuries, and elaborates on Foucault's belief that the majority of these rules and doctrines drew on the self-disciplines practiced by the Roman and Greek philosophers of antiquity.

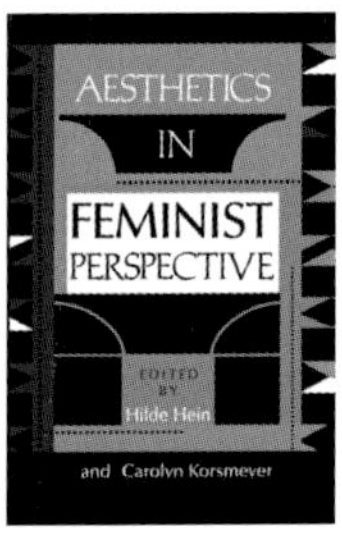

Hilde Hein, Carolyn C. Korsmeyer:
Aesthetics in Feminist Perspective
Indiana University Press, 1993

These essays examine the intellectual traditions related to the philosophy of art and aesthetics. Containing essays by scholars and the writer Marilyn French, the collection ranges from the history of aesthetic theory to a philosophical reflection on fashion. The contributions are unified by a sustained scrutiny of the nature of "feminist," "feminine," or "female" art, creativity, and interpretation.

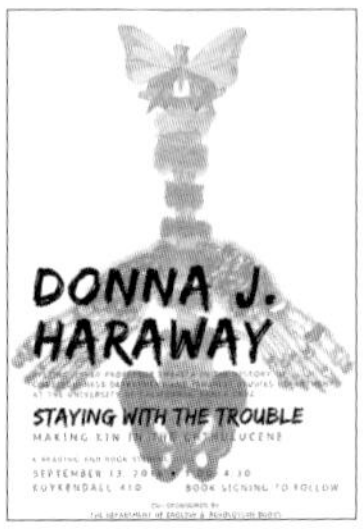

Donna J. Haraway:
Staying with the Trouble.
Making Kin in the Chthulucene
Duke University Press, 2016

In the midst of spiraling ecological devastation, multispecies feminist theorist Donna J. Haraway offers provocative new ways to reconfigure our relationship with the earth and its inhabitants. She eschews referring to our current epoch as the Anthropocene, preferring to conceptualize it as what she calls the "Chthulucene", as it more aptly and fully describes our epoch as one in which the human and nonhuman are inextricably linked. Theoretically and methodologically driven by the signifier SF—string figures, science fact, science fiction, speculative feminism, speculative fabulation, so far—*Staying with the Trouble* further cements Haraway's reputation as one of the most daring and original thinkers of our time.

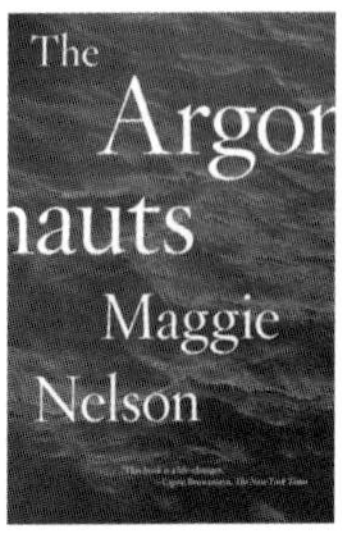

Maggie Nelson:
The Argonauts
Melville House, 2016

In episodic fragments, Nelson tells the story of her relationship with the artist Harry Dodge. Her words explore the intensity of their sexual connection, the keeping of their love and the journey they embarked on when sharing the project of making a home and building a family. In doing so Nelson joins "a long history of queers constructing their own families—be they composed of peers or mentors or lovers or ex-lovers or children or non-human animals."

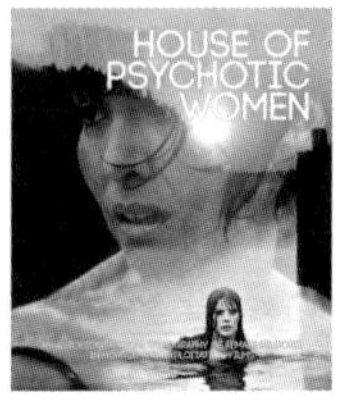

Kier-La Janisse:
House Of Psychotic Women.
An Autobiographical Topography of Female Neurosis in Horror and Exploitation Films
Fab Press, 2012

House of Psychotic Women is an autobiographical exploration of female neurosis in horror and exploitation films. Cinema is full of neurotic personalities, but few things are more transfixing than a woman losing her mind onscreen. Horror as a genre provides the most welcoming platform for these histrionics: crippling paranoia, desperate loneliness, masochistic death wishes, dangerous obsessiveness, and apocalyptic hysteria. Unlike her male counterpart—"the eccentric"—the female neurotic lives a shamed existence, making these films a rare place where her destructive emotions are so candidly explored.

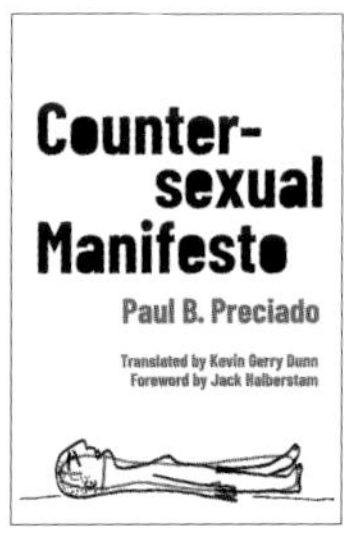

Paul B. Preciado:
Countersexual Manifesto
Columbia University Press, 2018

Countersexual Manifesto is an outrageous yet rigorous work of transgender studies, a definitively performative literary text, and an insistent call to action. Seeking to overthrow all constraints on what can be done to and with the body, Paul B. Preciado offers a provocative challenge to even the most radical claims about gender, sexuality, and desire.

Paul B. Preciado:
Testo Junkie. Sex, Drugs, and Biopolitics in the Pharmaco-pornographic Era
The Feminist Press at CUNY, 2013

What constitutes a "real" man or woman in the twenty-first century? Since the development of birth control pills, erectile dysfunction remedies, and synthetic testosterone and estrogen, the body someone is born with need no longer reflect the assumed gender identity of that person. In this penetrating analysis of gender, Preciado shows the ways in which the synthesis of hormones since the 1950s has fundamentally changed how gender and sexual identity are formulated, and how the pharmaceutical and pornography industries are in the business of creating desire.

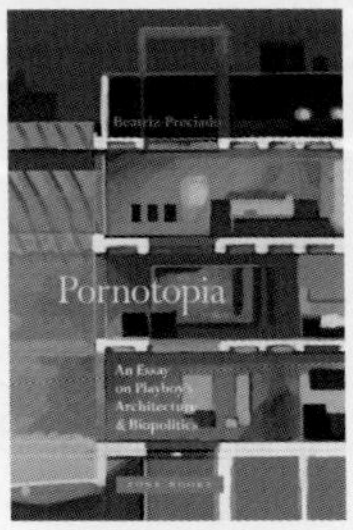

Paul B. Preciado:
Pornotopia.
An Essay on Playboy's Architecture and Biopolitics
Zone Books, 2014

In *Pornotopia*, Preciado examines popular culture and pornographic spaces as sites of architectural production.

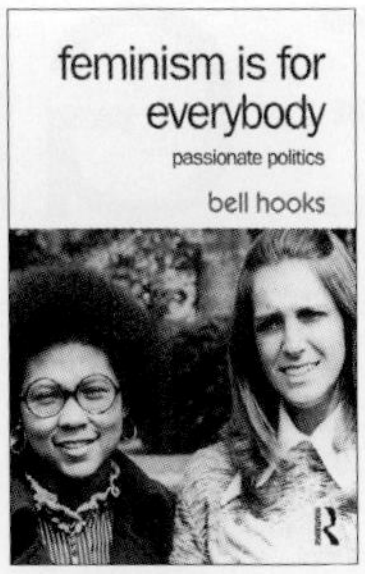

bell hooks:
Feminism Is for Everybody: Passionate Politics
Taylor & Francis Ltd, 2015

What is feminism? In this short, accessible and crucial piece of feminist literature, bell hooks explores the nature of feminism and its positive promise to eliminate sexism, sexist exploitation, and oppression. With her characteristic clarity and directness, hooks encourages readers to see how feminism can touch and change their lives—to see that feminism is in fact for everybody.

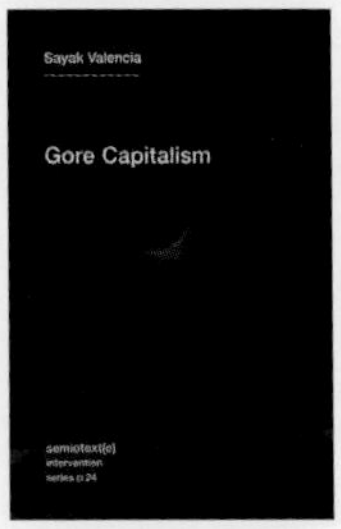

Sayak Valencia: *Gore Capitalism*
Semiotext(e), 2018

Gore Capitalism is an analysis of contemporary violence as the new commodity of the hyper-consumerist stage of capitalism we currently inhabit. Written by the Tijuanan intellectual activist Sayak Valencia, *Gore Capitalism* is a crucial essay positing a decolonial, feminist and philosophical approach to the outbreak of violence in Mexico and, more broadly, across the global South.

Ariana Reines: *The Cow*
Fence Books, 2006

"Anarchic, graphic, and literal, Ariana Reines' first book demonstrates the potential of poetry to cannibalize. She is a cow, grazing realms of experience explored by John Weiners, Hélène Cixous, Bernadette Mayer, Bruce Andrews, Alfred Döblin, and reality television. Beyond brilliant, *The Cow* is a manifesto of the paradoxical girl-state in which disappearance beckons through presence, and you are completely alert to a point where you can no longer stand it."
— Chris Kraus

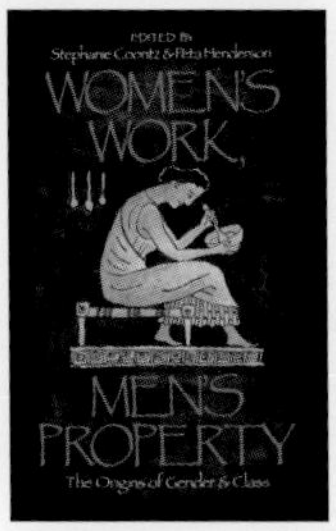

Stephanie Coontz:
Women's Work, Men's Property. The Origins of Gender and Class
Verso, 1986

Women's Work, Men's Property unites a group of French and American feminists whose work specializes in history and anthropology to examine the origins of the sexual division of labor, the nature of pre-state kinship societies, the position of women in societies that had slavery systems, and the specific forms taken by the oppression of women in Ancient Greece.

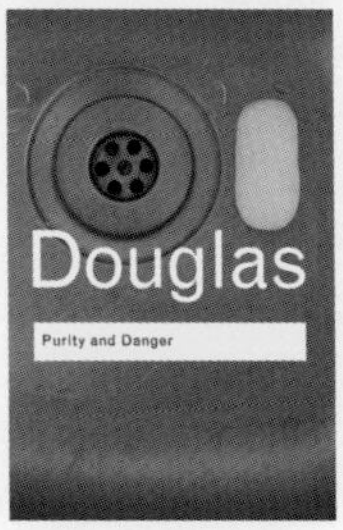

Mary Douglas:
Purity and Danger
Routledge, 2002

In *Purity and Danger*, Mary Douglas identifies the concern for purity as a key theme at the heart of every society. In lively and lucid prose, she unpacks the concept's relevance by revealing its broad impact on our attitudes to society, values, cosmology and knowledge.

SPICE GRRLZ, GORILLAZ GRRLS

Text
Year

Karl Holmqvist
2019

SPICE GRRLZ
GORILLAZ GRRLZ
SPICE GRRLZ
GORILLAZ GRRLZ
SPICE GRRLZ
GORILLAZ GRRLZ
GALERIES GRRLZ
SPICE GRRLZ
GORILLAZ GRRLZ
SPICE GRRLZ
GORILLAZ GRRLZ
SPICE GRRLZ
GORILLAZ GRRLZ
GALERIES GRRLZ
MY KIND OF GRRLZ
SPICE GRRLZ
GORILLAZ GRRLZ
SPICE GRRLZ
GORILLAZ GRRLZ
SPICE GRRLZ
GORILLAZ GRRLZ
SPICE GRRLZ
GORILLAZ GRRLZ
SPICE GRRLZ
GORILLAZ GRRLZ
SPICE GRRLZ
GORILLAZ GRRLZ
GALERIES GRRLZ
MY KIND OF GRRLZ
IF YOU WANT TO BE MY
LOVER
YOU GOTTA GET
WITH MY FRIENDZZ
LOVE WILL LASTS FOREVER
FRIENDSHIP NEVER ENDZ

SPICE GRRLZ
GORILLAZ GRRLZ
SPICE GRRLZ
GORILLAZ GRRLZ
SPICE GRRLZ
GORILLAZ GRRLZ
GALERIES GRRLZ
WEST COAST GRRLZ
EAST END GRRLZ
GALERIES GRRLZ
WEST COAST GRRLZ
SURF BOARD
EAST END GRRLZ
GALERIES GRRLZ
WEST COAST GRRLZ
EAST END GRRLZ
MY KIND OF GRRLZ
YOU'RE FROM TXXX, THAT'S
BEAUTIFUL...
IF YOU WANT TO BE MY
LOVER
YOU GOTTA GET
WITH MY FRIENDZZ
LOVE WILL LASTS FOREVER
FRIENDSHIP NEVER ENDZ

TELL ME WHAT YOU
WANT, WHAT YOU REALLY,
REALLY WANT
VICTORIA BECKHAM
COWGIRRLZ HALL OF
FAME
SPICE GRRLZ
GORILLAZ GRRLZ
SPICE GRRLZ
GORILLAZ GRRLZ
SPICE GRRLZ
GORILLAZ GRRLZ
MY KIND OF GRRLZ

WORKING WITHOUT THE
PRESSURE
OF SUCCE$$$$
SPICE GRRLZ
GORILLAZ GRRLZ
SPICE GRRLZ
GORILLAZ GRRLZ
SPICE GRRLZ
SEEING YOUR IDEAS LIVE ON IN
THE WERK OF OTHER$
GORILLAZ GRRLZ
SPICE GRRLZ
GORILLAZ GRRLZ
SPICE GRRLZ
GORILLAZ GRRLZZZ
TELL ME WHAT YOU
WANT, WHAT YOU REALLY,
REALLY REALLY REALLY
REALLY REALLY REALLY
REALLY REALLY REALLY
REALLY REALLY REALLY
REALLY REALLY REEALLLLY
REALLY REALLY REALLY
REALLY REALLY SRSLY
REALLY REALLY REALLY
REALLY REALLY REALLY
REALLY REALLY SRSLY
WANT
WHAT YOU WANT
IF YOU WANT TO BE MY
LOVER
YOU GOTTA GET
WITH MY FRIENDZZ
MEL B
MEL C JANE B
B C B C B C B C B C B C B
C B C B C B C B C B C B C B
C B C
B C B C B C B C B C B C B C
B C B C B C B C B C B C B C
B C B C B C B C B C B C B C
BIZZIE-BIZZIE
HAVING AN E$CAPE FROM ART
WORLD IN
YOUR 4 FREE-LANCE JOBS
MEL C
MEL B
NOT HAVING TO B $HOWN
WITH MEN
MEL C
MEL B
MEL C

LONG LINE— MATIAS FALDBAKKEN REVIEWED

Text Anne Gruber

The title character in Matias Faldbakken's book, *The Waiter,* works in Oslo at The Hill, an old and traditionally rich restaurant. "A place for the long line" as Widow Knipschild—a regular—describes it.

The Waiter's desire is to keep everything in order. He dresses the tables as they are always dressed. They shine white with pressed tablecloths, and are adorned with old and beautiful accessories. He guarantees habitual order by being "professionally and sensibly quiet" (as self-described), so that the guests can relish exercising their distinguished habits and tastes. He's a neurotic perfectionistic, trained to be exhaustingly emphatic.

The Waiter's inner monologues afford us an insight into how he analyzes the manners, interactions and habits of his fellow characters, as well as how he reflects on his own habitual behavior. His thoughts are rich in observation, detail, suspicion, and situated knowledge. The dismantling of the characters and situations decelerates the reading process, somewhat resembling the atmosphere these traditional restaurants often have.

Tradition, routine, taste and values play important roles for the Waiter. Surprises and changes are to be avoided or kept under control. But as strict routine is established, we become much more aware of the deviations. It is in these digressions that the story unfolds humorously. In a concatenation of incidents and emotional reactions, we accompany the Waiter as he loses sovereignty.

Though he is able to analyze and deconstruct his own habits en detail, he is unable to transform or adopt them into his interactions. In trying not to complicate the situation, he compensates for his "lack of tact" with grotesque actions.

When reading the text with a classical sociological perspective informed by Pierre Bourdieu, the descriptions of codes, habitual stereotypes, and interactions become very amusing. But even as Faldbakken unmasks these codes, the book remains in a reproductive state, missing the chance to widen or expand on these ideas; it ignores their active influence on inequality, normativity, and hegemony in society.

Matias Faldbakken (*1973) is a writer and visual artist living in Oslo. *The Waiter* was published in 2018 by Scout Press, with a German translation following suit in 2019, re-titled *The Hills* (Heyne Verlag).

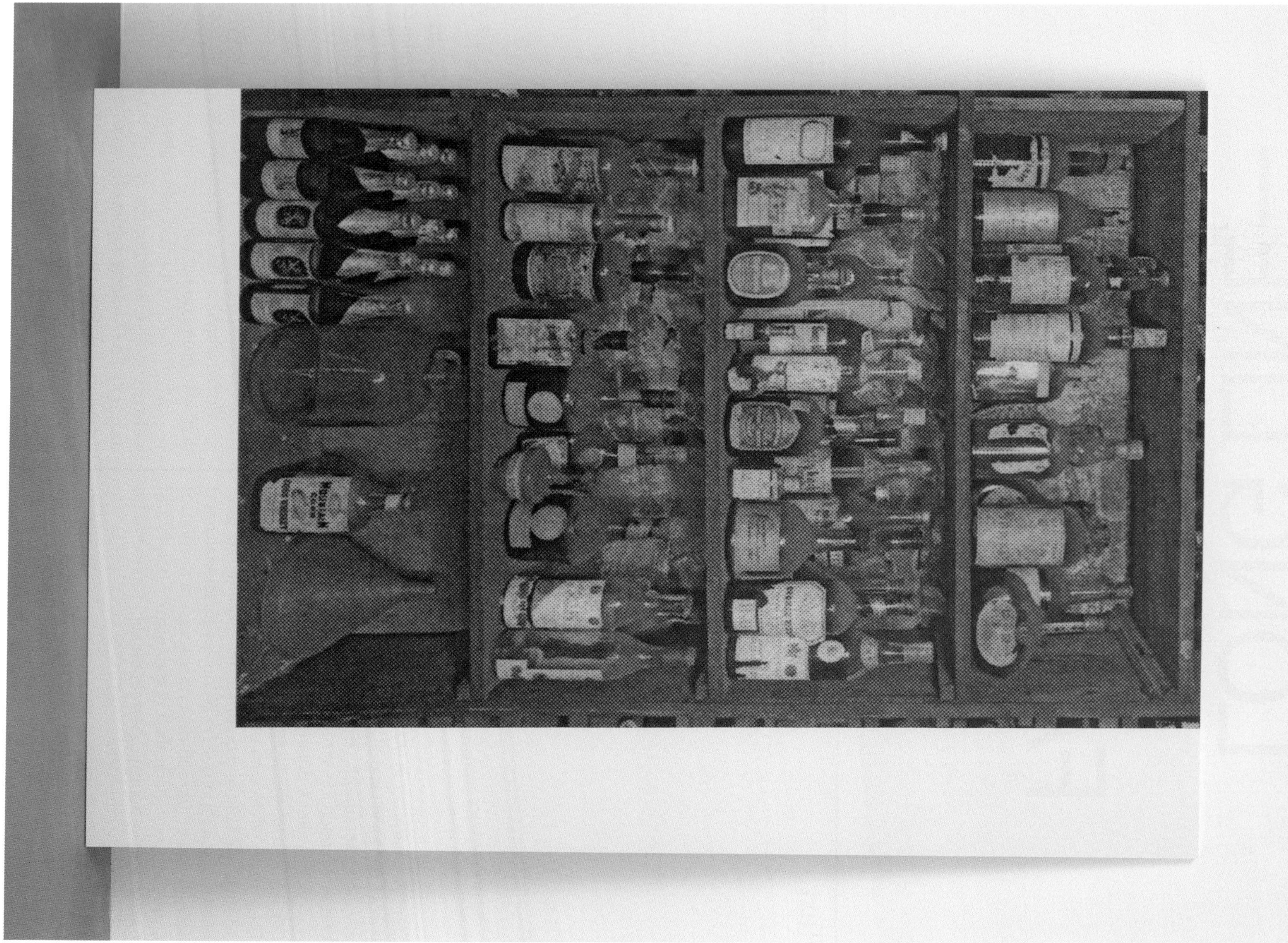

View of Mattias Faldbakken's 2012 exhibition "Shall I write it" at Eva Presenhuber, Zürich / Photo: Stefan Altenburger Photography, Zürich / Courtesy of Matias Faldbakken and Eva Presenhuber, Zürich and New York

DESIGN

A HOUSE TO START— CINZIA RUGGERI'S ART AROUND LIFE

Text Mariuccia Casadio

In "A house to Start: Cinzia Ruggeri's Art around Life" legendary fashion critic Mariuccia Casadio contributes to this publication with an experimental piece of writing dedicated to Italian fashion designer Cinzia Ruggeri. Casadio is a regular contributor to *Vogue Italia* and an advisor to Missoni; among the books she authored and edited are monographs on Emilio Pucci, Gianni Versace, and Fornasetti.

Cinzia Ruggeri doesn't particularly like talking about herself, even if she has a lot to say. She does it only when she feels like it, only with few people who are friends or understanding of her work, and only in her own way. If they ask questions, she answers as she likes, always giving priority to different matters, facts, experiences. Pertinent, but not necessarily determinant, easily minor, marginal memories, which, depending on the day, acquire overriding, unpredictable and always enchanting significance. A surreal quality that seem to concern her entire existence. Her present and her past time, her life as a celebrity in the years between the '60s and '90s, and her keeping away from the bustle of today. It is a very "Cinzia" way of being that began in 1960 as a one-person show, when she was just eighteen years old. It was introduced by the visionary artist and author Dino Buzzati, who wrote about musical notes fallen from the piano in the Ruggeri family's home, and which had been spread all over the floor and had taken the shape and consistency of stones.

It is an artistic beginning, which somehow epitomized her way of giving centrality, eloquence and humour and elegance and unicity to all things around us. To the most common objects and behaviours, affections and defects of our lives. Things that she revisits punctually in her designs, by putting them in a condition of talking and telling, like animated characters of a surreal and fascinating cartoon. Embellishing, for instance, the usual elongated and thin silhouette of a champagne goblet, with a dangling crystal drop, a fancy jewel that is clinking to all of our *cin cin*. Otherwise, transforming the enlarged shadows of a dove, "Colombra", or the one of a pissing pet schnauzer, "Cane Pipì", in black velvety, upholstered silhouettes, sofas to lay down and rest on. And furthermore, patenting liquid crystals thermo-sensitive textile, to make outfits that change color when warmed by the heat of one's body. Or either conceiving gowns, equipped with LEDs that can be turned on and off to externalize one's emotions and feelings.

BY THE WAY HER PROJECTUALITY IS IN A VARIETY OF WAYS REFERRING TO OUR HABITATS, OUR HOMES AND WAYS OF LIFE, EVOCATED, FROM FASHION TO INTERIOR-DESIGN AND ARCHITECTURE.

However, there is much more in the work of Cinzia, that in explicit or implicit ways, can be related to our dressing, behaving, and inhabiting. By the way her projectuality is in a variety of ways referring to our habitats, our homes and ways of life, evocated, from fashion to interior design and architecture. Our body inhabits a dress, a space, and a person that, like in her 1983 "Homage to Levi Strauss", can embody architecture's perpendicular lines and right angles, the zig-zagging of its staircases and ziggurats. The space of the dress therefore takes place in the space of our interiors, interacting with furnitures, ornaments and knick-knacks, aliments and materials, forms and functions of the late XX century lifestyle. A large mosaic of readymades, styles, meanings, inspirations, and suggestions that Cinzia resumes, alienates, overturns and enriches with unpredictable, surreal prerogatives. She envisages a postmodern totality of living. An ideal place to live and work, which she has often shaped, starting with her all-white first apartment, decorated with transparent perspex furnishing, and with her Milanese showroom in Via Crocefisso, which includes revolved volumes and a large pool inhabited by living shrimp and pink flamingos, as she recalls in conversations and interviews. An ideal place, eclectically designed, uniting art and fashion, architecture and interior decoration, which, in the '80s, generated complicities and collaborations with Studio Alchimia. Recently, it has become the topic of her exhibition "Home: A User's Manual" hosted by GTA in Zürich, and conceived like a confluence of various contributions. Cinzia Ruggeri, Alessandro Guerriero, Aldo Lanzini, Ugo La Pietra, Luigi Serafini and Wang Shuo conceived my contribution as a projected text which you can read below. It was a cut-up of homes in words, quoting Cinzia's recollection of her white apartment and Via Crocefisso's showroom, as well as other literary descriptions, that incidentally and indirectly evokes her visionary inventiveness, her transgressive taste, and her animist fairy-tale fantasies. From J. Karl Huysmans to Mies van der Rohe, and from "Our House" by Graham Nash, to the legendary Baba Yaga hut as passed on through the centuries by Eastern Europe's popular culture, and ultimately to my own personal projections and digressions on the show theme and topics.

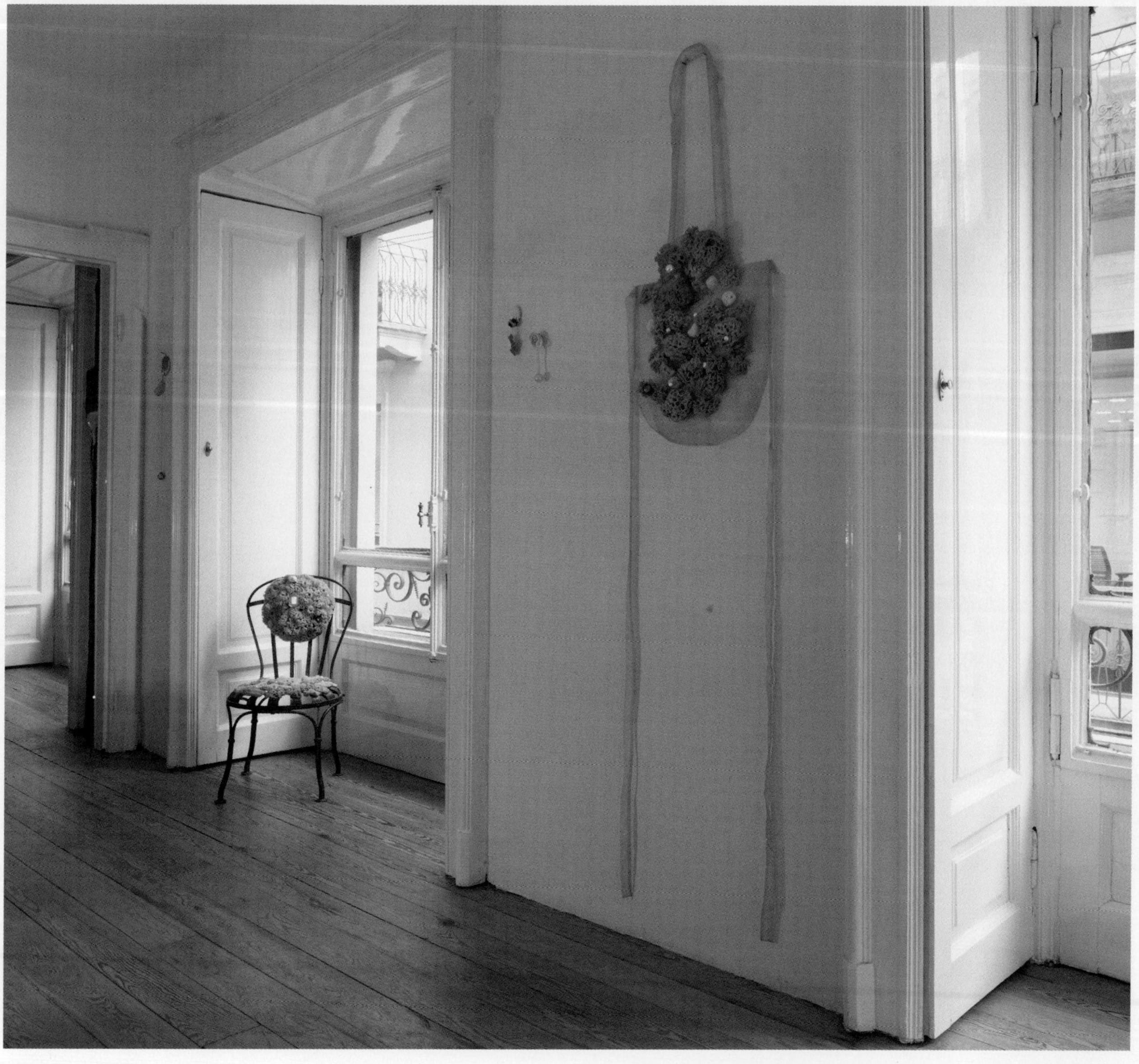

Photo: Santi Caleca / Courtesy of Cinzia Ruggeri and Galerie Federico Vavassori, Milano

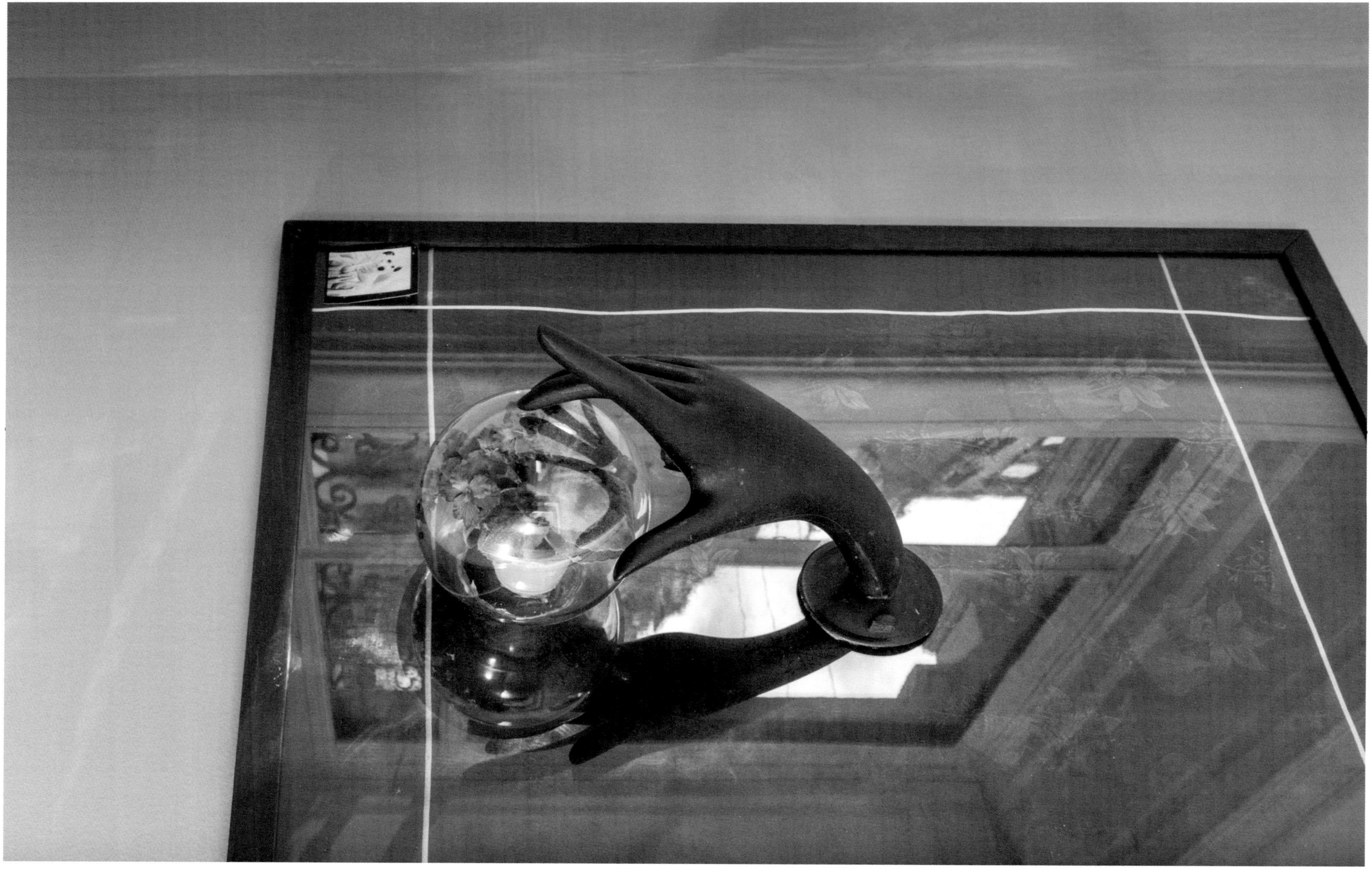

Photo: Santi Caleca / Courtesy of Cinzia Ruggeri and Galerie Federico Vavassori, Milano

At the end of the Sixties, just back from Paris, I meet a man I fall in love with; together we decide to get an apartment with a mutual agreement. We won't take with us anything belonging to our previous lives in order to restart from zero. We just get a bed and a mattress, but all the rest, all the furnishing has to be reinvented. We decide the house must be white, so we start from a flour white carpet on the floor and we just put a ping pong table on it.

Later on after a working period in Egypt we return to Milan with a bunch of caftans, we through a party at home and we give the caftans to our friends. They immediately wear them and the evening ends with all of them playing badminton with those caftans on.

My boyfriend and myself have then decorated the apartment with transparent perspex furnishings we had designed. No art on the walls, because you can't own what you love ... and we have thereby conceived our way of living.

Examining an Persian rug, one day, in reflected light, and following the silver gleams which fell on its web of plum violet and aladdin yellow, it suddenly occurs to him how much it would be improved if he could place on it some object whose deep color might enhance the vividness of its tints.

Possessed by this idea, he strolls aimlessly along the streets, when suddenly he finds himself gazing at the very object of his wishes. There, in a shop window on the Palais Royal, lays a huge tortoise in a large basin.

When I move my headquarters in the Milanese central via Crocefisso, the space is an ancient ex-convent with very high ceilings and wide open skylights. I have then an internal wooden balcony built, painted pink like the walls and rotated of 160 degrees. Behind the banister resuming the Roman Palazzo Farnese's ones, I do make appear the enlarged reproduction of an angel based on a Piero della Francesca's painting, a figure which unexpectedly looks out and controls the situation from above.

Over time I do contextualize into that space signs of any kind, like a very realistic lake I made with a basin inserted into the floor, lined with a plastic tarp and filled up with water. At the center of it emerges an old chair with legs sawn short, to create the illusion that the water is deeper. The lake doesn't miss to have some floating islands inhabited by living shrimps. I then set up the three bathrooms of the headquarter: in one you can perhaps find a gun resting on a pillow, in another a hen in the basin. It can also happen that I want to give to a pink flamingo, arrived from Sardinia and destined to the park of a famous Milanese residence, a more cheerful and unforgettable welcome. So, I'll take him to Via Crocefisso and let him free wallow in the water.

Decidedly, the black, the harsh sienna tone of this shell dulled the rug's reflections without adding to it ... The colors are not sufficiently subdued. He must reverse the process, dull the tones, and extinguish them by the contrast of a striking object ... He therefore decides to glaze the shell of the tortoise with gold ... At first he was enchanted with this effect. Then he reflected that that this gigantic jewel was only in outline, that it would not really be complete until it had been incrusted with rare stones.

There are no sketches or architectural projects, perhaps not even photographs or filmic frames, which, more than words, can make the experience of interiors and home angles exciting. Too technical, defined and detailed, they intimidate and bore, distancing and alienating from the freedom to imagine and to complete the design of places and furniture through imagination. The beauty and comfort of a living that speaks, evoking rooms and ante-rooms, furniture and ornaments. Keeping the design, the style and the idea alive, open and reconfigurable over time.

The glass walls open the inside of the house towards the external environment. The opacity of the structure is limited only by the horizontal partitions, two slabs enclosing the habitable environment. And they appear edged externally by visible steel bands white-painted. The house is raised from the ground, as if it levitates on eight H-profile pillars, also in white steel, connecting the floor to the ceiling. The building seems to float weightlessly above the surface of the ground. A third plate, slightly lowered than the level of the house, acts as a link between the ground and the small portico in front of the entrance.

The interior is a large open space, not structured, which can adapt to different needs. In the center, there is the "fulcrum" of the services, a conglomeration consisting of two wooden blocks containing a wardrobe, bathroom and kitchen. The rest of the space is characterized by the presence of movable elements, which allow a not rigid, versatile, and custom-made spatial division. It is a large single room endlessly configurable and reconfigurable.

Baba Yaga's hut is an elevated construction, that bases itself on two hen's legs. Protected by invisible guardians (a cat, a dog, a gate, and a tree) and by a door lock with sharp teeth, echoing the threatening jaws of a ferocious beast, it has the external walls coated with bones and it seems lacking of doors. It spins on itself revealing the access only to those who know the words of a precise magic formula.

The house floats in the space of dreams e thoughts. It rises up like a small elevator, but is wide and open like a playground. The content, a pathologic passion for the collection of works and objects, it's hidden in extractable shelves, organized per topic. As landscapes that show and retract themselves as I wish.

Our house is a very, very, very fine house! With two cats in the yard. Life used to be so hard but now everything is easy cause of you ... I light the fire and you place the flowers in the vase that you bought today.

Such a cozy room ...

THE POWER OF PRINT— ON BEA FEITLER

Text

Marte Eknæs
Nicolau Vergueiro

Bea Feitler (1938–82) was a Brazilian-born designer and art director best known for her work for *Harper's Bazaar*, *Ms. Magazine*, *Rolling Stone*, and the modern *Vanity Fair*. In the exhibition "Power of Print" at the Kölnischer Kunstverein (February 16–March 31, 2019), Marte Eknæs and Nicolau Vergueiro brought the vast scope of her practice and design strategies to public attention.

PROVENCE: How did you end up with the title "Power of Print?" Prima facie, the title seems rather generic. Is it a statement about printed media in general? Or would you consider it to be a specific reference?

Eknæs / Vergueiro: The title was taken from a *Harper's Bazaar* cover and spread titled "The Power of the Print", which featured boldly colorful, patterned clothing. We reinterpreted it to describe the powerful printed matter oeuvre of Bea Feitler. The title draws back to an era when most information—textual and visual—was communicated in print, and to the way in which Feitler was able to create an everlasting language in the editorial world as an art director and designer. Through her vibrant aesthetics, Feitler used the magazine as a mass vehicle to address and shape social issues; she had a profound understanding of how powerful images and layouts are in the process of disseminating progressive ideas.

PROVENCE: What would you consider as having been particular about Bea Feitler's approach and work during her time?

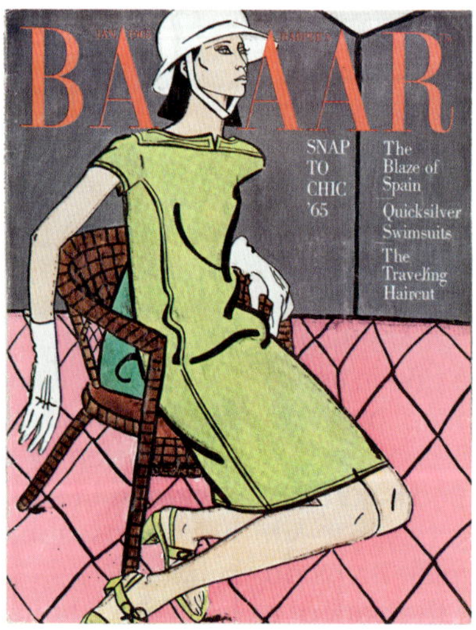

Harper's Bazaar cover, January 1965
Illustration by Katerina Denzinger

Eknæs / Vergueiro: Her expressive freedom is present in all her work and made her a much sought after professional at the time. She shifted the gaze from a male perspective—one that inevitably sexualized the female body—to one that focuses on exploring the potentials of the body as a form, both in identity and design, changing the commercial representation of the "modern woman". She also channeled and catalyzed the social changes of the times in her work. In January 1965, she famously featured the first African American supermodel on the cover of major fashion magazine *Harper's Bazaar*. Model Donyale Luna appeared as a racially ambiguous illustration by Katerina Denzinger. Later, in April 1965, Luna was once again featured in the iconic magazine, this time as the subject of an eight-page fashion spread, shot by Richard Avedon. This shoot was directly responsible for mass subscription loss as well as companies pulling their adverts from the magazine. Above all Feitler launched the seminal feminist magazine *Ms.*

Her work was the embodiment of the heterogeneity she's known for—her design combined gender, race, typography, methods, and style. She also elevated the juxtaposition of commercial and editorial images to an art form through her close collaboration and relation with artists, photographers et cetera. Her game-changing Calvin Klein campaigns from 1975 and 1976, for example, are still referred to as being the first to use art fashion photographers to shoot commercial advertisements. Feitler also featured the photography of Diane Arbus, a close friend of hers, in a 1969 editorial at *Harper's Bazaar*.

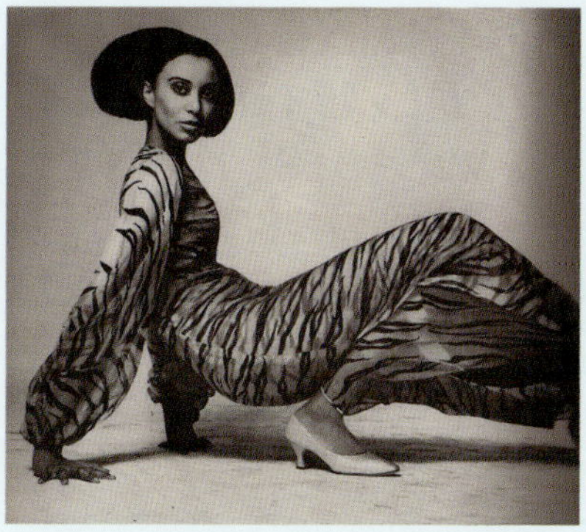

Harper's Bazaar April 1965
Photos by Richard Avedon

FEITLER HAD A PROFOUND UNDERSTANDING OF HOW POWERFUL IMAGES AND LAYOUTS ARE IN THE PROCESS OF DISSEMINATING PROGRESSIVE IDEAS.

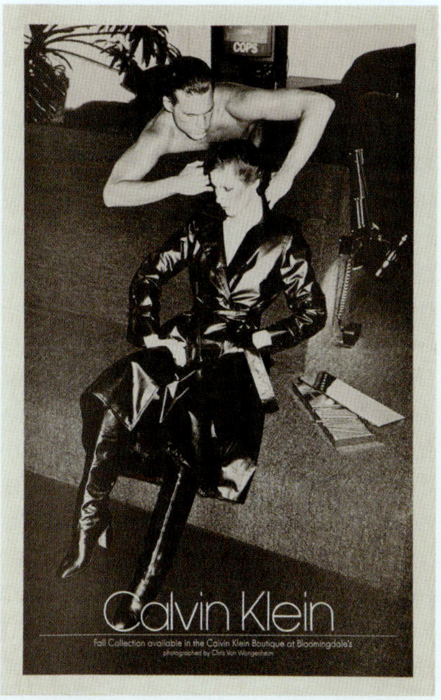

Calvin Klein newspaper print ad, 1975
Photo by Chris von Wangenheim

PROVENCE: Are there any points you would like to specify as being crucial to the way you approached her material?

Eknæs / Vergueiro: Rather than viewing it chronologically, we understood the material through the thematic design principles Feitler employed. Her use of the human silhouette stands out and threads her oeuvre—abstracting the body whilst bringing it into focus. She transforms the body into a generic and genderless sign, bridging the gap between the individual woman and the female collective.

Her use of the magazine's gutter centerfold as compositional device, typography, playing with scale and collage reimagined the relationship between body, text, and graphic design in terms of both layout and the sensory magazine experience. This guided us as to how we should transpose her work into an exhibition setting through a strategy principle from our collaborative practice, of creating content-based environments.

FEITLER TRANSFORMS THE BODY INTO A GENERIC AND GENDERLESS SIGN, BRIDGING THE GAP BETWEEN THE INDIVIDUAL WOMAN AND THE FEMALE COLLECTIVE.

PROVENCE: What made you decide to translate the archival material into a spatial setting, and show her work in an exhibition format?

Eknæs / Vergueiro: Our collaborative practice was inspired by revealing the invisible systems that construct the public realm and experience. When we first encountered her work en masse, we realized that she was behind so many archetypal pop culture im-

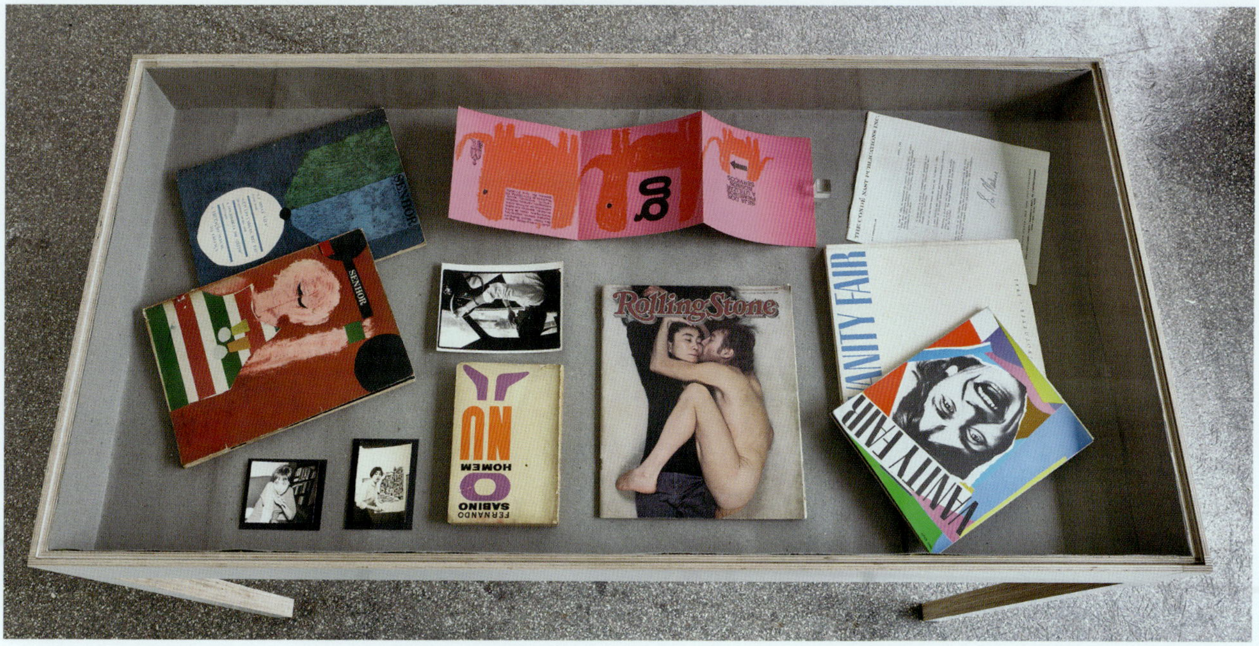

Vitrine in "Power of Print—The Work and Life of Bea Feitler",
Kölnischer Kunstverein, Cologne, 2019 / Photo: Simon Vogel

ages that went on to typify an era. Be it the *Harper's Bazaar* "pink helmet" cover, John Lennon and Yoko Ono's *Rolling Stone* cover, or Helmut Newton's *White Women* book; it is really striking to conceive of her invisible hands at work in so many iconic and disparate publications. We didn't want a historicized installation, but rather to realize a space that allows you to physically enter her work. We wanted people to feel as if they were walking into a magazine. The exhibition space allowed for this experience in which the blown up, to-scale, interactive flip frames and wallpapers literally immerse the viewer in her work.

PROVENCE: Why Bea Feitler now? What connects her to magazines of our times?

Eknæs / Vergueiro: It really is illuminating to look back at her work in the post-internet era. The process of hands-on graphic creation reveals the golden age of analogue artistry epitomized by Feitler. Another captivating aspect is to realize how progressive her work—and media in general—actually was in the 1960s and 1970s. She crafted an influential new language that became the foundation for contemporary concerns regarding diverse representation in the mainstream. It is important to acknowledge Feitler as an under-recognized precursor, and to reintroduce her vision and iconic imagery to the way we commit the issues of today to print.

Feitler played an important part in creating new standards in publication that are still upheld today. Her work for *Ms.* is indicative of "zine culture", which in turn points to blogs. In *Rolling Stone*, she really mastered the overlay of images to convey pictorial essays. She understood and stated that books and magazines should be 50/50 in terms of text and images—this is the case now more than ever.

IT IS REALLY STRIKING TO CONCEIVE OF HER INVISIBLE HANDS AT WORK IN SO MANY ICONIC AND DISPARATE PUBLICATIONS.

"ANY WOMAN WHO IS COMMITTED TO BEING AN INDIVIDUAL IS A FEMINIST. ANY WOMAN WHO IS INTELLIGENT IS FEMINIST. ANY WOMAN WHO VALUES HERSELF HAS TO BE FEMINIST. I WAS NEVER INVOLVED IN THE MOVEMENT. I THINK I WAS LIBERATED BEFORE ANY WOMEN'S LIBERATION."

Quote: Bea Feitler in *O Design de Bea Feitler* by Bruno Feitler and André Storlarski (São Paolo: Cosac Naify, 2012), translated from Portuguese by Nicolau Vergueiro.

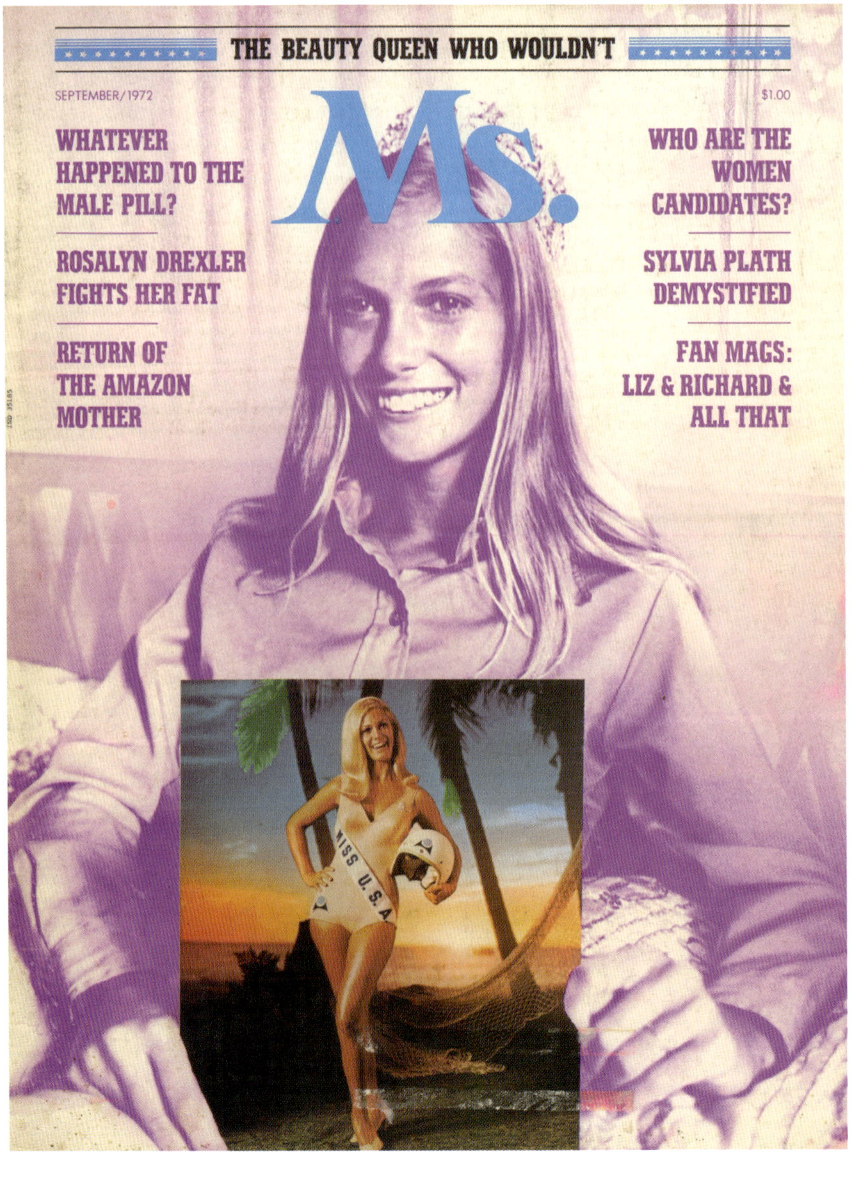

Ms. magazine cover, September 1972 / Photo by Mary Ellen Mark

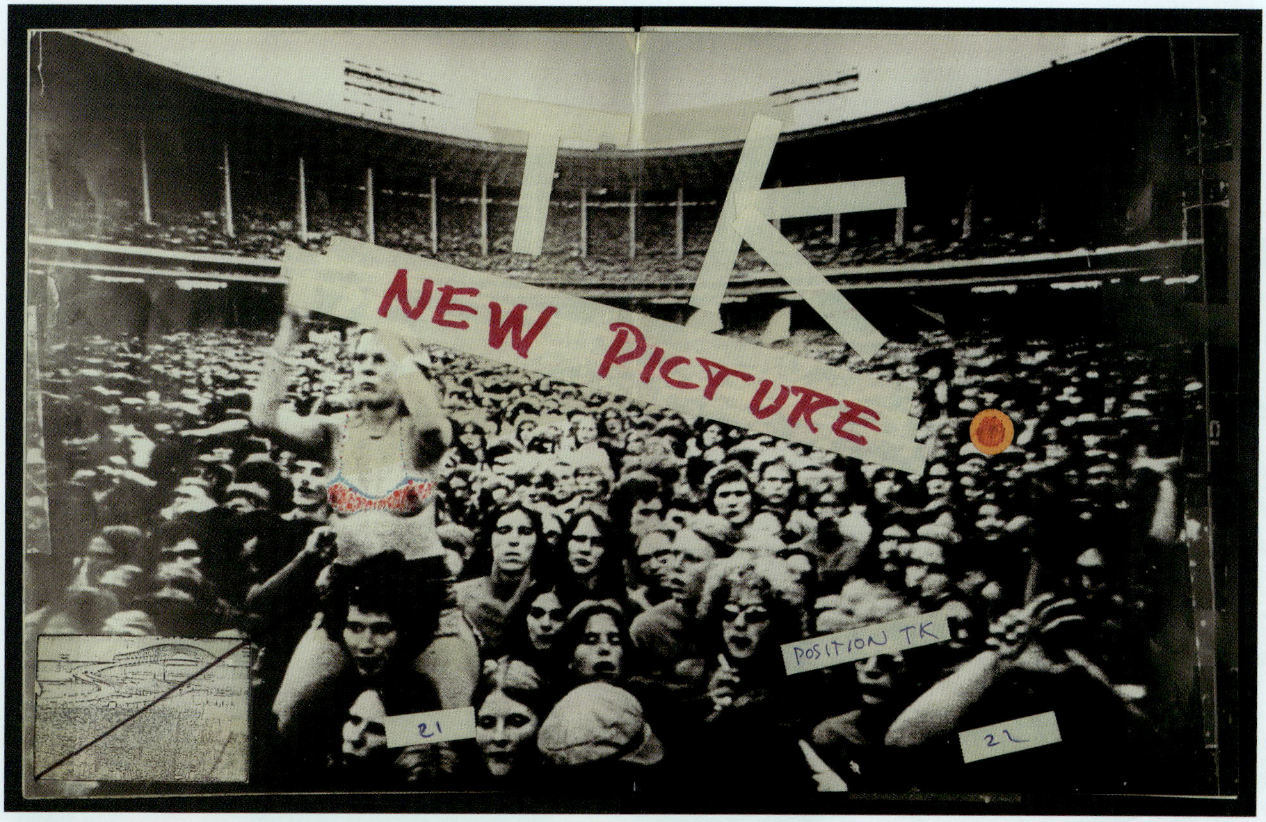

Mock-up for *Rolling Stone*'s "Snap Judgments. A Rock & Roll Retrospective 1969–1977", 1977, with photos by Annie Leibovitz / New School Archives and Special Collections Digital Archive

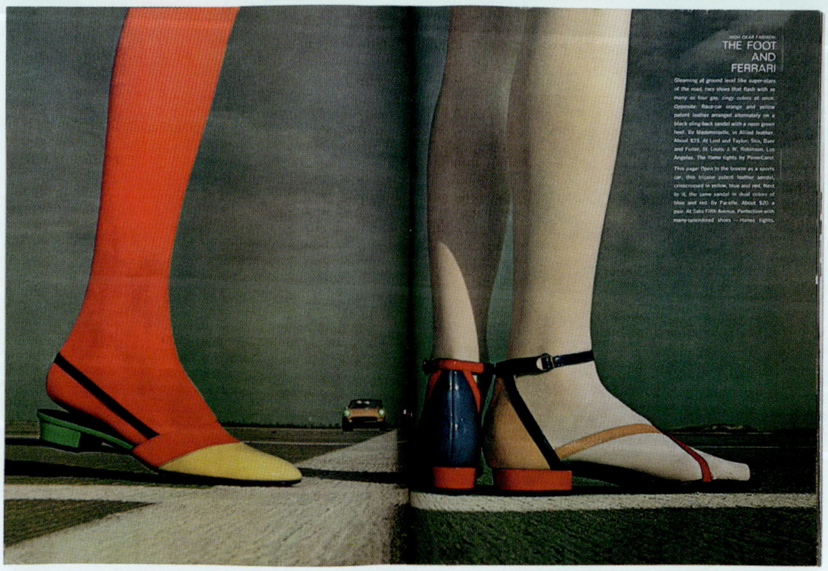

The Foot and Ferrari spread, *Harper's Bazaar*, March 1967
Photos by Bill Silano

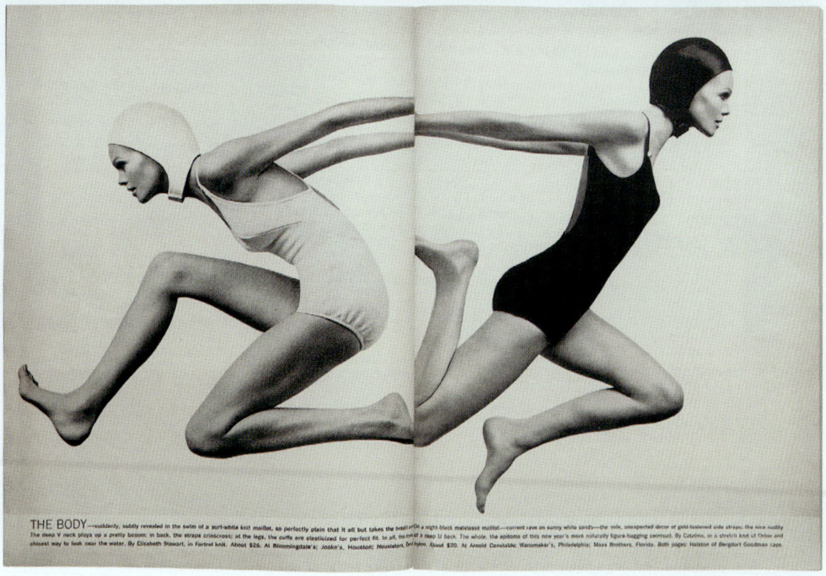

The Body spread, *Harper's Bazaar*, January 1968
Photos by Hiro

"THE MOCK LAYOUTS, ENERGETICALLY AND WILLFULLY ANNOTATED AND MARKED, DEMONSTRATE WELL HOW METICULOUS BEA WAS WITH THE MONTAGE, RE-ELABORATION AND REFINEMENT IN THE PHOTO SELECTIONS AS WELL AS IN THE DIALOGUE BETWEEN THE IMAGES. [...] BEA CONSTRUCTS A SECOND-LAYER DISCOURSE."

Quote: André Storlarski in *O Design de Bea Feitler* by Bruno Feitler and André Storlarski (São Paolo: Cosac Naify, 2012).

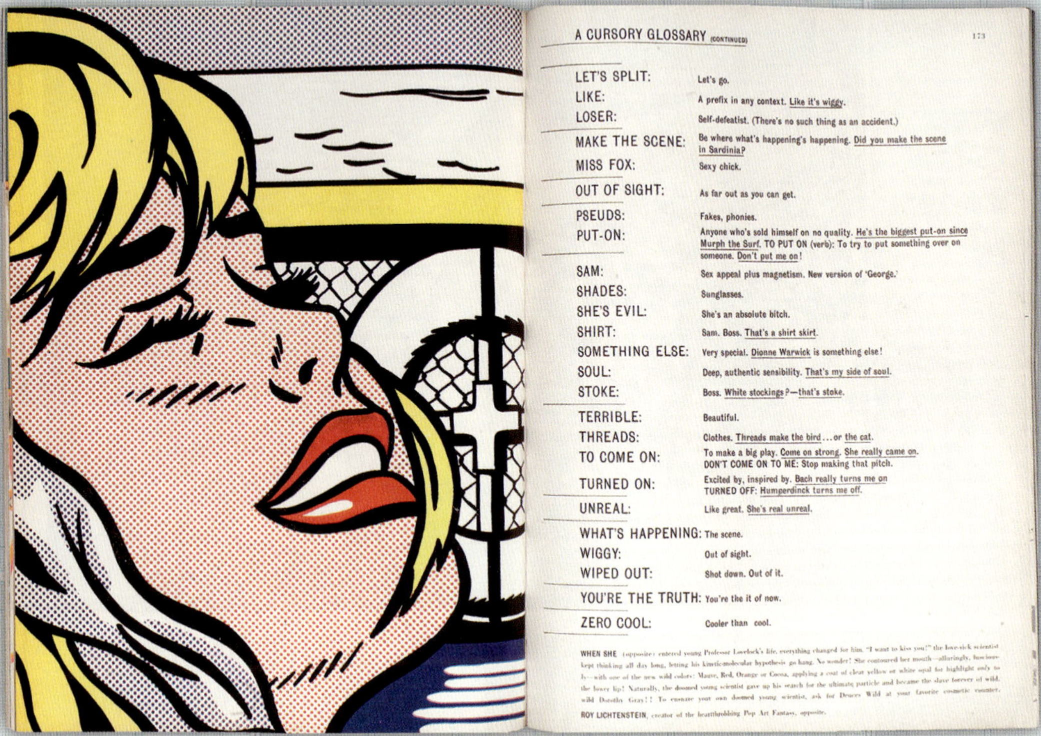

A CURSORY GLOSSARY (CONTINUED) 173

LET'S SPLIT:	Let's go.
LIKE:	A prefix in any context. Like it's wiggy.
LOSER:	Self-defeatist. (There's no such thing as an accident.)
MAKE THE SCENE:	Be where what's happening's happening. Did you make the scene in Sardinia?
MISS FOX:	Sexy chick.
OUT OF SIGHT:	As far out as you can get.
PSEUDS:	Fakes, phonies.
PUT-ON:	Anyone who's sold himself on no quality. He's the biggest put-on since Murph the Surf. TO PUT ON (verb): To try to put something over on someone. Don't put me on!
SAM:	Sex appeal plus magnetism. New version of 'George.'
SHADES:	Sunglasses.
SHE'S EVIL:	She's an absolute bitch.
SHIRT:	Sam. Boss. That's a shirt skirt.
SOMETHING ELSE:	Very special. Dionne Warwick is something else!
SOUL:	Deep, authentic sensibility. That's my side of soul.
STOKE:	Boss. White stockings?—that's stoke.
TERRIBLE:	Beautiful.
THREADS:	Clothes. Threads make the bird...or the cat.
TO COME ON:	To make a big play. Come on strong. She really came on. DON'T COME ON TO ME: Stop making that pitch.
TURNED ON:	Excited by, inspired by. Bach really turns me on TURNED OFF: Humperdinck turns me off.
UNREAL:	Like great. She's real unreal.
WHAT'S HAPPENING:	The scene.
WIGGY:	Out of sight.
WIPED OUT:	Shot down. Out of it.
YOU'RE THE TRUTH:	You're the it of now.
ZERO COOL:	Cooler than cool.

ROY LICHTENSTEIN, creator of the heartthrobbing Pop Art Fantasy, opposite.

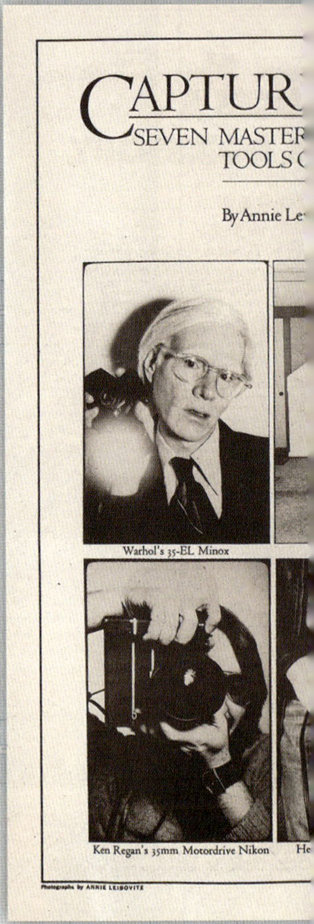

Warhol's 35-EL Minox

Ken Regan's 35mm Motordrive Nikon

Photographs by ANNIE LEIBOVITZ

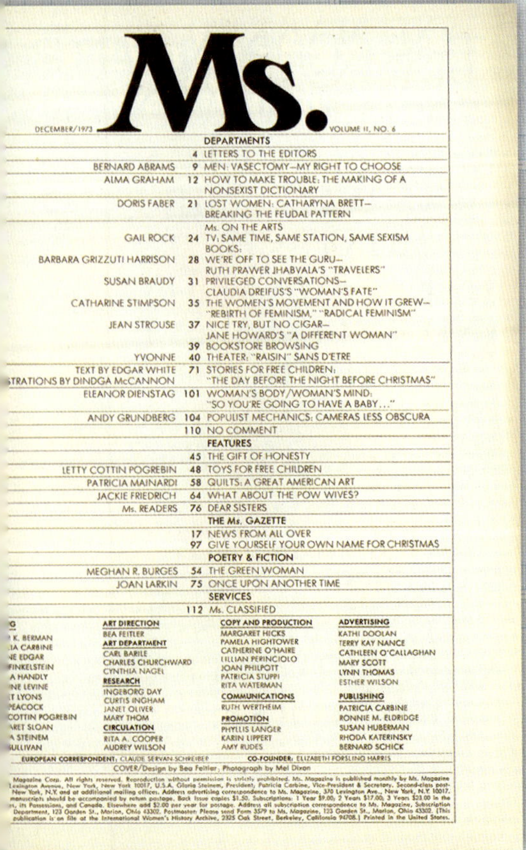

Ms.

DECEMBER/1973 VOLUME II, NO. 6

K. BERMAN / IA CARBINE / NE EDGAR / FINKELSTEIN / A HANDLY / NE LEVINE / T LYONS / PEACOCK / COTTIN POGREBIN / RET SLOAN / A STEINEM / SULLIVAN

ART DIRECTION: BEA FEITLER
ART DEPARTMENT: CARL BARILE, CHARLES CHURCHWARD, CYNTHIA NAGEL
RESEARCH: INGEBORG DAY, CURTIS INGHAM, JANET OLIVER, MARY THOM
CIRCULATION: RITA A. COOPER, AUDREY WILSON

COPY AND PRODUCTION: MARGARET HICKS, PAMELA HIGHTOWER, CATHERINE O'HAIRE, LILLIAN PERINCIOLO, JOAN PHILPOTT, PATRICIA STUPPI, RITA WATERMAN
COMMUNICATIONS: RUTH WERTHEIM
PROMOTION: PHYLLIS LANGER, KARIN LIPPERT, AMY RUDES

ADVERTISING: KATHI DOOLAN, TERRY KAY NANCE, CATHLEEN O'CALLAGHAN, MARY SCOTT, LYNN THOMAS, ESTHER WILSON
PUBLISHING: PATRICIA CARBINE, RONNIE M. ELDRIDGE, SUSAN HUBERMAN, RHODA KATERINSKY, BERNARD SCHICK

EUROPEAN CORRESPONDENT: CLAUDE SERVAN-SCHREIBER CO-FOUNDER: ELIZABETH FORSLING HARRIS

COVER/Design by Bea Feitler, Photograph by Mel Dixon

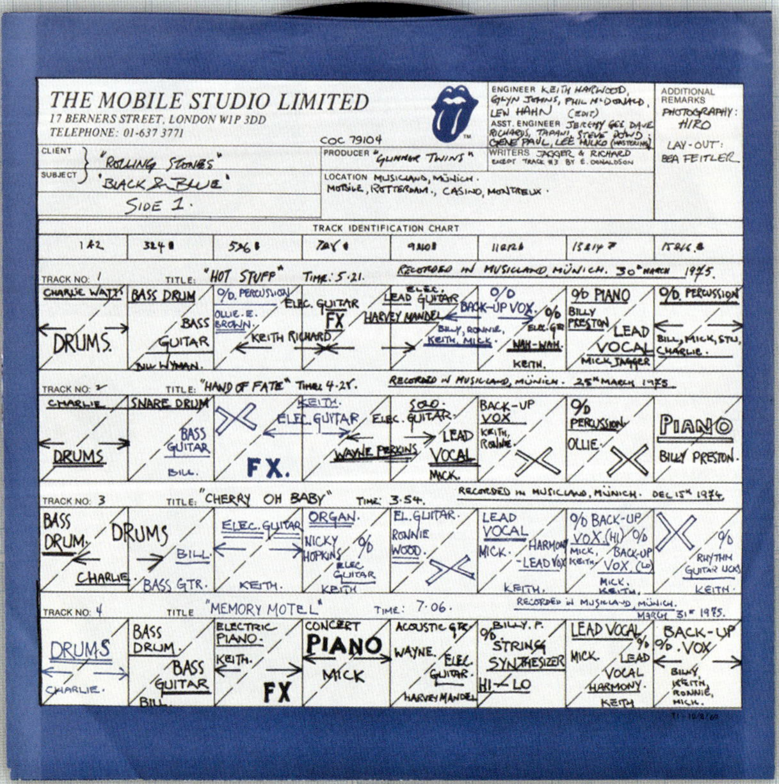

THE MOBILE STUDIO LIMITED
17 BERNERS STREET, LONDON W1P 3DD
TELEPHONE: 01-637 3771

COC 79104

ENGINEER KEITH HARWOOD, GLYN JOHNS, PHIL McDONALD, LEW HAHN (EDIT)
ASST. ENGINEER JEREMY GEE, DAVE RICHARDS, TAPANI, STEVE DOWD, GENE PAUL, LEE HULKO (MASTERING)

ADDITIONAL REMARKS
PHOTOGRAPHY: HIRO
LAY-OUT: BEA FEITLER

CLIENT / SUBJECT: "ROLLING STONES" 'BLACK & BLUE' SIDE 1.

PRODUCER "GLIMMER TWINS"

WRITERS JAGGER & RICHARD EXCEPT TRACK #3 BY E. DONALDSON

LOCATION MUSICLAND, MÜNICH. MOBILE, ROTTERDAM., CASINO, MONTREUX.

TRACK IDENTIFICATION CHART

TRACK NO: 1 TITLE: "HOT STUFF" TIME: 5·21. RECORDED IN MUSICLAND, MÜNICH. 30th MARCH 1975.

TRACK NO: 2 TITLE: "HAND OF FATE" TIME: 4·27. RECORDED IN MUSICLAND, MÜNICH. 25th MARCH 1975.

TRACK NO: 3 TITLE: "CHERRY OH BABY" TIME: 3·54. RECORDED IN MUSICLAND, MÜNICH. DEC 15th 1974.

TRACK NO: 4 TITLE: "MEMORY MOTEL" TIME: 7·06. RECORDED IN MUSICLAND, MÜNICH. MARCH 31st 1975.

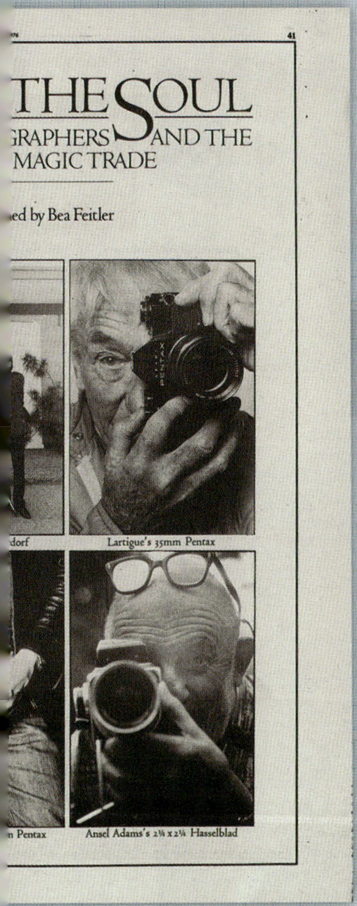

41

THE SOUL

GRAPHERS AND THE MAGIC TRADE

ed by Bea Feitler

dorf — Lartigue's 35mm Pentax

Pentax — Ansel Adams's 2¼ x 2¼ Hasselblad

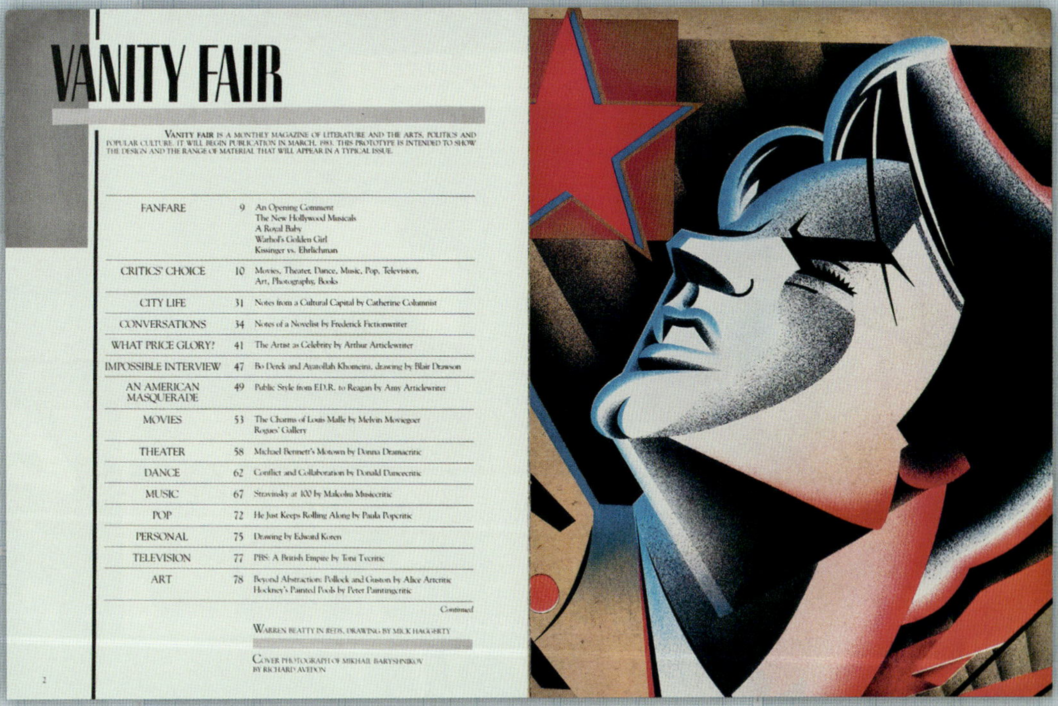

VANITY FAIR

VANITY FAIR IS A MONTHLY MAGAZINE OF LITERATURE AND THE ARTS, POLITICS AND POPULAR CULTURE. IT WILL BEGIN PUBLICATION IN MARCH, 1983. THIS PROTOTYPE IS INTENDED TO SHOW THE DESIGN AND THE RANGE OF MATERIAL THAT WILL APPEAR IN A TYPICAL ISSUE.

Continued

WARREN BEATTY IN REDS, DRAWING BY MICK HAGGERTY

COVER PHOTOGRAPH OF MIKHAIL BARYSHNIKOV BY RICHARD AVEDON

2

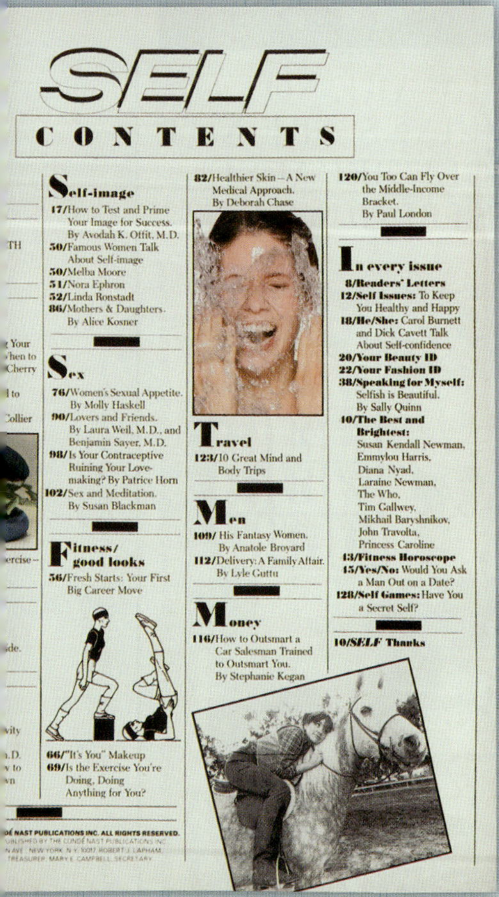

SELF

CONTENTS

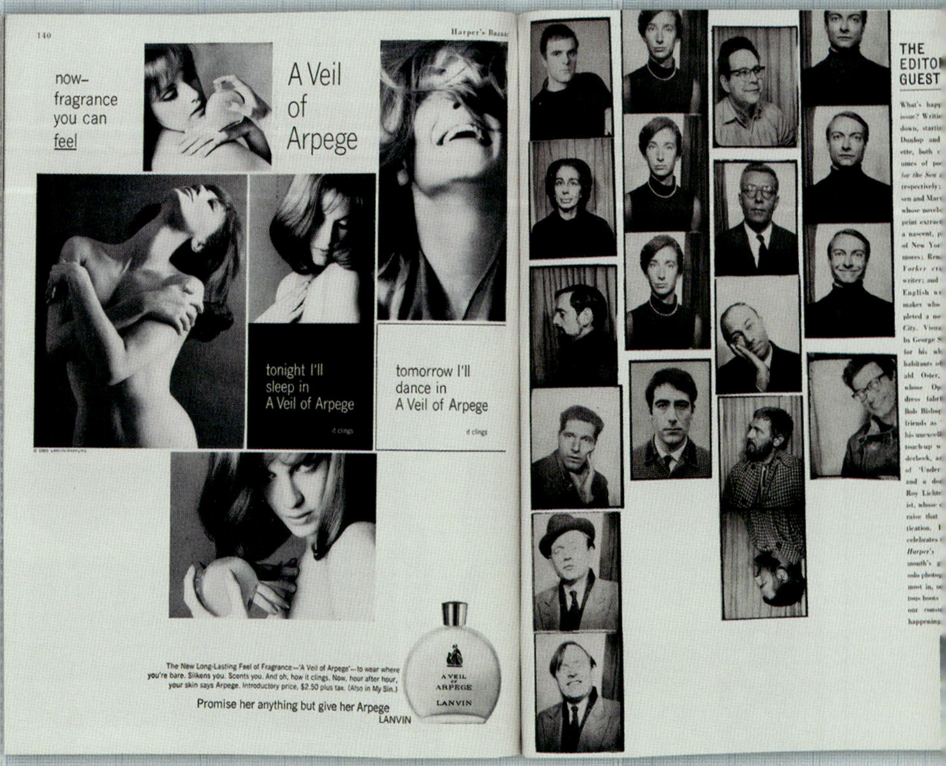

140 — Harper's Bazaar

THE EDITO[R'S] GUEST

Ms.

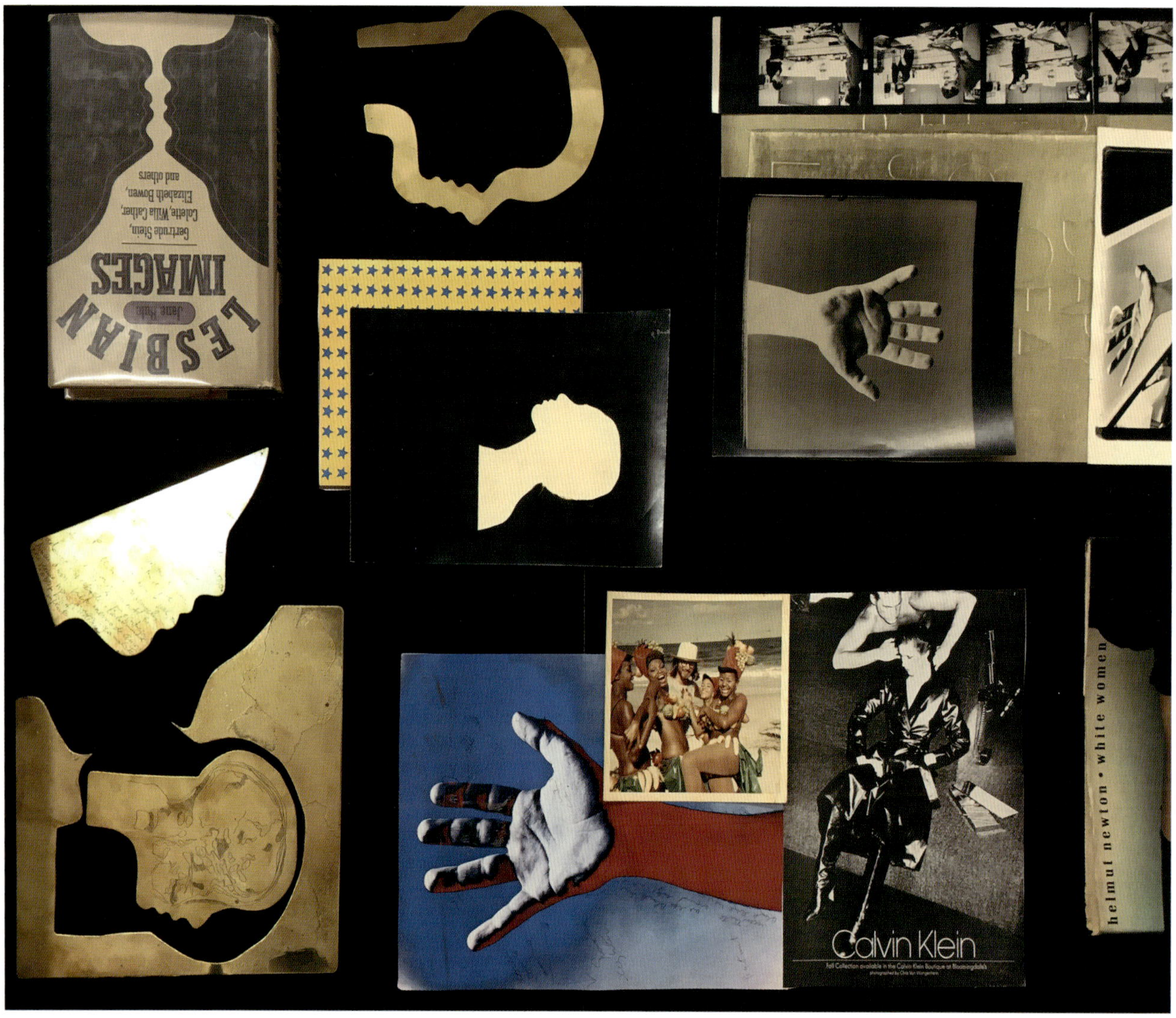

Previous spread: index poster for “Power of Print—The Work and Life of Bea Feitler”, Kölnischer Kunstverein, Cologne, 2019
Vitrine with silhouettes in “Power of Print—The Work and Life of Bea Feitler”, Kölnischer Kunstverein, Cologne, 2019

“MOST WRITERS AND EDITORS GENERALLY ARE NOT VISUAL PEOPLE, HOWEVER, MOST HUMAN BEINGS ARE NOT VISUAL. DESIGNERS WILL ALWAYS STRUGGLE BECAUSE EVERY WONDERFUL PAGE LAYOUT IS A STRUGGLE.”

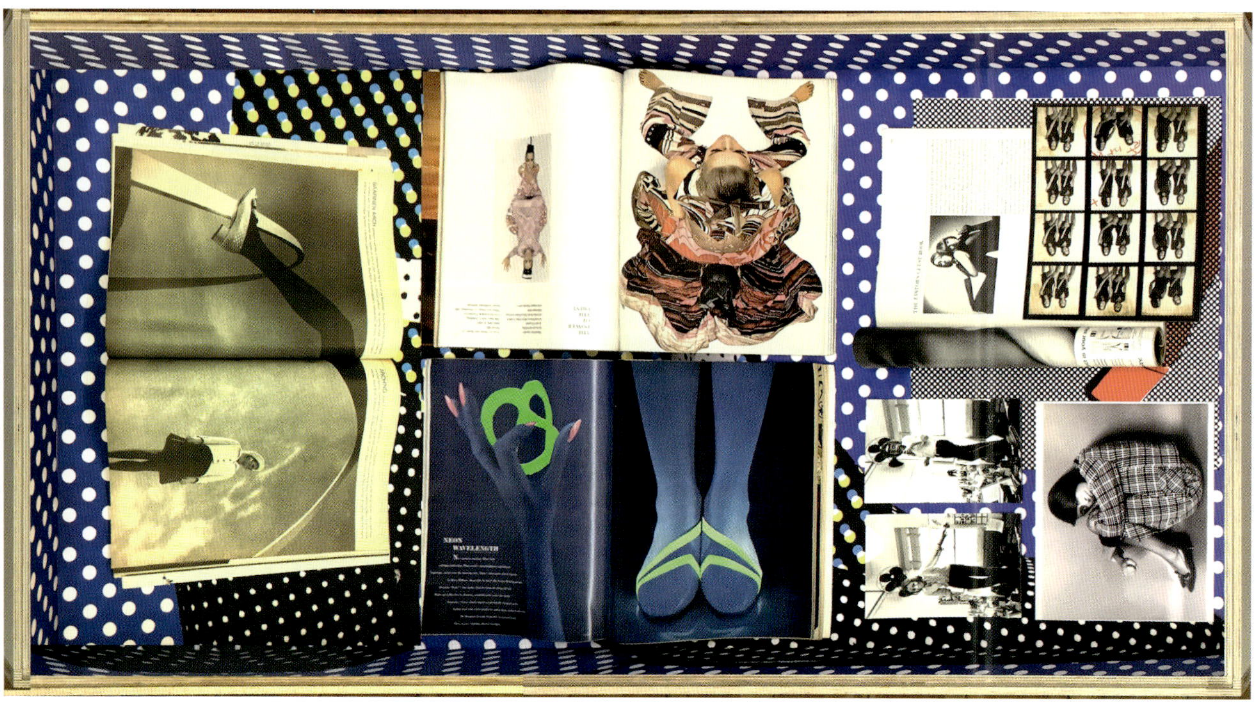

Vitrine on *Harper’s Bazaar* in “Power of Print—The Work and Life of Bea Feitler”, Kölnischer Kunstverein, Cologne, 2019

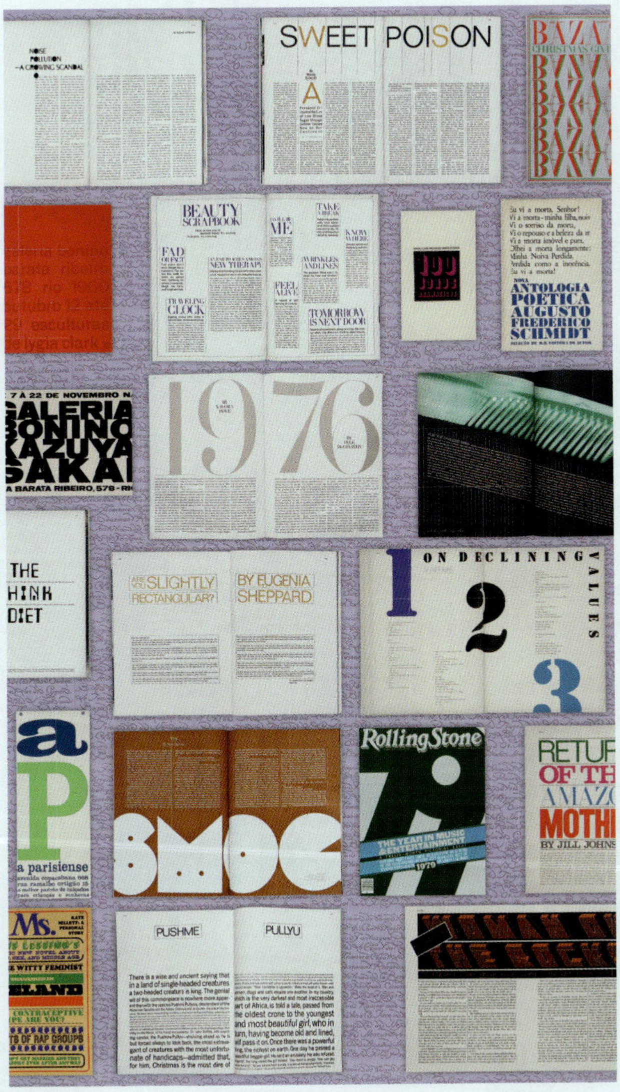

Typography poster for “Power of Print—The Work and Life of Bea Feitler”, Kölnischer Kunstverein, Cologne, 2019

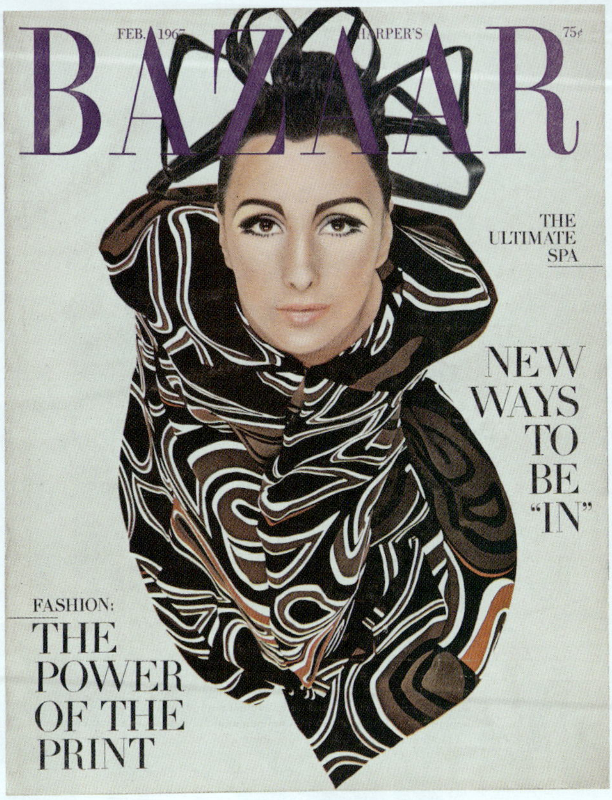

Harper's Bazaar cover, February 1967 / Photo by Hiro

POWER OF PRINT— THE WORK AND LIFE OF BEA FEITLER

Kölnischer Kunstverein
February 16 – March 31, 2019
Organized by Marte Eknæs and Nicolau Vergueiro
in collaboration with Kölnischer Kunstverein

The exhibition “Power of Print” focused on the recurrent themes of Feitler's work—the human silhouette, typography, solarization, the centerfold gutter as compositional device, collage—through which she reimagined the relationship between the body and graphic design in both layout and sensorial terms.

Guided by Feitler's design vision, we translated her work from publication form to exhibition space, reimagining her design as wallpapers, showing magazine covers and spreads in interactive flip frames, enlarging covers and placing them in windows to face the public space of the street, designing topical wall posters and vitrines containing original material. We wanted to ask ourselves what it felt like to walk into a magazine. How could we emulate the flow of an editorial spread in an exhibition format? How can the magazine content be negotiated into a physical space?

Feitler described herself as a “natural collaborator”, which is reflected in the exhibition through the inclusion of original pieces, by friends and collaborators, which were dedicated to her. Among original works and artifacts by Diane Arbus, Annie Leibovitz, Richard Bernstein, and Richard Avedon, “Power of Print” also included footage from the dance piece *Hidden Rites* by the Alvin Ailey Dance Theatre, which Feitler created costumes for, and Andy Warhol's 1964 *Screen Test #100*, which depicted Feitler. Through a deep engagement with Feitler's oeuvre, we think of this project as a form of “collaboration” with her practice and world, bringing it forward into a contemporary context.

“[A MAGAZINE] SHOULD FLOW. IT SHOULD HAVE ITS UPS AND DOWNS. IT SHOULD HAVE A BEGINNING AND AN END. IT SHOULD NOT BE DESIGNED AS A SPREAD-BY-SPREAD CONCEPT. THE CLOSEST THING TO MOTION IS EDITORIAL DESIGN.”

Quotes this spread: Robert A. Propper in conversation with Bea Feitler, “Bea Feitler—Sense Ability”, in *Graphics Today*, vol. 2, no. 4 (July/August 1977): 23–32.

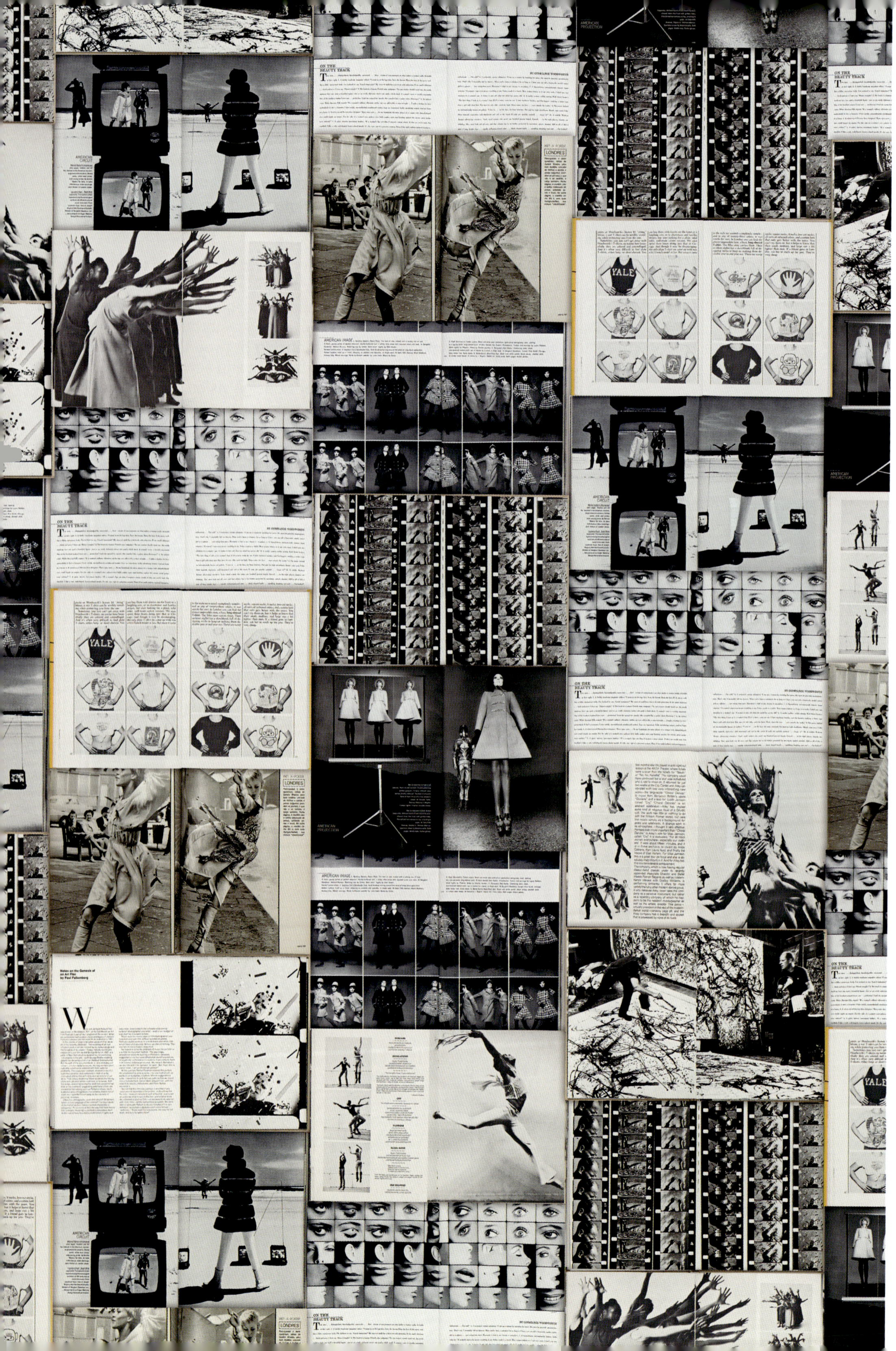

Collage poster (frame sequence) for "Power of Print—The Work and Life of Bea Feitler," Kölnischer Kunstverein, Cologne, 2019

gast räume

PUBLIC ART IN ZURICH
8.6 – 1.9.2019
#kioer

www.stadt-zuerich.ch/gastraeume

Stadt Zürich
Kunst im öffentlichen Raum

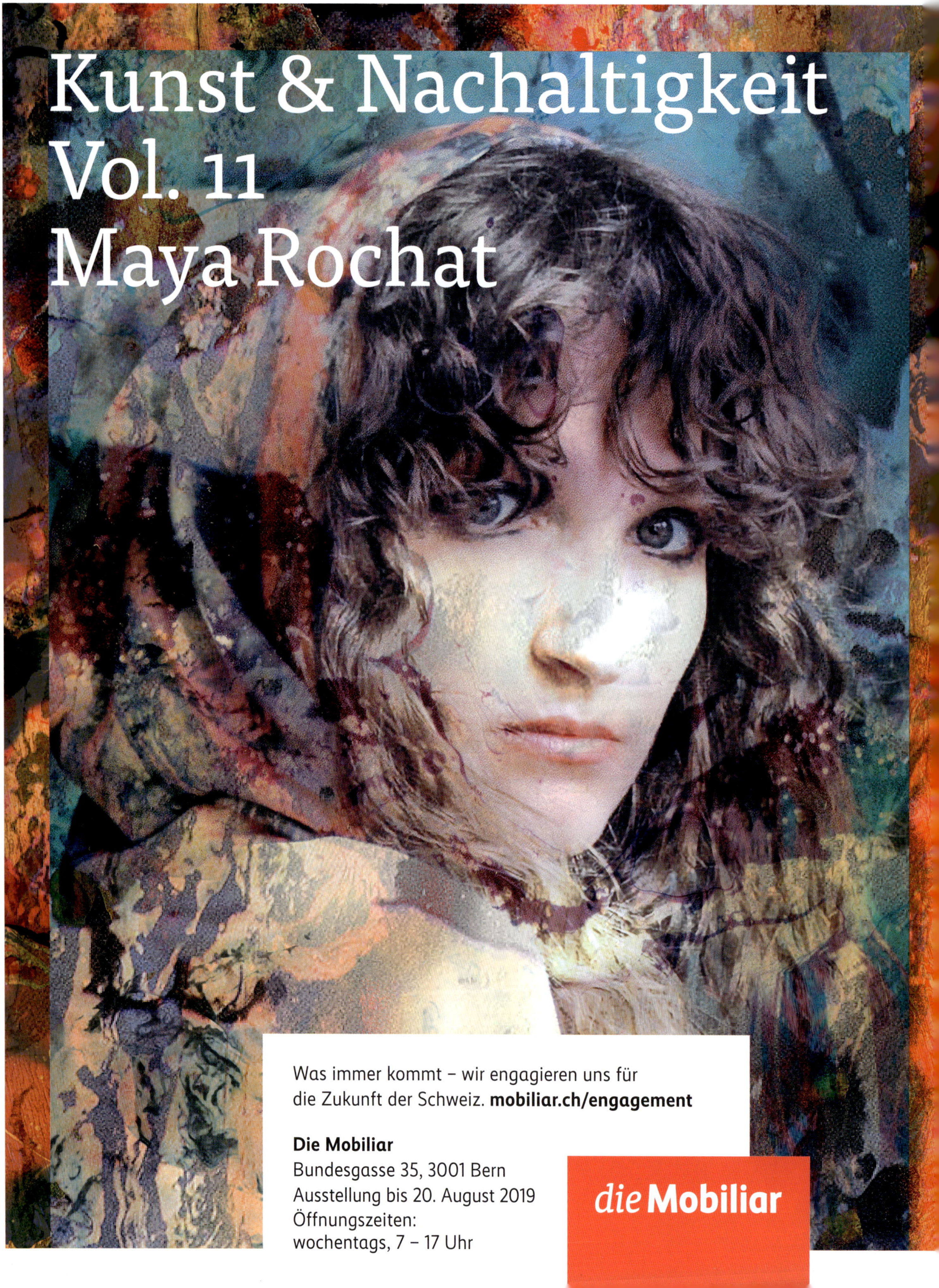
Kunst & Nachaltigkeit
Vol. 11
Maya Rochat
Was immer kommt – wir engagieren uns für die Zukunft der Schweiz. mobiliar.ch/engagement
Die Mobiliar
Bundesgasse 35, 3001 Bern
Ausstellung bis 20. August 2019
Öffnungszeiten:
wochentags, 7 – 17 Uhr
die Mobiliar